T0301622

Growth Theory and Sustainable Development

Growth Theory and Sustainable Development

Lucas Bretschger

Professor of Economics, University of Greifswald, Germany

Edward Elgar

Cheltenham, UK • Northampton, MA, USA

Published by
Edward Elgar Publishing Limited
Glensanda House
Montpellier Parade
Cheltenham
Glos GL50 1UA
UK

Edward Elgar Publishing, Inc.
136 West Street
Suite 202
Northampton
Massachusetts 01060
USA

A catalogue record for this book
is available from the British Library

Library of Congress Cataloguing in Publication Data

Bretschger, Lucas, 1958–
    Growth theory and sustainable development / Lucas Bretschger.
    Includes bibliographical references and index.
      1. Economic development. 2. Natural resources. 3. Sustainable
development. I. Title.
    HD87.B73 1999
    338.9—dc21   99–14862
                                      CIP

ISBN 1 84064 135 5

Printed and bound in Great Britain by Bookcraft (Bath) Ltd.

Contents

Figures

Tables

Variables

- A Total factor productivity, knowledge level
- A^K Capital productivity
- A^L Labour productivity
- a Input coefficient
- C Consumption
- c Per capita consumption
- c^R Extraction costs
- D Constant variable (in the production function)
- E Harvest costs
- g Growth rate
- H Human capital
- h Per capita transfer
- I Investment in physical capital
- K Capital stock
- k Capital intensity
- L Labour
- M Environment as a consumption good
- M^d Nominal money demand
- m Money supply per capita
- N Natural resource as an input
- n Number of designs or intermediate goods
- P Price level
- p Goods price
- Q Public services
- R Exhaustible resource
- r Interest rate
- S Total saving
- s Savings rate
- T Skilled labour
- t Time index
- U Utility
- U/L Utility per capita
- u Time-share of human capital in production
- V Stock of renewable natural resource
- v Capital coefficient
- W Wealth
- w Factor price
- X Input of resources of differentiated goods
- x Differentiated good

- Y Output, income
- Y^D Goods demand
- Y^H High-tech consumption good
- Y^L Labour income
- Y^S Goods supply
- y Per capita output, per capita income
- y_v Disposable per capita income
- Z Harvest
- z Market value of a design
- α Production elasticity of capital
- β Parameter for gains from specialisation (Section 7.3)
  Production elasticity of labour (Section 7.4)
- γ Reciprocal value of the elasticity of intertemporal substitution
- δ Depreciation rate
- ε Elasticity of substitution, price elasticity of demand
- ϕ Fixed parameter
- κ Knowledge capital
- λ Convergence speed
- μ Efficiency in education
- ν Parameter for externalities in consumption
- π Profit in the intermediate goods sector
- π^R Rent of resource owner
- θ Factor shares
- ρ Discount rate
- σ Elasticity of substitution
- ξ Fixed parameter
- ψ Parameter for externalities in production
- τ Tax rate
- ζ Fixed parameter

Abbreviations

- AC   Average costs
- CES   Constant elasticity of substitution
- GDP   Gross domestic product
- GNP   Gross national product
- GR   Golden rule
- KR   Keynes–Ramsey
- MC   Marginal costs
- MPK   Marginal product of capital
- MR   Marginal Revenue
- OECD Organisation for economic co-operation and development
- OLS   Ordinary least squares
- R&D   Research and development

Preface

The explanation of long-term economic development has always been a major issue in economic theory. The 'wealth of nations' today is the result of specific growth paths in the past. As is well known, the present situation is characterised by huge international differences in living standards. Contributing to the explanation of this pervasive observation is a challenge for any modern theory of economic growth. Another important task is to evaluate the conditions under which the present development will be sustainable in the future. The limited supply of natural resources has an impact on the growth of economic activities in the long term.

This book combines the issue of economic growth with the topic of sustainability. It aims to show that the understanding of growth theory is an important key to predict the sustainability of long-term development. The text gives a broad survey of growth theory in general and of recent topics in particular. The explanations range from the standard textbook models of the 1960s to the so-called 'new' growth theory, in which the long-term growth rate of an economy becomes an endogenous variable. Endogenous growth is based on a broadened concept of accumulated capital and on non-market interactions in the accumulation process. The theoretical foundation is then used to consider the issue of growth under environmental restrictions. Thereby, the text builds on recent developments in economic theory and in empirical studies which have significantly improved the theoretical analysis.

The text is designed for the level of first-year graduate students. At several European universities it also corresponds to the advanced undergraduate or intermediate level, where it can be used for elective courses. The book is suitable for lectures on economic growth, development economics, macroeconomics and sustainable development. In addition, it can be used for parts of other courses such as the dynamic part of environmental or resource economics. It is also relevant for economists from other fields who wish to learn about recent dynamic theory.

To understand growth theory, a certain amount of analytical exposition is indispensable. However, this textbook aims to keep the level of mathematics at the minimum necessary to present the important issues. For example, intertemporal optimisation is first derived in an easy-to-follow two-period model; also, the form of the production functions is always chosen so as to be as simple as possible. This procedure has proved to be successful in classes at different levels. A select bibliography is given at the end of each chapter; specific extensions, theoretical explanations, and empirical applications are presented in separate boxes.

The textbook is divided into twelve chapters. After an introduction to the general topic and some empirical facts in Chapter 1, a concise examination of the early formal models of Harrod and Domar follows in Chapter 2. Chapter 3 covers the basic neo-classical growth model and adds recent extensions such as the theory of the growth bonus and the convergence issue. In Chapter 4, intertemporal optimisation is introduced in a step-by-step procedure, concentrating first on a limited time range for didactic reasons.

Chapter 5 introduces the important concept of positive spillovers, which opens the analysis of the findings in recent growth theory. In Chapter 6, three basic models of endogenous growth with private investments, public services, and human capital are laid out in detail. Chapter 7 introduces research and development in multi-sector models of endogenous growth, building on the expansion-in-varieties approach of recent contributions. In the following two chapters, the open economy is introduced and several extensions of growth theory are discussed.

Finally, sustainable development is considered in the last three chapters. Chapter 10 gives a general survey of sustainability and its connection with the theory of endogenous economic growth. In Chapter 11, the dynamic consequences of negative externalities and the use of renewable or non-renewable natural resources are comprehensively examined. Chapter 12 concludes with a general summary and some implications for theory and policy.

The preliminary work for this book dates back to a one-year academic stay at Princeton University in 1991. Earlier manuscripts have been used for teaching at the Universities of Zurich, Constance, Greifswald and La Paz. In response to the feedback in the classroom, the text was continuously improved in terms of content and exposition. In several research projects on economic geography and on sustainable development, simpler versions of the theory were applied to current political problems, which helped to clarify the content and accuracy of the present text.

The author wishes to thank Hansjörg Schmidt, Daniel Kalt and Patrick Schüepp for their helpful suggestions based on preliminary versions, and Frank Hettich, Reto Schleiniger and Michael Breuer for their valuable comments on the present manuscript. Many thanks go also to Monica Klingler and Chris Ricketts for translating and correcting the text respectively, and to Hannes Egli for providing careful editorial assistance.

1. Long-term Development in Perspective

1.1 FACTS AND STYLISED FACTS FOR DIFFERENT COUNTRIES

a) Facts

World-wide, we observe substantial differences in the levels of per capita income as well as in the regionally achieved growth rates. In the industrialised countries, growth was greater in the last two centuries than in any previous period. In many countries of the Third World, however, no comparable development can be seen.

In these and the following comparisons, it must be taken into consideration that the per capita income data shown in statistics are not complete indicators of individual welfare, but they remain the best possibility for quantitative international comparisons to date. The combination of these income data with qualitative indicators and measures of the state of the natural environment and of income distribution, however, is normally useful.

In the period between 1960 and 1990 (see Figure 1.1), the average real growth rates of per capita income in individual countries lay between slightly negative values and 7 percent a year. In particular, newly industrialised countries in the Southeast Asian regions as well as Japan experienced a period of remarkable growth. In the period after the Second World War, the developed market economies attained a growth rate of real per capita income of about 3 percent a year. The countries of Western Europe, the USA, Canada, Japan and Australia belong to this group. The countries with the greatest wealth at the beginning of this period, the USA and Switzerland, achieved rather below average growth. Some of the less developed countries showed clearly higher growth rates.

A much smaller per capita income and lower growth rates were attained by the countries of the former 'Eastern bloc'; however, direct comparison is difficult because of data problems. A stagnation is recorded in the economies of many South American countries between 1975 and 1990 after an initial growth phase in the post-war period. Asia, on the other hand, had a low income level at the beginning of the period and then was mostly able to realise higher growth rates later on.

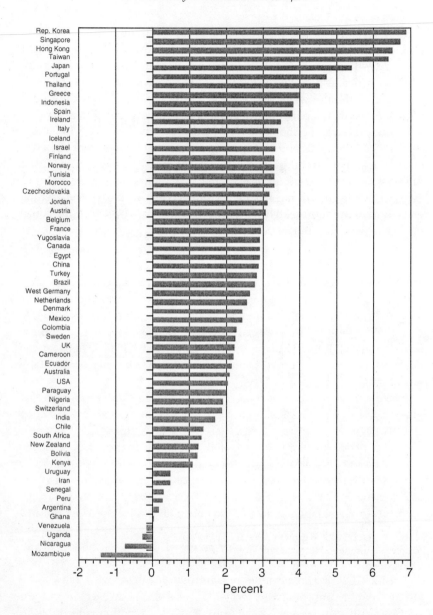

Note: Average GDP growth rates: real, per annum, per capita and in %.
Source: Summers/Heston, Penn World Table 5.6.

Figure 1.1 Comparison of growth rates, 1960–1990

More recently, the increases have been especially high in China; however, this development is taking place on a very low level. India showed lower growth rates with a still lower income level in the same time period, while in Africa, especially during the second half of the period, 1975–90, the real growth rates were decreasing in many countries. Today the economies of Sub-Saharan Africa show the lowest levels of per capita income.

In the post-war period, different phases can be observed for many countries. In the 1950s and 1960s, the average growth rates were higher in many places than after the big recession in the mid-1970s. In Figure 1.2, we can see this development in the example of Japan and to a lesser extent of the USA, while growth rates in the UK showed less variation. The average growth rates are represented for the five business cycles which the countries have gone through from 1950 to 1992.

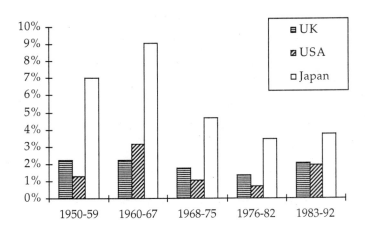

Note: Average GDP growth rates: real, per business cycle and in %.
Source: Summers/Heston, Penn World Table 5.6.

Figure 1.2 GDP growth rates for three countries

b) Stylised Facts

In economics, the expression 'stylised facts' describes those economic contexts which are supported by many observations – for example, in different countries or at different moments. The simplification, which finds its expression in the stylisation of reality, is a first step towards formulating a theory. The first six of the following stylised facts go back to Kaldor (1965), and the remaining points were added by Romer (1989) and other authors.

- Output per worker shows continuing growth; there is no tendency for the rate of productivity increase to decline.
- Capital per worker is characterised by continuing growth.
- The rate of return to capital stays constant over time.
- The relation between capital and the entire production is constant over time.
- Labour and capital each receive a constant share of the total income.
- Wide differences exist in the rate of productivity growth of different countries.
- In an international cross-section, the population growth rate is negatively correlated with the growth rate of per capita income.
- High percentages of skilled labour of the total labour force influence growth positively.
- In an international cross-section the increases in volume of foreign trade are positively correlated with the growth rates of per capita income.
- There is no simple connection between the income level at the beginning of a period and the subsequent growth rates, that is, poorer countries do not necessarily grow faster than rich ones.

Regarding Kaldor's stylised facts, it should be noted that the statements partially overlap. The first five statements could actually be reduced to three, since two stylised facts result directly out of the other three.

We shall now also note the following: the sixth point, relating to the different productivity development, is closely bound to the statement of Figure 1.1, for the productivity development per working place is largely responsible for the development of the per capita income. With respect to points seven and eight, corresponding graphics together with theoretical explanations for the influence of population growth and education (human capital) will be presented in Chapters 6 and 9. With regard to the relationship between foreign trade and growth, the positive correlation says nothing about the causality of the relationship; this will be explained further in Chapter 8. The relative growth chances of poorer countries in comparison with richer countries are the subject of the discussion on convergence in Chapter 3.

Further, in the international cross-section, countries with a high investment share have above average growth rates. Figure 1.3 shows a positive correlation between the two entities for a cross-section of countries. The connection between investing or saving and growth represents a central foundation stone of macroeconomic growth theory.

1.2 METHODOLOGICAL ISSUES

Different methodical paths to capture long-term economic development in theory can be found in the literature; these paths can be classified as follows:

- sociological–economic field analysis
- historical–evolutionary theories
- empirical–statistical analysis
- exact model theory.

In sociological–economic field analysis, the efforts to seek an explanation remain as close as possible to reality. Many growth-relevant facts will be described for many countries and for different moments in time. These statements do not represent a self-contained theory but can be used as a basis for forming overlapping theories. Lewis (1955), for instance, represents this view.

The history of economics deals with historical–evolutionary theories. Here a theory is formulated on the basis of a wide historical perspective. Different research programmes following this direction are strongly interdisciplinary in their orientation. The theory of evolution in economics (see Section 9.4) is a kind of contra-position to the neo-classically oriented growth theories, which are our primary concern in this book.

We understand the term 'empirical–statistical' analysis to mean a refined data analysis. This can range from simpler methods to refined statistical research. The formulation of the stylised facts discussed above, is a first step in this kind of analysis.

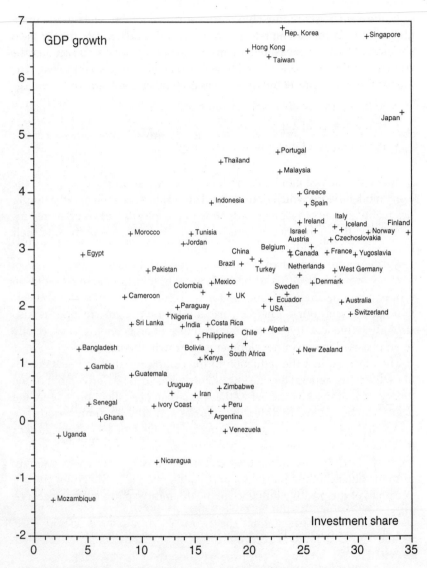

Note: Average GDP growth rates: real, per annum, per capita and in %;
           Investment share as average of the whole period.
Source: Summers/Heston, Penn World Table 5.6.

Figure 1.3 Average growth rates, 1960–1990, and average investment share

In the term 'exact model theory', the attribute 'exact' refers to the models and not to the attempt to represent reality exactly. The theory used should be based on consistent, that is, non-contradictory assumptions; the results should be deduced exclusively from the models employed. The methodical paths presented differ from each other, for example:

- in the degree of abstraction from reality
- in the degree of aggregation
- in the degree of generality of the results.

In modern macroeconomic theory and thereby also in this book, it is the exact model theory which dominates. This kind of research greatly simplifies reality; it leads to a great 'reduction of complexity', of complex reality. The notion that good theories are simple, that is, theories reduces to their base essentials, is widespread in economics.

Furthermore, one often argues on the highly aggregated level in macroeconomics. It needs to be said, though, that the aggregation of an economy to one single product sector is useful only when looking at certain specific questions. The fact that the long-term growth path is also strongly influenced by the sectoral structure of an economy is especially re-emphasised in newer developments of growth theory.

The more explicit the reduction of the complex reality in macroeconomics, the more general are the statements which can be derived out of the theory. Put differently: the better the applied models, the more widely the results can be applied to different countries and different time periods.

An individual research programme in the field of long-term growth processes does not necessarily have to be limited to one of the four method paths. For example, the exact model theory can benefit strongly from the other method paths and partly integrate them. The following are examples of the positive influence of the other three paths on macroeconomics:

- The creation of stylised facts which are found by empirical–statistical methods.
- The examination of fundamental changes in development, for example in the period of the 'industrial revolution' where historical–evolutionary theories are an important condition and addition for macroeconomic analysis.
- The completion of case studies which are close to the real situation and where, based on fundamental macroeconomic knowledge, concrete problems can be studied using a field analysis. An example of

this is the examination of competitiveness of a regional economy and the analysis of structural strengths and weaknesses of an industrial location which accompany it.

1.3 HISTORY OF GROWTH THEORY

Long-term economic development has been studied by classical economists such as Smith, Ricardo, Malthus and Marx. The investigation of the reasons for long-term economic growth was a central concern of these leading economists of the 18th and 19th centuries.

In the first half of the 20th century, the question of growth no longer attracted the same attention. The microeconomic discussion shifted progressively to the analysis of partial or general equilibrium systems.During the Great Depression and when Keynes was making his scientific contributions, unemployment and the possibilities of compensatory economic policy stood at the forefront of macroeconomic research.

At about the same time but at first attracting little attention, Schumpeter was already writing important contributions to the new theory of dynamic economic development. His theory of 'creative destruction' stresses innovations as a growth motor and thus enhances the usual approaches of the time. In the second half of the 20th century, Schumpeter's basic thoughts served as the basis of at least three research directions, as shown in Figure 1.4.

In industrial organisation, the connection between market forms and innovation activity became a dominant theme, initially within the descriptive and empirical but then progressively also within an analytical-mathematical context.

A second development took place with Arrow's contribution (1962), which also became an important main pillar of the new growth theory. Here the knowledge factor is no longer identified exclusively as input for economic processes, but equally as output of a learning process (see Chapters 5 and 6). The economic theory of sector-specific 'learning by doing', 'doing' initially meaning investment activities, introduced the element of activities with so-called positive spillovers (see Chapter 5) into the theory, an element which became decisive in the newer ideas. Kennedy (1964) pursues the idea of technical knowledge as input and applies it to a macroeconomic production function with separate influence possibilities for capital and labour productivity.

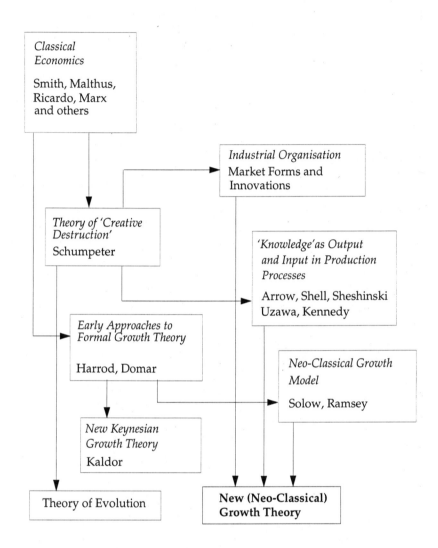

Figure 1.4 History of growth theory

In his paper, Shell (1967) emphasises that it is not only the knowledge factor but also other resources which are decisive in the production of new knowledge. According to his statements, knowledge is a consciously produced output from a separate research sector.

Sheshinski's contribution (1967) leads us in a slightly different direction. He shows that positive spillovers decisively influence the level of optimum capital accumulation. However, since the author assumes decreasing marginal products in factor accumulation, the decisive step towards the 'new growth theory' is not (yet) taken. The first representative of the new generation of growth theorists, Romer (1986), argues that the marginal product of the factors accumulated under market conditions approximates a positive constant, and so does not approach zero as is assumed in the traditional theory. Now, growth rates which do not decline over time can be explained theoretically. Furthermore, Uzawa (1965) has already stressed the meaning of human capital for growth processes, which is further developed in the newer theory.

The evolutionary theoretical approaches to economic growth are based quite directly on Schumpeter and less on neo-classical models. With reference to models in natural science, the dynamic economic development is understood as a process upon which no complete prediction can be made (see Section 9.4).

The second main line of research development in growth theory generates the most widely known post-war growth models; it neither refers to Schumpeter nor is the knowledge factor treated as an endogenous variable. As in the Keynesian multiplier analysis, the starting point of the Harrod/Domar growth model (see Chapter 2) is a constant savings rate. The work of these authors has a significant effect on the neo-classical growth theory of Solow (1956), which in its turn has greatly influenced the more recent developments (see Chapter 3).

A further development of the neo-classical growth model took place in the so-called Ramsey–Cass–Koopmans model (see Section 4.4). This theory is based on an older approach by Ramsey (1928) concerning interest-dependent saving activity in combination with the neo-classical production technique.

In the neo-classical as well as in the new growth theory, the form of the aggregate production function plays an important role. On the other hand, the Cambridge school and, for instance Kaldor as a representative of the neo-Keynesian growth model, categorically reject the aggregate production function as an analytical construction. The problem of the non-guaranteed adaptation to the balanced growth rate which is expressed by Harrod and Domar is solved by an adaptation of the distribution of income in the Kaldor model.

In conclusion as regards the new developments in growth theory, it can be stated that apart from the neo-classical growth model, industrial organisation and macroeconomic contributions to the knowledge factor are the main pillars of the so-called new growth theory, which will be discussed extensively from Chapter 5 on.

1.4 GROWTH THEORY AND RELATED FIELDS

a) Environmental Economics

A decisive issue for long-term development is the limited supply of natural resources. The relation between economic growth and the ecosystem has to be examined theoretically. The central theme in this field is sustainable development (see Chapters 10–12).

b) Business Cycle Theory

The comparison between the two theories can be made with the help of the following criteria (compare also with Section 9.2):

- Explanation of long-term economic development versus explanation of cyclical fluctuations: This characterisation best defines the difference between the growth theory and the business cycle theory.
- Explanation of the long-term trend versus explanation of the deviation from the trend: This characterisation is not basically wrong but delicate since the corresponding decomposition of income data is theoretically and empirically disputed.
- Explanation of the supply side versus explanation of the demand side of an economy: This characterisation was often used; it is, however, unsatisfactory, since modern theories consider the supply side as well as the demand side in both fields.

c) Other Theories

At the heart of growth theory is the explanation of long- and middle-term economic growth, helped by a few central determinants. However, particularly interesting statements are also possible in relation to other fields of theory. For example:

- Trade theory: Statements about the long-term effect of free trade agreements, about economic integration and competitiveness of regions and economies (see Chapter 8).
- Labour market theory: statements about the long-term employment prospects in a growing economy.

- Business cycle theory: statements about whether recessions provoke growth weaknesses or – on the contrary – can have a healing effect in the long term.

d) Economic Policy

Questions about economic implications or suitability of governmental interference and appropriate instruments arise with each approach of the growth theory. While the different aspects of market failure play the main role in these questions, the limitations of the political decision-makers must also be taken into account, as far as economic advice is concerned.

In times of growing globalisation of the world economy and intensifying competition among industry locations, the question of competitiveness is a point of prime importance in the political discussion. However, sustainability and long-term expectations on the labour market are also fields in which answers to present and concrete questions are extensively sought in the theory.

When applying the theory, it can be seen that in the field of growth, it is not only direct instruments such as the subsidising of research which must be considered; it is also important to bear in mind that many fields of policy influence growth through infinite interdependence and are therefore relevant to growth.

SELECTED READING

- ARROW, K.J. (1962), 'The Economic Implications of Learning by Doing', *Review of Economic Studies*, **29** (1),155–73.
- DOMAR, E.D. (1946), 'Capital Expansion, Rate of Growth, and Employment', *Econometrica*, **14** (2), 137–47.
- HARROD, R.F. (1939), 'An Essay in Dynamic Theory', *Economic Journal*, **49** (193), 14–33.
- KALDOR, N. (1965), 'Capital Accumulation and Economic Growth', in F. Lutz (ed.), *Theory of Capital*, London: Macmillan.
- KENNEDY, C. (1964), 'Induced Bias in Innovation and the Theory of Distribution', *Economic Journal*, **74**, 541–7.
- LEWIS, W.A. (1955), *The Theory of Economic Growth*, London: Allen & Unwin.
- MALTHUS, T.R. (1798), *An Essay on the Principle of Population*, Original: London 1798, Reprint: London 1986: Pickering.

- MARX, K. (1867), *Das Kapital, Band I–III*, Reprint: Berlin, 1987: Dietz.
- RAMSEY, F.P. (1928), 'A Mathematical Theory of Saving', *Economic Journal*, **38**, 543–59.
- RICARDO, D. (1817), *On the Principles of Political Economy and Taxation*, Original: 1817, Reprint: Cambridge 1951: Cambridge University Press.
- ROMER, P.M. (1986), 'Increasing Returns and Long-run Growth', *Journal of Political Economy*, **94** (5), 1002–37.
- ROMER, P.M. (1989), 'Capital Accumulation in the Theory of Long-run Growth', in R.J. Barro (ed.), *Modern Business Cycle Theory*, Cambridge Mass.: Harvard University Press.
- SCHUMPETER, J.A. (1934), *The Theory of Economic Development*, Cambridge Mass.: Harvard University Press.
- SHELL, K. (1967), 'A Model of Inventive Economic Activity and Capital Accumulation', in K. Shell (ed.), *Essays on the Theory of Optimal Economic Growth*, Cambridge Mass.: MIT Press.
- SHESHINSKI, E. (1967), 'Optimal Accumulation with Learning by Doing', in K. Shell (ed.), *Essays on the Theory of Optimal Economic Growth*, Cambridge Mass.: MIT Press.
- SMITH, A. (1776), *An Inquiry into the Nature and the Causes of the Wealth of Nations*, Original: 1776, Reprint: New York 1937: Random House.
- SOLOW, R.M. (1956), 'A Contribution to the Theory of Economic Growth', *Quarterly Journal of Economics*, **70** (1), 65–94.
- UZAWA, H. (1965), 'Optimum Technical Change in an Aggregative Model of Economic Growth', *International Economic Review*, **6**, 18–31.

2. Early Approaches to Formal Growth Theory

2.1 CAPACITY AND INCOME EFFECT (DOMAR SOLUTION)

The starting point for the early approaches to the formal growth theory, besides classical representations of the long-term economic development, was the macroeconomic theory of Keynes (1936). Here the studies of Harrod (1939) and Domar (1946) are of first importance. The goals of these studies consist mainly in explaining in which circumstances an economy can grow and whether the markets (especially the labour market) are in equilibrium during the growth process.

Domar stresses that positive net investments are not compatible with a constant capital stock, a simplifying assumption often found in business cycle models. According to Domar, demand or income and the capital stock must increase equally in time for capacities to be fully employed.

To simplify matters, we shall here assume a closed economy, in which the government will not be considered separately. In addition, all variables are real; the consequences of the money aspect will be considered in the next chapter in Section 3.9.

Notation:

- Y^S Goods supply (potential output)
- Y^D Goods demand
- K Capital stock
- L Labour
- v Capital coefficient (K/Y^S)
- I Investments
- g_x Growth rate of variable x ($g_x = \dfrac{dx(t)/dt}{x(t)}$)
- s Savings rate
- S Total saving
- t Time index.

Domar's theory consists of two elements. The first element concerns the so-called capacity effect, which describes the enlargement of the production potential of an economy that is reached by investments in physical capital. Here, an increase in the amount of physical capital creates an exactly proportional enlargement of the production potential. If no depreciation is assumed, net and gross investments do not need to be considered separately. The change in the capital stock follows out of:

$$I(t) = dK(t) \tag{2.1}$$

It is not imperative here for the extra capital stock to be utilised. The capacity effect of investments I therefore counts for the increase of potential production dY^S and can by use of the capital coefficient v be represented as:

$$dY^S(t) = \frac{1}{v} \cdot I(t) \tag{2.2}$$

The second element of the theory concerns the income effect, which represents the increase in income following investments. As in the Keynesian business cycle model, the savings rate s is given as constant and exogenous in Domar's approach. From $s \cdot Y^D = I$ follows:

$$dY^D(t) = \frac{1}{s} \cdot dI(t) \tag{2.3}$$

The expression $1/s$ is the Keynesian multiplier of the investments in the simplest model version (without money holdings, government, foreign countries and so on). Since $0 < s < 1$ is true for the savings rate, an autonomous investment increase enlarges the income $Y^D(t)$ by more than the original investment. This shows that investments influence the production side as well as the demand side of an economy.

For the solution of the model, we adopt the following definition which is generally used in growth theory: growth is assumed to be balanced when the condition $Y^D = Y^S$ is fulfilled at every moment in time. In this dynamic balance, all variables grow at a constant rate. The state of constant growth of the variables is also called 'steady state'.

The steady state is calculated by equating dY^S from (2.2) with dY^D from (2.3). This results in:

$$\frac{dI(t)}{I(t)} = \frac{s}{v} = g_Y \qquad \text{with } g_Y = \frac{dY(t)}{Y(t)} \tag{2.4}$$

Steady-state growth is thus defined by the quotient of the exogenous parameters s and v. In Figure 2.1, the growth's dependency on s and v is graphically represented. The slopes of the straight lines $S(Y^D)$ and $Y^S(K)$ define the growth rate g_Y. Depreciation, that is, differentiation between gross and net investments, will only be introduced in Section 2.4. A disinvestment and the consequent capital stock loss are therefore not possible here.

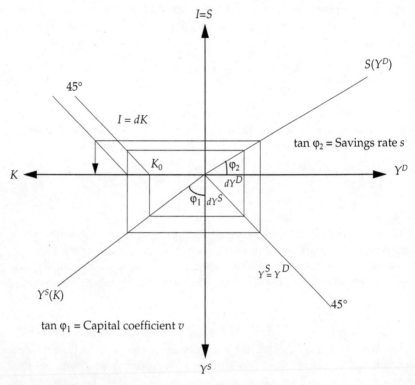

Figure 2.1 Steady-state growth according to Domar

2.2 ACCELERATOR AND SAVINGS FUNCTION (HARROD SOLUTION)

Harrod (1939) treated the same problem from a slightly different angle. To him, in contrast to Domar, it is not the investments that stand at the beginning of the theory, but the total demand. From that point, he then explains how total demand influences investments and savings. In order to formulate the model, he employs the accelerator 'theory' of investments and a specific savings function.

The following basic idea leads to the so-called accelerator assumption: enterprises normally respond to a growing demand of goods with an increase in production. Assuming fully utilised capacities ($Y^S = Y^D$), this demands buying new machines, that is, an enlargement of the capital stock. This means that investments are dependent on demand fluctuations:

$$I(t) = v \cdot dY^D(t) \tag{2.5}$$

The relation between the two entities $I(t)$ and $Y^D(t)$ is constructed via the capital coefficient v. The equation (2.5) is based on the simplifying assumption that enterprises react immediately to demand fluctuations and that the enlargement of the capital stock connected to the investment happens without time loss.

The next element of the theory regards the savings function of households. A constant part of the income is assumed to be saved:

$$S(t) = s \cdot Y^D(t) \tag{2.6}$$

Thus the steady state can now be calculated. The assumption of steady-state growth and the identity of saving and investing, that is, $S = I$, result in:

$$g_K = g_Y = \frac{s}{v} \tag{2.7}$$

In this way, it is shown that notwithstanding different basic ideas, Harrod and Domar still arrive at the same result. This is mostly due to the simplified conditions on which both models are based.

2.3 CONSEQUENCES FOR EMPLOYMENT

As mentioned at the beginning of the chapter, the consequences of growth for the employment of the labour force are of special interest besides the steady-state growth rate. For this we need an explicit production function. Since Harrod as well as Domar abstained from formulating an explicit production function, this element has to be added from a modern perspective.

To this end, most authors use the 'Leontief production function' (with a constant input relation of the production factors), since it seems to correspond best to Harrod's and Domar's conception. Thus:

$$Y = \min[A^L \cdot L(t), A^K \cdot K(t)] \qquad (2.8)$$

where A^X describes the (exogenous) productivity of the variable X.

A substitution of capital for labour and vice versa is not possible in this fixed-proportions production function, which is represented in Figure 2.2. The isoquants run at right angles; only the production at the corner points is efficient.

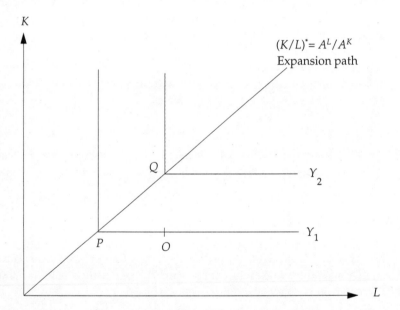

Figure 2.2 The Leontief production function

The expansion path which connects the efficient points distinguishes itself by a constant factor input relation $(K/L)^*$. If in the economy considered the amounts of labour and the amounts of capital do not correspond to the optimal input relation, this has a negative effect in the conditions represented: either a part of the capital remains underutilised or unemployment arises. For example, in point O, the quantity $\overline{OP}$ of the population is unemployed. Only when the quantity $\overline{OQ}$ of new capital is accumulated, will the state of full employment be reached.

Population growth is another decisive factor for the situation on the labour market. Especially in poor countries, population growth g_L is important. From the given production function it follows that the capital stock must grow at the same rate as the population in order to arrive at balanced growth:

$$g_K = \frac{s}{v} = g_L \tag{2.9}$$

The growth rate s/v is also known as the 'warranted rate of growth', and the measure g_L as 'natural' growth rate. Unemployment can be avoided if the warranted rate of growth corresponds to the natural rate of growth during the growth process.

Up to now, the quantities have been considered on an aggregate level, which influences individual welfare indirectly. As a next step, we shall consider per capita entities which express the position of the (average) individual directly and therefore play an important role in many growth models.

By dividing the above equations by L, we arrive at the per capita expression. All per capita variables will be represented by small letters.

Notation:

- y Per capita income (Y/L)
- k Capital intensity (K/L).

The per capita production function is:

$$y(t) = \min[A^L, A^K \cdot k(t)] \tag{2.10}$$

This connection can also be represented graphically as in Figure 2.3. From this figure, it becomes evident that with a capital stock which is smaller than in the steady state, the per capita output and consequently the per capita income are limited by the short supply of the capital factor. In the inverse case, the per capita income is limited by the available quantity of labour.

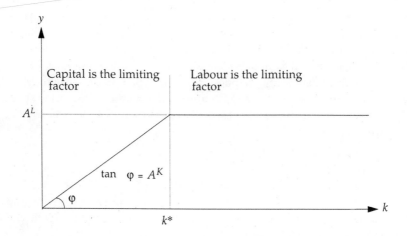

Figure 2.3 The Leontief per capita production function

Based on the figure, the production function can be rewritten as follows:

$$y(t) = A^L \qquad\qquad \text{for } k(t) > k^* \qquad (2.11)$$

$$y(t) = A^K \cdot k(t) \qquad\qquad \text{for } k(t) < k^*$$

2.4 ADJUSTMENT OF THE CAPITAL INTENSITY

Writing down the relations in per capita terms shows that the capital intensity is an important variable for the determination of per capita income. In order to demonstrate the dynamic properties of the system, it will therefore be considered how capital intensity changes in time. For the derivative of a variable with respect to time, we subsequently use the form with a dot, for example:

$$\frac{dk}{dt} = \dot{k}$$

Taking logarithms of the capital intensity and differentiating with respect to time results in:

$$\ln(k(t)) = \ln(K(t)) - \ln(L(t)) \qquad\qquad (2.12)$$

$$\frac{1}{k} \cdot \dot{k} = \frac{1}{K} \cdot \dot{K} - \frac{1}{L} \cdot \dot{L} \qquad (2.13)$$

$$g_k = g_K - g_L \qquad (2.14)$$

The simplification that no depreciation is necessary will now be disregarded. A part of the capital stock will be deducted in each period; with the depreciation rate being represented by δ, the result is:

$$\dot{K} = s \cdot Y(t) - \delta \cdot K(t) = \quad \text{net investments} \qquad (2.15)$$

Inserting (2.15) in (2.14) yields for each period ($dt = 1$):

$$g_k = \frac{s \cdot Y(t)}{K(t)} - \delta - g_L = \frac{s \cdot y(t)}{k(t)} - \delta - g_L \qquad (2.16)$$

Depending on whether labour or capital is the limiting factor in determining total output, a different expression for Y must be inserted in this equation. This yields the following two relations (2.17) and (2.18):

$$g_k = \frac{s \cdot A^L}{k} - (\delta + g_L) \qquad \text{if } k > k^* \qquad (2.17)$$

In this case capital stock changes have no influence on the per capita income. The reverse situation occurs for $k < k^*$:

$$g_k = s \cdot A^K - (\delta + g_L) \qquad \text{if } k < k^* \qquad (2.18)$$

Here we have $k^* = A^L/A^K$. Following (2.18) three cases can be distinguished, depending on whether ($s \cdot A^K$) is smaller, equal to, or bigger than $(\delta + g_L)$.

In Figures 2.4 to 2.6, the three cases are represented. The $(s \cdot y)/k$ curve can be divided into the two segments $k < k^*$ and $k > k^*$ (see Figure 2.3). Depending on the size of the capital intensity k, the labour factor or the capital factor determines the amount of output per capita. If $k < k^*$, then capital and output change at the same rates, and the gross investment share stays constant. If, however, k surpasses the optimal factor input relation k^*, then the capital does change, but not the output, since labour limits the production.

1. Case $s \cdot A^K < (\delta + g_L)$ in k_0

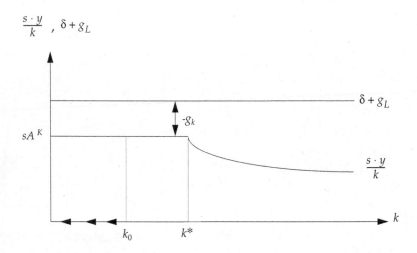

Figure 2.4 Decreasing capital intensity

In this case, no steady-state growth path exists. The gross investments do not suffice to equip the growing population with capital and simultaneously make the necessary depreciation. Starting from k_0, the capital intensity falls by g_k and in the long term tends towards zero. Unemployment already exists with $k*$; it gets worse over time, since the relation between capital and labour converges towards zero.

2. Case $s \cdot A^K = (\delta + g_L)$ in k_0

In contrast to the preceding example, an economy in the case of $s \cdot A^K = (\delta + g_L)$ and $k_0 < k*$ is capable of replacing the capital stock with the rate δ, and of enlarging it at the same time at the height of population growth. It is, however, not possible to do more than that. The gross investment share allows no increase in capital intensity k.

In the case of $k' > k*$, the country is confronted with a falling capital intensity k, which in the long term approaches the optimum $k*$. In this scenario, the exogenous parameters are given in such a way in this scenario, that the economy develops towards a steady state, in which there is no lack of employment.

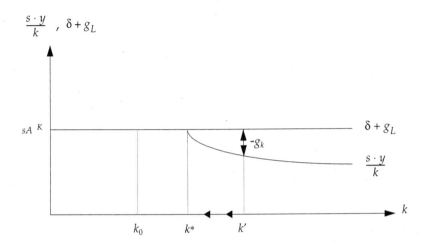

Figure 2.5 Stationary economy

3. Case $\quad s \cdot A^K > (\delta + g_L)$ in k_0

In the case of $k_0 < \tilde{k}$, the capital intensity grows in the beginning phase until the point of intersection of the curves in $\tilde{k}$ is reached. Should k_0 be bigger than $\tilde{k}$, then k will fall to $\tilde{k}$. In this situation, the long-term steady state (where the capital stock is not fully utilised) is not influenced by the first input relation. Only the exogenous model parameters δ, s, A^K and g_L are decisive.

According to this third scenario, different rates of steady-state growth for different countries can be explained by different depreciation rates, savings rates, capital productivity and population growth rates. It is to be noted that zero growth of the per capita variables is reached in the steady state. Total output grows at the same rate as the population. In addition, it is possible to introduce an exogenous technical progress into the model, but this will be done only in Chapter 3.

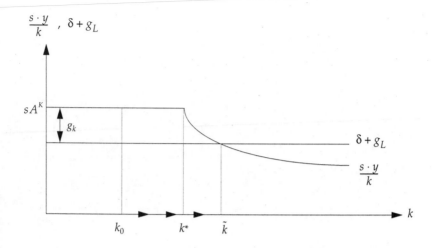

Figure 2.6 Growth of the capital intensity

2.5 ASSESSMENT AND CRITIQUE

Harrod's and Domar's contributions are a central starting point for many of the following studies in growth theory. This can be seen in the established place which is dedicated to these authors in textbook literature. Similarly, the questions of the meaning of unbalanced states for growth processes as well as the influence in the inverse direction remain relevant in theory and practice. However, it must be said that there are not many recent contributions to this specific theme of the growth theory.

Harrod's and Domar's theoretical results have been criticised in many ways, and today's final deductions are in part strongly contradictory to early approaches of the formal growth theory. The points of critique can be summed up as follows:

- The Harrod/Domar model assumes an inflexible production technique. In the short term, the Leontief production function might correspond to reality, however; growth theory, in contrast to business cycle theory, concentrates on the long term. Then, the possibility of substitution of input factors is at least partly given.

- Full employment is 'incidental' because it can arise only under favourable circumstances. None of the model parameters which are relevant to growth is endogenous, that is, explained by theory.

- Because the balance of growth is unstable under most conditions, the term 'growth on the cutting edge' was introduced for this approach.
- A constant savings rate does not correspond to the theory of inter-temporal optimisation, according to which the variable s is dependent on the interest rate.
- The factor productivity is constant or grows at a rate which is unexplained by the model.

This critique, as well as other factors, has been taken into account in the growth theories which have been developed since Harrod and Domar. This will become clear in the following chapters.

SELECTED READING

- DOMAR, E.D. (1946), 'Capital Expansion, Rate of Growth, and Employment', *Econometrica*, **14** (2), 137–47.
- HARROD, R.F. (1939), 'An Essay in Dynamic Theory', *Economic Journal*, **49** (193), 14–33.
- KEYNES, J.M.(1936), *The General Theory of Employment, Interest and Money*, London: Macmillan.

3. The Neo-classical Growth Model

3.1 BASIC ASSUMPTIONS

The neo-classical growth model of Solow (1956) has three building blocks: an aggregate savings function, an aggregate financing relation and an aggregate production function. This three-part pattern was adopted in many subsequent models.

- Savings: As is the case for Harrod/Domar, the savings rate is constant.
- Financing: As is the case for Harrod/Domar, savings and investments are identical.
- Production: In contrast to Harrod/Domar, the substitution of labour and capital in production is allowed. This leads to a variable capital coefficient, the size of which depends on relative factor prices.

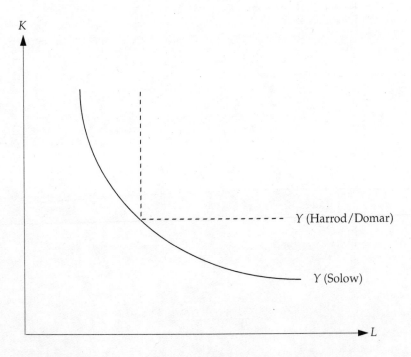

Figure 3.1 Production functions in comparison

In Figure 3.1, the different assumptions on production technique are represented. In the neo-classical growth model, contrary to Harrod/ Domar, a given output Y can be produced with different combinations of the production factors labour L and capital K under the assumption of full employment of both factors.

Further assumptions of the neo-classical growth model are perfect competition in goods and factor markets as well as constant returns to scale in the aggregate production function. If it is taken into consideration that in this model, the process assumed towards the steady state on factor markets takes a certain time, the angular isoquant in the above figure can be understood as an assumption for the short term, and the neo-classical production function can be seen as a representation of the longer term.

3.2 DERIVATION OF THE STEADY STATE

The production (without technical progress, see Section 3.3) is given by the following production function:

$$Y(t) = F(K(t), L(t)) \tag{3.1}$$

The output Y is defined by a function F, the arguments of which are K and L. Here, again, the variables are dependent on time t. The function has constant returns to scale in K and L. And so, in per capita notation and with k for capital intensity, the relation is:

$$y(t) = f(k(t)) \tag{3.2}$$

Contrary to the aggregate notation, we use f for the functional character in the per capita notation. The following properties are assumed for this function f:

$$f' > 0, f'' < 0, f'(0) = \infty, f'(\infty) = 0$$

f' designates the first derivation of the function f; for greater distinctness, it will, in some instances, also be represented as $f'(k)$. The four represented requirements (sometimes also only the last two) are known as 'Inada conditions'. In this way, $f(k)$ takes the form represented in Figure 3.2.

Without technical progress, the per capita income is on the steady-state level when the capital intensity has reached a constant value. For this reason, the change in time of the capital intensity can be considered in order to define the steady state. For the derivation of a variable with respect to time, we shall again use the form with a dot, for example:

$$\frac{dk}{dt} = \dot{k}$$

In the Solow model, the analytical expression for the change in capital intensity over time results from using the savings, financing and production functions. Again, we assume a constant depreciation rate δ for the capital which gives us:

$$S(t) = s \cdot Y(t) = s \cdot F(K(t), L(t))$$

$$= I(t) + \delta K(t) = \dot{K}(t) + \delta K(t) \tag{3.3}$$

By equating and remodelling the bold expressions on the right-hand side, we arrive at:

$$\frac{\dot{K}}{L} = s \cdot f(k(t)) - \delta \cdot k(t)$$

Now if numerator and denominator on the left-hand side are multiplied by L and the term $(\dot{L} \cdot K)/L^2$ is subtracted on both sides, we get:

$$\frac{L \cdot \dot{K}}{L^2} - \frac{\dot{L} \cdot K}{L^2} = s \cdot f(k(t)) - \delta \cdot k(t) - g_L \cdot k(t)$$

Since the left-hand side of this expression corresponds exactly to the change in time of the capital intensity, the following is true for this model:

$$\dot{k} = s \cdot f(k(t)) - (\delta + g_L) \cdot k(t) \tag{3.4}$$

This is the key equation of the Solow model. In order to arrive at the first version of a graphical representation of this fundamental relation, we divide the expression by the savings rate. In this way, the adjustment of the capital intensity can be represented as the difference between the per capita production and a straight line, which is given as $((g_L + \delta)/s) \cdot k$ in the graph. Analytically speaking, the difference d, marked by an arrow means:

$$d = \frac{\dot{k}}{s} = f(k(t)) - \left(\frac{\delta + g_L}{s}\right) \cdot k(t)$$

If the capital intensity is smaller than the steady-state value, then k and y increase steadily. In the steady state with k^*, the per capita income stagnates, because the capital equipment per working place no longer increases ($\dot{k} = 0$).

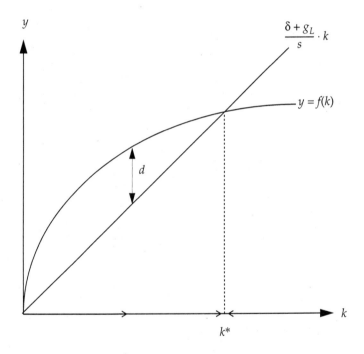

Figure 3.2 *Growth and the steady state in the Solow model*

The represented steady state is uniquely determined and stable because of the conditions which are assumed for the function f. Assuming constant parameters for g_L, δ and s, only a constant upward shifting of the production function can produce long-term growth. Such a shift is possible, for example, through technical progress.

3.3 ADJUSTMENT AND STEADY-STATE GROWTH

Only in the phase of adjustment to the long-term steady state can the Solow model explain the growth rate of an economy dependent on structural parameters such as the savings rate and population growth. In the long run, that is, on the steady-state growth path, the income in the model increases only if exogenous technical progress is also assumed.

For the level of technical knowledge, the variable A is introduced into the production function. The function is now:

$$Y(t) = A(t) \cdot F(K(t), L(t)) \tag{3.5}$$

or, in per capita notation:

$$y(t) = A(t) \cdot f(k(t)) \tag{3.6}$$

Technical progress leads to growth in the variable A. Change in time in the capital intensity is defined as follows:

$$\dot{k} = s \cdot A(t) \cdot f(k(t)) - (\delta + g_L) \cdot (k(t)) \tag{3.7}$$

As in Figure 3.2, the two terms on the right-hand side of this equation, after division by s, are represented in Figure 3.3.

The two arrows in Figure 3.3 show the difference between adjustment growth and steady-state growth, which is central to an understanding of the Solow model. The exogenous technical progress shifts the production function upwards. In the represented case, an enlargement of A to A' occurs.

In a second, much used variant of representation of the same circumstances, the growth of capital intensity becomes directly discernible as the difference of two geometrical loci. In this case, we use the 'Cobb–Douglas' form for the production function:

$$Y(t) = A(t) \cdot K(t)^\alpha \cdot L(t)^{1-\alpha} \tag{3.8}$$

In per capita notation, this is:

$$y(t) = A(t) \cdot k(t)^\alpha \tag{3.9}$$

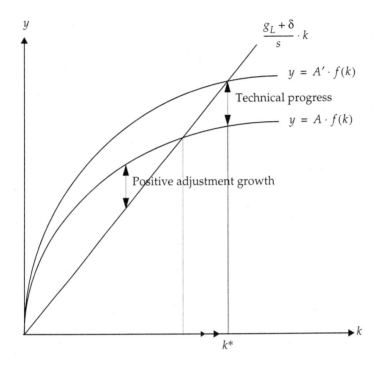

Figure 3.3 Exogenous technical progress

Here, the following explanation is helpful as regards parameter α. The production elasticity of the capital stock is defined as $(dy/dk)/(y/k)$. The following is true for the Cobb–Douglas function (3.9):

$$\frac{dy/dk}{y/k} = \frac{\alpha \cdot A \cdot k^{\alpha-1}}{\dfrac{A \cdot k^{\alpha}}{k}} = \alpha$$

The production elasticity of capital in the Cobb–Douglas function is then exactly equal to α. In the neo-classical theory, a value of about a third is assumed for the size of this elasticity (see Box 3.1). The production elasticities of labour and capital complete each other exactly to one in the neo-classical growth model. In the newer theory, however, this assumption is no longer valid (see from Chapter 5 on).

From (3.7) and applying (3.9), the growth of capital intensity gives:

$$g_k = s \cdot A(t) \cdot k(t)^{\alpha-1} - (\delta + g_L) \tag{3.10}$$

This leads to the graphical representation of Figure 3.4 for the growth of capital intensity.

In this representation and in the other explanations we have $k = K/L$. As mentioned already in Chapter 2, taking logarithms and differentiating with respect to time results in:

$$g_k = g_K - g_L.$$

Equating to zero and dissolving equation (3.10) leads to steady-state capital intensity with constant technical knowledge A ($g_A = 0$):

$$k^* = \left[\frac{\delta + g_L}{s \cdot A}\right]^{\frac{1}{\alpha-1}} \tag{3.11}$$

In the literature, capital intensity is sometimes represented as capital per efficiency unit $A^L \cdot L$, which we define as $\hat{k}$. Here, technical progress has an effect on the labour factor; the difference from the preceding representation will be explained in the following section.

If $\hat{k} = (K/(A^L \cdot L))$, the growth rate of this kind of capital intensity becomes:

$$g_{\hat{k}} = g_K - g_{A^L} - g_L$$

In the long-term steadystate with steady technical progress, $\hat{k}$ is constant, that is, $g_{\hat{k}} = 0$.

Corresponding to the above, we can look for the steady-state value for $\hat{k}$; with this kind of technical progress, the following is true:

$$\hat{k}^* = \left[\frac{\delta + g_L + g_{A^L}}{s}\right]^{\frac{1}{\alpha-1}} \tag{3.12}$$

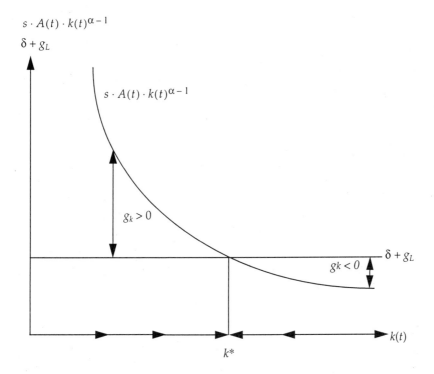

Figure 3.4 Neo-classical adjustment growth

3.4 CLASSIFICATION OF TECHNICAL PROGRESS

In the neo-classical model, a growth which exceeds adjustment to the optimum capital intensity and which is steady becomes possible only through exogenously given technical progress. As has already been seen in the above explanations, one talks of technical progress in this context whenever an enlargement of technical knowledge allows an increase in the output, without an increase in the employment of production factors being necessary. Technical progress can have the same effect or different effects on the two factors, labour and capital. This is why the classification which will now be described was introduced into the literature.

Box 3.1: Empirical Determination of the Income Level

The difference in income levels of different countries can be explained with the help of the neo-classical growth model. In the first part of an empirical study by Mankiw/Romer/Weil (1992), it is assumed that the studied countries are in the long-term steady state. The steady-state capital intensity in expression (3.12) of the main text is the starting point. When the steady-state capital intensity is introduced into the per capita production function of the Cobb–Douglas form (3.9), the following estimation equation results after taking logarithms:

$$\ln y = \text{const} + (\alpha/(1-\alpha)) \ln s - (\alpha/(1-\alpha)) \ln (\delta + g_L + g_A) + \varepsilon$$

Here ε is the error term. This equation has been empirically estimated in an international data set for different samples. The data for the per capita incomes are to be found in the international data set by Summers/Heston, for the savings rates, investment shares are used which were, like the population growth, taken from the same data set. For the sum of depreciation rate and technical progress, the value of 0.05 was assumed.

In a cross-section of 98 countries, from which countries with a high oil export were excluded, the following result was found for the period 1960–85:

$$\ln y = 5.48 + 1.42 \ln s - 1.97 \ln (\delta + g_L + g_A)$$
$$(1.59) \quad (0.14) \quad (0.56)$$

OLS estimation, standard errors in brackets, R^2 (corrected) 0.59

The estimated coefficients for savings rate and population growth have the expected sign and are highly significant. The hypothesis that the two estimated coefficients show the same size (with inverse signs) cannot be rejected either. According to the authors, the differences in savings rates and population growth explain a large part of the international differences in income level. The authors themselves do, however, state that the implied value for α of 0.6 is nearly twice as big as would actually be expected with neo-classical assumptions. They therefore postulate that the accumulation of human capital must also be taken into consideration in the theory. With an additional savings rate for human capital, which is analogous to the physical capital, the model is estimated again in the aforementioned study. This yields results which are also satisfying as regards the capital share.

The results show that the empirical content of the neo-classical model is bigger than generally assumed. However, these results are valid only for income levels. Also, the estimations for the subsample of the important OECD countries are much less satisfying. In addition, the assumption that technical progress is exactly the same in all countries is rather far from reality. Furthermore, if the technical progress in the individual countries depends on the investment share, the chosen estimation method is no longer appropriate. If it is accepted that technical innovations are central for growth, then they must be explained. This, among other things, is the subject of the new growth theory (see from Chapter 5 on).

a) Hicks Neutrality

According to Hicks, technological innovations are to be regarded as 'neutral' if the relation of the marginal products of the two factors stays constant over time with a given capital intensity ($k = K/L$), that is:

$$\frac{F_{K,0}}{F_{L,0}} = \frac{F_{K,t}}{F_{L,t}} = \text{constant} \tag{3.13}$$

Here the ts are time indices and $F_{K,0}$ denotes the marginal product of capital at moment 0. Hicks-neutral technical progress is also called 'product augmenting'; it implies an income distribution on the two factors which is constant over time.

The production function then has the already familiar form:

$$Y(t) = A(t) \cdot F(K(t), L(t)) \tag{3.14}$$

It is, however, conceivable that technical innovations have different effects on the factor productivity of capital and labour. We shall therefore now look at situations where technical progress has either a labour-augmenting or a capital-augmenting effect.

b) Harrod Neutrality

In the presence of factor-augmenting rather than product-augmenting technical progress, the production function can be written as:

$$Y(t) = F(A^L(t) \cdot L(t), A^K(t) \cdot K(t)) \tag{3.15}$$

The arguments $A^L(t) \cdot L(t)$ and $A^K(t) \cdot K(t)$ of this production function are called factor efficiency units. In the following, we assume constant returns to scale and consider the case of purely labour-augmenting technical progress ($A^K(t)$ is constant, and $A^L(t) \cdot L(t)$, that is, efficient labour, increases).

If it is now assumed that the relation $A^L(t) \cdot L(t)/K(t)$ stays constant, then the relation of the factor amounts needed for the production of a certain amount of output $L(t)/K(t)$ decreases in the same measure as the efficiency of the labour factor $A^L(t)$ can be increased through technical progress.

If L is reduced in the same measure as A^L increases, then the marginal product of capital which is dependent only on the relation

$A^L(t) \cdot L(t) / K(t)$ also stays constant. For this reason, labour-augmenting progress is sometimes also called 'labour saving'. A proportional increase in the input then leads to an increase in the output of same size. So the capital coefficient v ($v = K(t)/Y(t)$) stays constant.

After these reflections, Harrod neutrality can be defined as technical progress which changes neither the return on capital ($= F_k$) nor the capital coefficient ($v = K(t)/Y(t)$). Furthermore, the relation of the incomes factor stays unchanged. So the production function assumes the following form:

$$Y(t) = F(K(t), A(t) \cdot L(t)) \tag{3.16}$$

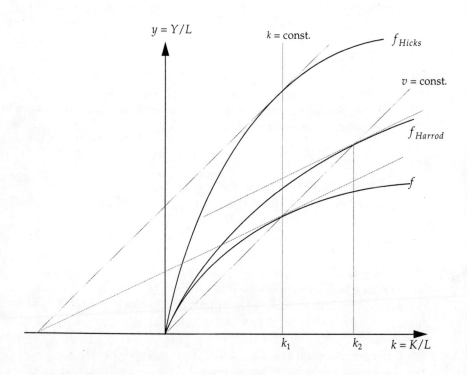

Figure 3.5 Harrod neutrality and Hicks neutrality

Figure 3.5 stresses the difference between the two concepts of Harrod neutrality and of Hicks neutrality. In the case of Harrod neutrality, the basic production function $f(k)$ is shifted upwards through technical progress in such a way that the slope of the production function (and so also capital return f_k) stays constant at the point of intersection with the straight line $v = \text{const.}$

It becomes clear that with labour-augmenting technical progress, capital intensity, that is, the relation between capital and 'pure' labour L, increases, while in the case of Hicks neutrality, the capital intensity stays constant.

c) Solow-Neutrality

Analogous to Harrod neutrality, technical progress is called purely capital augmenting or Solow neutral, when with a constant labour coefficient L/Y the marginal productivity of labour does not change. This implies the following production function, see (3.16):

$$Y(t) = F(A(t) \cdot K(t), L(t)) \tag{3.17}$$

Technical progress has an effect on capital productivity only. Therefore, in order to augment total economic output, the capital input must be raised less in the measure in which technical progress $A(t)$ augments the capital productivity.

d) Progress and the Steady State

Finally, it will be shown that with general production functions only progress in the Harrod sense is compatible with the concept of steady-state growth. From Chapter 2, we know that the following applies in the steady state:

$$g_Y = g_K = \frac{s}{v} = \text{constant} \tag{3.18}$$

This condition can be fulfilled only if – given a constant savings rate – v stays constant over time. This means, however, that technical progress cannot have any capital-augmenting effect whatsoever, since otherwise $v = K/Y$ would augment. With the production function chosen as general, technical progress is therefore compatible with the steady-state concept only if it is Harrod neutral or purely labour augmenting. In addition, it should be noted how well the definition of Harrod-neutral progress corresponds to the stylised facts of growth described by Kaldor (see Chapter 1).

The Cobb–Douglas production function is an important exceptional
case as regards the question of technical progress; with this function, the
different kinds of technical progress can be directly transferred into each
other. For this production function, the three kinds of Hicks-, Harrod- and
Solow-neutral technical progress are:

$$Y = \tilde{A}_{Hi} \cdot K^{\alpha} \cdot L^{1-\alpha}$$

$$Y = K^{\alpha} \cdot (A_{Ha} \cdot L)^{1-\alpha} = A_{Ha}^{1-\alpha} \cdot K^{\alpha} \cdot L^{1-\alpha} = \tilde{A}_{Ha} \cdot K^{\alpha} \cdot L^{1-\alpha}$$

$$Y = (A_{So}K)^{\alpha} \cdot L^{1-\alpha} = A_{So}^{\alpha} \cdot K^{\alpha} \cdot L^{1-\alpha} = \tilde{A}_{So} \cdot K^{\alpha} \cdot L^{1-\alpha}$$

There is no qualitative difference between these functions, so the Cobb–
Douglas production function is independent of the definition of technical
progress.

3.5 ROLE OF ECONOMIC POLICY

According to welfare theory, decisions of economic policy should be
directed to the welfare of the households. Neither output nor investments
are direct measures of welfare. In microeconomic theory, it is consumption
(besides arguments such as wealth, state of the natural environment and
others) which is decisive for the utility level. In the context of the neo-classical growth model, therefore, reaching the highest possible consumption
in steady-state growth represents an optimal welfare goal.

In steady-state growth, per capita investments are equal to the sum of
the depreciation rate and population growth multiplied by capital intensity:

$$g_k = 0 \qquad => (\delta + g_L) \cdot k^* = s \cdot y^* = s \cdot A \cdot f(k^*) \qquad (3.19)$$

Per capita consumption in steady-state c^*, which is to be maximised,
results from the difference between per capita output y^* and per capita
investments (= per capita savings):

$$c^* = A \cdot f(k^*) - s \cdot A \cdot f(k^*) \qquad (3.20)$$

Inserting (3.19) into (3.20) gives:

$$c^* = A \cdot f(k^*) - (\delta + g_L) \cdot k^*$$ (3.21)

Totally differentiating (3.21) gives:

$$dc^* = \underbrace{(f(k^*) \cdot dA)}_{1.} + \underbrace{(-k^* \cdot d\delta)}_{2.} + \underbrace{(-k^* \cdot dg_L)}_{3.}$$

$$+ \underbrace{((Af'(k^*) - \delta - g_L) \cdot dk^*)}_{4.}$$ (3.22)

The four terms 1, 2, 3 and 4 can be further elaborated as follows:

- **1.** Technical progress, expressed by dA, is given exogenously and therefore cannot be influenced by the government in this model; it is a present which 'falls like manna from heaven'.
- **2.** and **3.** According to the assumptions of the Solow model, the depreciation rate and population growth are exogenous and constant ($d\delta = dg_L = 0$).
- **4.** Capital intensity is the only factor over whose size the government has a certain measure of decisional power. Instruments such as investments by the government or savings promotion as well as different taxation of the labour and capital input factors can be employed in order to have an impact in this field.

The influence of k on c^* according to (3.22) is:

$$\frac{dc^*}{dk} = Af'(k) - (\delta + g_L)$$

In order to maximise consumption c^*, $dc^*/dk = 0$ must be true. This leads to the golden rule, which is also called the 'Phelps golden rule of capital accumulation' after its inventor:

$$Af'(k) = \delta + g_L$$ (3.23)

or: $$\frac{dy}{dk} = \delta + g_L$$

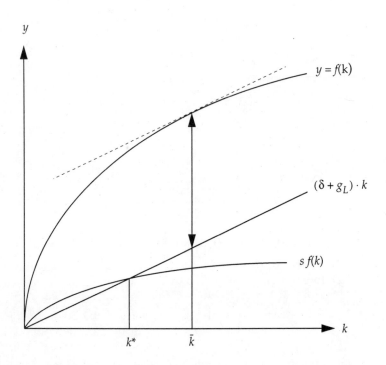

Figure 3.6 Maximum per capita consumption

For maximum per capita consumption, according to this stipulation, the marginal product of capital should be equal to the sum of the depreciation rate and the rate of population growth. This result can be very nicely visualised graphically (see Figure 3.6). Point k^* represents the steady state in the diagram (see expression 3.4). The per capita consumption, however, is biggest where the slope of the two geometrical loci $f(k)$ and $(\delta + g_L) \cdot k$ is the same; in the figure, this is the case at point $\bar{k}$.

In order to arrive at maximum per capita consumption, policy must therefore succeed in shifting the curve $sf(k)$ in such a way that k^* comes to lie exactly at the same place as $\bar{k}$. How can this goal be reached? An example will be presented in the following discussion.

Notation:

- w_L wage rate, that is, wage per worker
- w_K return per unit of capital with which capital owners are compensated for the supply of capital.

As we have up to now, we shall base our argument on the two production inputs, capital and labour; to simplify matters, the time index will be omitted. The income of the amount Y gained through selling the produced goods is paid out in full to the capital owners and the employees:

$$Y = w_L \cdot L + w_K \cdot K$$

In per capita notation, the following is true:

$$y = w_L + w_K \cdot k$$

In addition to the salary earned for its labour, an average household also receives a capital return of the amount of $w_K \cdot k$. In perfectly competitive markets, the capital return rate is equal to the marginal product of capital:

$$\frac{dy}{dk} = \frac{d(Y/L)}{d(K/L)} = \frac{dY}{dK} = w_K \tag{3.24}$$

Dividing (3.19) by k^* gives:

$$\delta + g_L = \frac{s \cdot Af(k)}{k} = \frac{s \cdot Y/L}{K/L} = s \cdot \frac{Y}{K} \tag{3.25}$$

Application of the golden rule gives:

$$s \cdot Y = w_K \cdot K \tag{3.26}$$

In the 'golden' steady state, the total savings are equal to the total capital returns. So the following basic rule can be postulated for this simplifying model: if a country invests, that is, saves its capital returns and consumes its salaries, it maximises per capita consumption.

3.6 GROWTH ACCOUNTING

In the context of growth accounting, economic growth is statistically dissected according to the contribution of the different factor quantity increases to output growth. Here, share factors find their role as weights. The amount of growth which cannot be 'explained' by the quantity increases of inputs is called Solow residual.

Notation:

- $\theta_{L,K}$ labour share and capital share
- F_X derivative of function F with respect to X.

We start from the production function (3.5) with technical progress in the form:

$$Y(t) = A(t) \cdot F(K(t), L(t))$$

The factor $A(t)$ is often called 'total factor productivity' in growth accounting. Differentiating with respect to time t (to simplify matters the time indices will be omitted in the following) we arrive at:

$$\dot{Y} = (F \cdot \dot{A}) + (A \cdot F_K \cdot \dot{K}) + (A \cdot F_L \cdot \dot{L})$$

Division by Y or $A \cdot F(\;\cdot\;)$ leads to:

$$\frac{\dot{Y}}{Y} = g_Y = \frac{(F \cdot \dot{A})}{A \cdot F(\;\cdot\;)} + \frac{(A \cdot F_K \cdot K)}{Y} \cdot \frac{\dot{K}}{K} + \frac{(A \cdot F_L \cdot L)}{Y} \cdot \frac{\dot{L}}{L}$$

Expressed in the notation for growth rates:

$$g_Y = g_A + \frac{(A \cdot F_K \cdot K)}{Y} \cdot g_K + \frac{(A \cdot F_L \cdot L)}{Y} \cdot g_L \qquad (3.27)$$

In the case of perfect competition on factor and goods markets, the wage rate w_L (= marginal costs of labour) is defined by the marginal product of labour $A \cdot F_L$:

$$w_L = A \cdot F_L$$

The wage share is given as:

$$\theta_L = \frac{w_L \cdot L}{Y} = \frac{(A \cdot F_L) \cdot L}{Y} \tag{3.28}$$

Since constant returns to scale are assumed for the aggregate production function, the sum of the share factors θ_L and θ_K yields unity, that is, all of Y goes to the owners of K and L:

$$Y = w_L \cdot L + w_K \cdot K$$

Expressed in shares, which are obtained by dividing by Y, this means:

$$\theta_K = 1 - \theta_L \tag{3.29}$$

In this way, from (3.27) we arrive at the formula used in growth accounting:

$$g_Y = g_A + (1 - \theta_L) \cdot g_K + \theta_L \cdot g_L \tag{3.30}$$

Normally, it should be possible to obtain the data for all variables of this expression – except for g_A – out of the national accounting, that is, official data sets. The growth of total factor productivity g_A then follows as residuum (Solow residual) and can be interpreted as technical progress. In growth-accounting language, a result is 'satisfying' given that the residual results as relatively small in a calculation.

For practical use, (3.30) calls for some enlargements:

- The expression 'capital' encompasses a great number of inhomogeneous kinds of capital; the quality aspect must be added.
- The labour factor is not homogeneous either; the difference in qualifications needs to be considered.
- The integration of additional production factors, for example land, is also important.

This already touches on a big problem of this method: the data in the statistics have to have the required qualities. Other points which can be criticised in growth accounting are:

- Production technique and market form are reproduced very restrictively. In reality, there are market imperfections as well as the possibility of increasing returns to scale in the aggregate production function.
- Equation (3.30) shows no causal relationships, it is a statistical identity. The mutual endogenous influence between capital formation and technical progress is completely neglected.

A more far-reaching and satisfying method of statistical research into the long-term development is empirical testing of theoretical models of recent growth theory with the aid of regression analysis (see Box 3.1 and from Chapter 5 on). Only with this kind of empirical test does it become possible to analyse causal relationships in the growth process.

3.7 GROWTH BONUS

Let us assume that the efficiency of an economy increases, for example, because of changes in economic policy. In recent years, the increase in the total economic efficiency due to participation in the programme of the Common European Market has been much discussed in this context (compare Cecchini et al. 1988). Other measures to bring about an increase in competition intensity or appropriate deregulation can, however, have the same effect.

How strongly does the per capita income increase in the long-term steady state, when assuming the Solow model? Following Baldwin (1989) the middle-term additional growth, which positively reinforces the static efficiency increase (for example calculated in Cecchini) in neo-classical growth theory, is called a 'growth bonus'.

A simple neo-classical production function in per capita notation with the usual designations and the Cobb–Douglas form as in Section 3.3 is assumed:

$$y(t) = A(t) \cdot f(k(t)) = A(t) \cdot (k(t))^\alpha \tag{3.31}$$

Taking logarithms and differentiating with respect to time results in:

$$g_y = g_A + \alpha \cdot g_k \tag{3.32}$$

According to (3.32), the growth of per capita income in a Cobb–Douglas function consists of two terms. Now if an increase in the total economic efficiency A occurs, then the steady state will change; an adjustment growth takes place in variable k, until the new steady state is reached. In the y/k-diagram the production function shifts upwards with an increasing A, as can be seen in Figure 3.7.

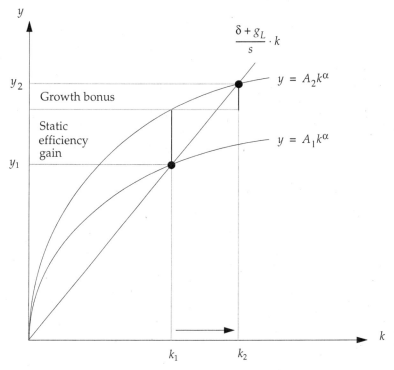

Figure 3.7 Growth bonus

The figure shows the two steps of income increase. With constant capital intensity, what occurs first is an increase in the per capita income, which is defined as 'static efficiency gain'. Here, however, the system is not on the steady-state growth path.

Only after an adjustment of the capital intensity is the long-term steady-state reached again. How much does the growth of the capital intensity depend on the growth of the efficiency increase in A?

Here, we propose the following reflection. The share of the capital incomes in the total income is:

$$\theta_K = \frac{w_K \cdot K}{Y} = \alpha \tag{3.33}$$

Then for the capital return w_K the following is true:

$$w_K = \alpha \cdot y/k \tag{3.34}$$

Since α (by assumption) and y/k (in long-term steady state) are constant, the marginal product of capital and, therefore, also the capital return w_K must be constant in the long-term steady state. The marginal product of capital is:

$$w_K = \frac{dY}{dK} = \frac{dy}{dk} = \alpha \cdot A \cdot k^{\alpha-1}$$

Taking logarithms and differentiating with respect to time gives:

$$\frac{\dot{w}_K}{w_K} = \frac{\dot{A}}{A} + (\alpha-1) \cdot \frac{\dot{k}}{k} \tag{3.35}$$

If w_K is constant in the steady state, then $\dot{w}_K/w_K$ must be equal to zero. Then, expressed in growth rates, the following is true for (3.35):

$$g_A = (1-\alpha)g_k$$

Here we find that the wanted growth rate for k is dependent on the efficiency gain:

$$g_k = \frac{1}{1-\alpha} \cdot g_A \tag{3.36}$$

Inserting (3.36) into (3.32) gives:

$$g_y = g_A + \frac{\alpha}{1-\alpha} \cdot g_A = g_A\left(1 + \frac{\alpha}{1-\alpha}\right) \tag{3.37}$$

The number one, in brackets on the right-hand side, stands for the efficiency gain; the second term in the brackets is the growth bonus. Herewith the growth bonus, which is also represented in Figure 3.7, is equal to:

$$\frac{\alpha}{1-\alpha} \tag{3.38}$$

The higher the postulated value for the production elasticity of the capital α lies, the higher is the fortifying effect of the induced capital formation for the income on the steady-state growth path. So the growth bonus is dependent on the stipulated production function.

If one assumes positive externalities in the formation of capital (see Chapter 6), then the production elasticity of capital is bigger than in the case of neo-classical assumptions. The same is true if the concept of capital also encompasses human capital (see Box 3.1). In the context of the new growth theory, further points are also of importance for the effect of a one-time increase in efficiency (see from Chapter 6 on, especially Chapter 8).

3.8 CONVERGENCE

In the neo-classical growth theory, income level and productivity level converge into a stable long-term steady state. In this steady state, the relevant entities (per capita production and capital intensity) no longer grow by more than the exogenously given rate of technical progress. In the transition dynamics towards a steady state, backward countries and regions, however, grow faster than those which lie closer to or even in their steady state (see Figure 3.4).

In this way, the convergence process leads to less capital-rich countries and regions catching up with already further developed ones. If – independent of economic parameters such as savings rate, level of technology, population growth and so forth – the income levels and the capital intensities of different countries or regions converge in time, one speaks of 'absolute' convergence.

Figure 3.8 shows, for an international cross-section, that no absolute convergence can be observed in reality. Those countries which showed a low productivity in 1960 did not necessarily grow faster in the following thirty years than the wealthier countries.

In any case, the neo-classical growth model does not predict an absolute, but much more a so-called 'conditional' convergence. Only if all parameters of the model are the same over all countries, do they converge to the same steady state, and only in this case is a clear catching-up of the poorer regions with the richer ones predicted. Statistically speaking: according to neo-classical theory, an absolute convergence is to be observed only if the model parameters are held constant.

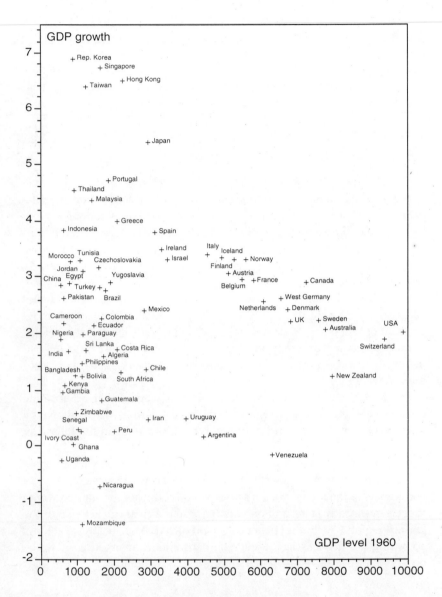

Note: GDP growth rates: real, per annum and per capita, in %; level 1960: real and
           per capita, in US $, at 1985 prices.
Source: Summers/Heston, Penn World Table 5.6

Figure 3.8 Average growth rates, 1960–1990, and income level, 1960

A hypothetical example shows how a richer country (R) can show higher adjustment growth than a poor country (P). The graphs from Figure 3.4 are inserted for both countries in Figure 3.9. Notwithstanding higher capital intensity, country R has a bigger growth rate, because it is further away from its own steady state than country P. In this example, this is caused by differences in the population growth rate, the depreciation rate, the savings rate, and – possibly – in the technology parameter. This is realistic in so far as in reality poorer countries do register a lower per capita capital stock and at the same time a higher population growth. In this way it can be explained in the context of neo-classical theory why Western countries, while rich in capital, can still partly show higher per capita growth rates than certain developing countries.

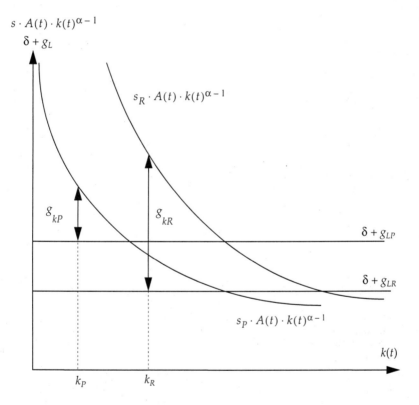

Figure 3.9 *Conditional convergence*

Box 3.2: Empirical Results on Convergence

In the second part of the aforementioned empirical study by Mankiw/Romer/ Weil (1992), it was assumed that the studied countries are in a phase of adjustment to the long-term steady state. In a first attempt, the authors tested for unconditional convergence, that is, the growth rates g_y of the per capita income in the time period 1960–1985 were brought into relationship with the initial level of the per capita income y (1960). In a cross-section with 98 countries, the following estimated result was found:

$$g_y = -0.27 + 0.094 \ln y \ (1960)$$
$$(0.38) \ \ (0.049)$$

OLS estimation, standard error in brackets, R^2 (corrected) 0.03

As has already been seen in Figure 3.8, there is no unconditional convergence of income levels which can be confirmed world-wide. For this sample, the estimation explains nothing about the real development; the coefficient for the initial level even shows the 'wrong' sign. For the sample of the OECD countries, however, the result of this same estimation is quite satisfying, as mentioned in the main text, since these countries show similar economic characteristics.

For the large sample with 98 countries, however, the situation is different if the empirical test concerns conditional convergence as it is predicted for reality by the neo-classical growth model. Also in the same study, the accumulation of human capital (see Box 3.1) was additionally defined by a variable *SCHOOL*. The result of this estimation is:

$$g_y = 3.04 - 0.289 \ln y \ (1960) + 0.524 \ln s - 0.505 \ln (g_L + g_A + \delta)$$
$$(0.83) \ (0.062) (0.087) (0.288)$$
$$ + 0.233 \ SCHOOL$$
$$ (0.060)$$

OLS estimation, standard error in brackets, R^2 (corrected) 0.46

The estimated coefficients have the expected sign and are all significant. The size ranges of the coefficients are also very plausible. The model explains nearly half of the differences in international growth rates; with such big differences between the individual countries, this is a good result. This same model possesses an even greater power of explanation for the conditional convergence of the OECD sample. An R^2 of 0.65 resulted from that estimation.

All in all, the results regarding conditional convergence are quite convincing, although the critique already mentioned in Box 3.1 is valid here, too. Furthermore, it must be mentioned that the enlargement of the neo-classical model by human capital is also an important postulate of the new growth theory (see Chapter 6). It becomes clear that the results shown here do not conflict with the newer theories, if we bear in mind the fact that the new growth theory's goal is to explain endogenously the still exogenous long-term growth rate. On the contrary, it is proved that the variables which are used here are central in all attempts to explain long-term economic development.

The convergence hypothesis has been explored empirically in many different ways. The most prominent paper is by Mankiw, Romer and Weil (1992, see Box 3.2). Here and in many other international cross-section studies, a significant negative relation between the initial level of productivity and subsequent growth has been demonstrated. In order to do this, however, certain model parameters and factors which influence the individual steady state of the countries had to be held constant. Apart from the initial income for example, savings rates (represented by the investment shares) as well as population growth, the depreciation rate and exogenous technical progress are to be regarded as variables which explain growth in the regressions.

This, however, precisely confirms the prediction of conditional convergence, that is, a convergence which is dependent on the model parameters. For the countries of the OECD, an unconditional convergence can be confirmed, as can be supposed by a glance at this group of countries in Figure 3.8. In these countries, the clearly negative connection between initial level and growth probably stems from the strong resemblance shown during the entire time period considered in their savings shares, population growth rates and so forth.

In this context, the convergence speed is also interesting, that is, the speed at which the remaining gap to the long-term steady state is closed. How fast can a country which has not yet reached the steady state or which has been removed from it by a shock (re)reach the steady state?

The convergence speed of per capita capital stock can be determined as follows for the production function $y(t) = A(t)k(t)^\alpha$, which is the Cobb–Douglas form. The change in capital intensity in period t is given by:

$$\dot{k} = s \cdot A(t) \cdot k(t)^\alpha - (\delta + g_L) \cdot k(t) \tag{3.39}$$

The functional form of $\dot{k}$ is reproduced in Figure 3.10. The convergence speed λ is the relation of the change of k in period t to the remaining gap towards the steadystate:

$$\lambda = \frac{\dot{k}_t}{k^* - k_t} \quad (= \tan\varphi) \tag{3.40}$$

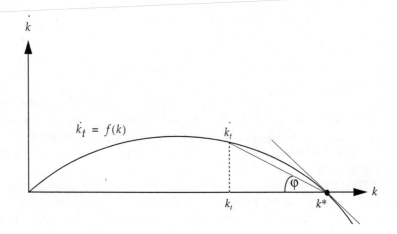

Figure 3.10 Convergence speed

As an approximation, that is to say assuming that the country considered is close to the steady state, the convergence speed can be calculated as the (negative) slope of the $\dot{k}$-function at point k^*. For the production function supposed here, k^* is according to Section 3.3:

$$k^* = \left[\frac{\delta + g_L}{s \cdot A}\right]^{\frac{1}{\alpha - 1}}$$

After insertion of this expression, the (negative) derivative of (3.39) with respect to k yields for k^*:

$$\tilde{\lambda} = (1 - \alpha)(\delta + g_L) \tag{3.41}$$

For example, for the parameter values $\alpha = 0.4$ and $(\delta + g_L) = 0.04$, this would result in a convergence speed of 0.024, that is, the gap to the steady state would close with 2.4 percent of the remaining stretch in every period. Many empirical estimations for convergence, as, for example, that already mentioned one by Mankiw, Romer and Weil, actually do imply a (conditional) convergence speed of about 2 percent.

The percentage share x of the remaining stretch to the long-term steady state is travelled in a certain time T. This time can be defined by dissolving the following formula:

$$(k^* - k_t)(1 + \lambda)^T = (k^* - k_t)(x/100)$$

or,

$$T = \frac{\ln(x/100)}{\ln(1 + \lambda)}$$

The so-called 'half-life of convergence', that is, the time that it takes for half the initial gap to be eliminated ($x = 50$), amounts, for example, with a convergence speed of 2 percent, to about 35 years.

Finally, the fact must be considered that in the Solow model convergence is explained solely by capital accumulation; in reality, however, apart from the adjustment of capital intensities, catching-up processes and convergence processes caused by the adjustment of the technology levels, that is, the variable $A(t)$, do arise as well.

Apart from this, foreign trade, which can be very important for a faster development or higher convergence speed for poorer countries, is not considered in the Solow model (compare with Chapter 8).

3.9 ADDING THE MONETARY SECTOR

The growth models discussed up to now are distinctive because the existence of a monetary sector is not explicitly taken into consideration in the modelling. The reason for this is the hypothesis of long-term neutrality of money. Already in earlier literature, however, money has been represented by certain authors as a factor which has a positive value for economic agents. The demand for money must then be assumed to stem from real needs. Keynes was also of the opinion that certain problems of modern money economies cannot be explained by the assumption of neutrality of money. Integrating a monetary sector into already existing growth models and analysing its effect on the growth process has therefore been attempted in different approaches.

a) The Tobin Model

In the Tobin model, money and physical capital are understood as alternative forms of assets. The neo-classical growth model by Solow with the per capita production function (without time indices) is the starting point:

$$y = f(k) \tag{3.42}$$

The change in capital intensity over time happens according to the already known equation

$$\dot{k} = s \cdot f(k) - (g_L + \delta) \cdot k \tag{3.43}$$

Notation:

- M^d nominal money demand
- m^d real per capita money demand
- P price level
- r nominal interest rate
- m real per capita money supply
- f_k derivative of f with respect to k.

The integration of the monetary sector into this model frame occurs by formulating a money demand function which is correlated positively with per capita income (transactions demand for money) and negatively with the size of the nominal interest rate (speculative demand for money). The real per capita money demand is then:

$$\frac{M^d}{P \cdot L} = m^d(y, r) \tag{3.44}$$

In this money demand function, y corresponds to the per capita output $f(k)$, and the nominal interest rate r is composed of the net marginal product of the capital $(f_k - \delta)$ and the inflation rate g_P. Since it is assumed that the economic agents in this neo-classical model have perfect foresight, the expected inflation always corresponds to the actual inflation. (3.44) can therefore be rearranged in the following way:

$$\frac{M^d}{P \cdot L} = m^d(f(k), f_k - \delta + g_P) = m^d(k, g_P) \tag{3.45}$$

On the steady-state growth path, where the real interest rate $(f_k - \delta)$ remains constant, money demand is then (negatively) dependent on the inflation rate g_P and (positively) on capital intensity k. After taking logarithms of and differentiating this expression with respect to time, changes in the real per capita money supply $m = M/(P \cdot L)$ give:

$$\dot{m} = (g_M - g_P - g_L) \cdot m \tag{3.46}$$

Here, g_M is the growth rate of the nominal amount of money. In the money market equilibrium, the money supply m corresponds to the money demand $m^d(k, g_P)$, and the amount of money held per capita is constant by assumption. Consequently, equation (3.46) can be equalled to zero, and the following condition must apply:

$$g_P = g_M - g_L \tag{3.47}$$

It is assumed that the increase in the money supply occurs through government (per capita) transfer payments, which are denoted by h_T:

$$h_T = g_M \cdot m = \frac{\dot{M}}{P \cdot L} \tag{3.48}$$

The transfer payments augment the available income y_v of the economic agents. This income increase is, however, accompanied by an inflation effect which reduces the cash balances. The actually available per capita income is therefore composed as follows:

$$y_v = f(k) + h_T - g_P m \tag{3.49}$$

Inserting (3.48) gives:

$$y_v = f(k) + (g_M - g_P)m \tag{3.50}$$

By using (3.47) we finally arrive at:

$$y_v = f(k) + g_L \cdot m \tag{3.51}$$

This is the available income on which individuals base their consuming and savings decisions. Income can be further differentiated as regards its use as gross investments and as consumption:

$$Y/L = I/L + C/L \tag{3.52}$$

The gross per capita investments (I/L) can be divided into net investments $\dot{k}$ and a part $(g_L + \delta)k$ for depreciation δk and for the capital equipment of the newly arrived population $g_L k$. So (3.52) becomes:

$$f(k) = \dot{k} + (g_L + \delta) \cdot k + (1 - s) \cdot y_v \tag{3.53}$$

Since $\dot{k} = 0$ in the steady state, inserting (3.51) into (3.53) and transforming yields the following condition:

$$s \cdot f(k) = (g_L + \delta) \cdot k + (1 - s) \cdot g_L \cdot m \tag{3.54}$$

b) Comparison of Tobin and Solow Models

The equation (3.54) corresponds – up to the last term – to the steady-state condition for k in the Solow model. Figure (3.11) renders very clearly the difference between the neo-classical growth model and the model in which the monetary sector is added.

Here attention has to be paid to the fact that, in Figures 3.2 and 3.3, the expressions which are analogous to (3.54) were divided by the savings rates, so that only $f(k)$ remained on the left-hand side. It is, however, immediately apparent that the variant chosen here demands the same process for finding the steady state (see Figure 3.6).

The steady state $k*^S$, which is known from the Solow model, results from the point of intersection between the $sf(k)$ curve and the $(g_L + \delta)k$ straight line. In equation (3.54), it can be seen that the straight line $(g_L + \delta)k$ is shifted upwards by $(1 - s) \cdot g_L \cdot m$ in the Tobin model. Therefore, in the case of real money balances of the size of m_0, there will be a steady-state capital intensity of $k(m_0)^T$.

An expansive monetary policy through transfer payments (g_M increases) now allows inflation and, consequently, also the nominal interest rate to augment, according to (3.47). Following (3.45), this leads to a reduction of the real cash balances to m_1 and, as a consequence, to a new (higher) capital intensity $k(m_1)^T$. So, in this model, an increase in the money supply growth rate actually does have real consequences, which manifest themselves in an increase in capital intensity and in aggregate economic output.

Now, if the money supply increases with constantly growing rapidity and consequently inflation augments constantly, then according to (3.45) the real cash balances will strive towards zero in the limit. Money loses its meaning completely, and the Tobin model 'converges' towards the Solow model.

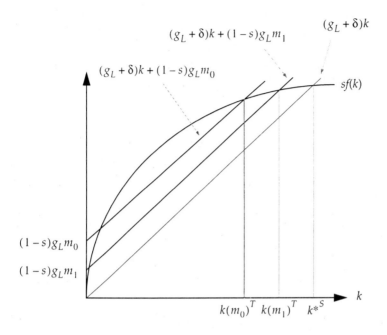

Figure 3.11 Comparison of Tobin and Solow growth models

However, the monetary growth model by Tobin is subject to the following contradiction: the model-conform statement, according to which an economy which is enriched by a monetary sector shows a lower capital intensity than a simple trade economy without money, does not correspond to our expectations. The existence of a financial sector normally leads to a higher efficiency of the capital allocation and should therefore influence the formation of capital positively. The paradoxical result of the Tobin model can be traced to the fact that, besides the integration of money as an additional savings form, the initial assumptions of the Solow model were also simply taken over. Money has no productive function and, moreover, it absorbs savings.

The recognition that money actually does produce a profit when transaction costs are reduced leads to the development of models which take money into consideration as an argument in the utility function or as an input in the production function. With the help of these models, it has been possible to show that the growth path of a monetary economy dominates the growth path of a pure exchange economy without money.

Apart from the enlargements inside a neo-classical model frame, various other models have been developed, mainly models in the Keynesian tradition, allowing for dynamic disequilibria. The Keynesian critique was mainly aimed at the a priori assumed identity of saving and investing in the neo-classical model. This is why independent savings functions and investment functions are formulated in the so-called Keynes–Wicksell models. It is true that in these models it is also assumed that in the long term, savings and investments can be balanced; however, in the short term, for example, assuming an adaptive expectation formation, unexpected price-level fluctuations can lead to market disequilibria. The consequences of these are unemployment and an underutilisation of the capital stock (see Section 9.1).

SELECTED READING

- BALDWIN, R.E. (1989), 'The Growth Effects of 1992', *Economic Policy*, **9**, 247–81.

- BARRO, R.J. and X. SALA-I-MARTIN (1992), 'Convergence', *Journal of Political Economy*, **100** (2), 223–51.

- BARRO, R.J. and X. SALA-I-MARTIN (1995), *Economic Growth*, New York: McGraw-Hill.

- CECCHINI, P. et al. (1988), *The European Challenge 1992*, Aldershot: Gower.

- MANKIW, G., D. ROMER and D. WEIL (1992), 'A Contribution to the Empirics of Economic Growth', *Quarterly Journal of Economics*, **107** (2), 407–37.

- SOLOW, R.M. (1956), 'A Contribution to the Theory of Economic Growth', *Quarterly Journal of Economics*, **70** (1), 65–94.

- TOBIN, J. (1965), 'Money and Economic Growth', *Econometrica*, **33**, 671–84.

4. Intertemporal Optimisation

4.1 SAVINGS DECISION

As already shown in Chapters 2 and 3, savings play an important role in middle-term economic development. In the following discussion, this role will become even more important, since in the context of the newer theories, the saving process can influence the long-term growth path directly (see from Chapter 5 on).

Figure 4.1 shows, for the USA, Japan, Western Germany, France, Italy, the UK and Canada, that in the international cross-section big differences in savings shares can be noted. Japan, for example, traditionally has a high savings activity, while the USA, just as traditionally, is to be found at the lower end of the scale. A savings share with the tendency to decline, however, is common to most of the industrialised countries in the post-war period. Economic, sociological, demographic and institutional facts can be taken as explanations for these observations.

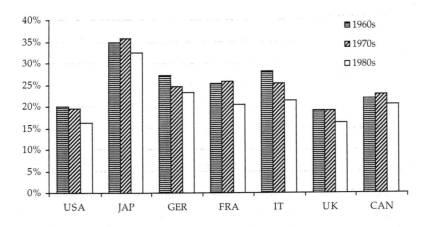

Source: B. Kauffmann 'Microaspects of Saving', in A. Heertje (ed.), *World Savings*, Oxford: Blackwell, 1993.

Figure 4.1 Country-specific differences in savings shares

Accordingly, many influence factors for savings are discussed in the literature. These factors can range from country-specific bequest behaviour to socio-political stability. In the context of the macroeconomic growth theory, for the savings, it is of the greatest importance that individuals choose their intertemporal consumption path through the savings decision. The optimal decision of the households depends upon saving motivations, individual preferences and the economic attractiveness of saving. As regards preferences, two parameters, which have to be held clearly apart, are important: the discount rate and the elasticity of intertemporal substitution (compare with the following Section 4.2).

A large share of the saving is done by the households, either directly by personal saving or indirectly as saving by enterprises which are owned by the households. As Table 4.1 shows using the example of the UK, public savings are relatively small. This is why as a next step the optimisation problem of the private households will be analysed.

Table 4.1 Structure of savings in the example of UK

Gross savings as a ratio of GNP	1960s	1970s	1980s
Savings of the households	5.4%	6.1%	6.0%
Savings of the firms	9.4%	9.2%	10.4%
Public savings	3.6%	2.6%	0.1%
Total savings rate	**18.4%**	**17.9%**	**16.6%**

Source: J. Elmeskov et al., Saving Trends and Measurement Issues, OECD Working Paper No. 105, Paris, 1991.

4.2 UTILITY OF CONSUMPTION IN TIME

In the steady state, the growth rate of consumption is equal to the growth rate of output and savings. By calculating the optimum consumption growth, one can therefore deduce the growth of income. It is for this reason that intertemporal optimisation of the consumption is of the greatest importance for the growth theory.

With rational individuals, saving decisions and consumption decisions take place over many periods. However, for analytical simplification, the economic context can be represented in a two-period model. In Section 4.3, the generalisation for many periods is derived from the two-period representation. The optimisation over an infinite number of time periods is dis-cussed in Box 4.1. In the main text, the following assumptions are made for the time being:

- The optimisation comprises two time periods. A positive wealth at the end of the second time period does not yield any utility; the households therefore use up all their savings in the second period.
- Households supply a fixed amount of labour for a constant wage in both periods. This leads to the fact that the labour incomes of both periods are given exogenously.
- Money can be invested as well as borrowed at a given market interest rate. The household must be able to pay back its credits completely in the second period.

Notation:

- C_1 consumption in the first period
- C_2 consumption in the second period
- r interest rate
- Y_1^L labour income in the first period
- Y_2^L labour income in the second period
- W_1 wealth at the beginning of the optimisation.

In the two-period model, consumption growth is:

$$g_C = \frac{\Delta C}{C} = \frac{C_2 - C_1}{C_1} = g_Y = \frac{\Delta Y}{Y} = \frac{Y_2 - Y_1}{Y_1}$$

The following is also true:

$$\frac{C_2}{C_1} = (1 + g_C)$$

a) The Budget Constraint

In the first period, the household considered receives a labour income of the amount Y_1^L. Besides this, it disposes of an initial wealth W_1. The future labour income Y_2^L is already known, for example, through a fixed contract.

For the derivation of the budget restriction, two variants are possible. Variant 1: If the household consumes less in the first period than its labour income Y_1^L and its property W_1 would allow, then it will invest the rest $Y_1^L + W_1 - C_1$ in the bank. In this way, in the second period, besides its work income Y_2^L, the savings of $(1 + r) \cdot (Y_1^L + W_1 - C_1)$ are at its disposal. Variant 2 on the other hand would be the following case: if wealth W_1 and labour income Y_1^L are not enough for the household, it will have to take out a credit of $C_1 - Y_1^L - W_1$. This will have to be paid back in the second period with an interest of $(1 + r)$, so that for consumption C_2 only $Y_2^L - (1 + r)(C_1 - Y_1^L - W_1)$ remains at its disposal.

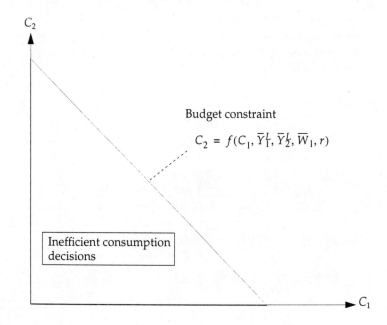

C_2

Budget constraint

$$C_2 = f(C_1, \overline{Y}_1^L, \overline{Y}_2^L, \overline{W}_1, r)$$

Inefficient consumption decisions

C_1

Figure 4.2 Intertemporal budget constraint

With the assumption that in both cases the household uses up in the second period the amounts which are at its disposal for consumption, we arrive at the following relationship for the two variants:

$$C_2 = (Y_1^L + W_1 - C_1)(1 + r) + Y_2^L \qquad (4.1)$$

The dependence of future consumption on the consumption in the first period can be represented as budget constraint in the C_1/C_2 space, see

Figure 4.2. The resulting budget constraint is defined, apart from the interest rate r, by the exogenous variables Y_1^L, Y_2^L and W_1.

The slope of the budget constraint is calculated by differentiating function (4.1) with respect to C_1:

$$\frac{dC_2}{dC_1} = -(1 + r) \tag{4.2}$$

Because of (4.1), the household is constrained in its consumption decision, but this alone does not allow for any explanation of the consumption choice. The optimum is definable only by consulting a utility function.

b) The Discount Rate

In economics, one assumes that individuals value future consumption less than present consumption. This so-called discount has different causes:

- Impatience: Individuals are not inclined to wait long for consumption. Today's consumption means more to them than future consumption.

- Time horizon: Individuals cannot plan for the long term; they have a limited time horizon. The further in the future a consumption stream lies, the less it is included in present decisions.

- Uncertainty: It is a fact that planning for the future always involves uncertainty.

On an aggregate level, that is, from the view point of society as a whole, however, the justification of the discount is strongly disputed. Many scientists (for example Ramsey 1928, from whom the discussion in this chapter stems), think that a positive discount rate is ethically indefensible for society as a whole (see also Chapter 10).

What influence does the discount have on consumption growth? The consumption utility of the second period is discounted with rate ρ. In this way, one compares the utility of the two consumption streams which are different in time at the beginning of the optimisation, and one decides how much will be saved or used in the first period.

Notation:

- $U(C_t)$ utility in period t from consumption in period t

  And so: $U(C_1)$: today's utility of today's consumption
  $U(C_2)$: future utility of future consumption
  $U(C_2)/(1+\rho)$: today's utility of future consumption

- ρ discount rate.

In order to show clearly the difference between the discount rate and the other elements of the utility function, an auxiliary line is introduced into Figure 4.3. A straight line corresponding to the budget constraint is drawn for discount rate ρ, always assuming that the discount rate is smaller than the market interest rate.

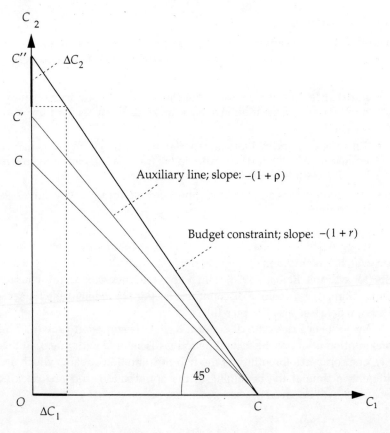

Figure 4.3 Discount rate

The household subjectively values consumption amount OC in the first period as the same as the (bigger) amount OC' in the second period. It can also be observed that the household demands a compensation in the second period of CC' for a consumption renunciation in the first period; the market, however, offers CC''. If the discount rate were the only problem for intertemporal optimisation, then the household would save the entire consumption for the second period and place itself on point C'' because the interest rate is bigger than the discount rate. However, no household will act in this way. Why?

c) Decreasing Utility of Consumption

An additional consumption unit brings an additional utility unit to every household. A decreasing marginal utility of consumption is assumed in economics. This means that the lower the consumption level a household affords to attain, the bigger it will perceive the additional utility. From this follows:

The marginal utility is positive: $U'(C) > 0$
The slope of the marginal utility curve is decreasing: $U''(C) < 0$

In Figure 4.4, the decreasing marginal utility is expressed in the concave course of the utility function, in which utility U appears as a function of consumption C.

In this figure the answer to the question posed in the preceding paragraph is clarified. If a household chose point C'' in Figure 4.3, it could increase its utility if it shifted a part of its consumption from period 2 (ΔC_2) to period 1 (ΔC_1), since $\Delta U_2 < \Delta U_1$, even if $\Delta C_2 > \Delta C_1$. So it can be surmised that there must be an optimum, in which we have $\Delta U_2 = \Delta U_1$ meaning that a shift of consumption from one period to the other does not pay off for a household. This optimum will be discussed in Section 4.3.

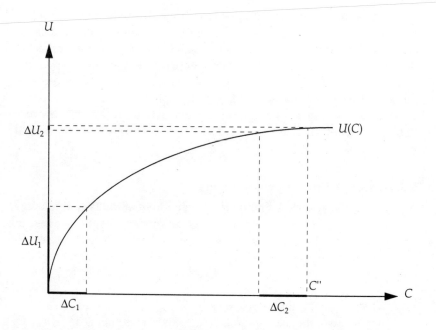

Figure 4.4 Decreasing marginal utility

d) Elasticity of Intertemporal Substitution

A simple utility function results from the addition of the utility in the first and second periods. For simplicity, in this subsection, the discount rate will be zero, to differentiate it from Subsection b). In Section 4.3, all elements of the optimisation will then be brought together. Disregarding the discount rate, the utility function is:

$$U = U(C_1) + U(C_2) \qquad (4.3)$$

In this (additive separable) function, it is supposed that the utility level $U(C_1)$ of consumption C_1 is independent of the size of C_2. This is obviously a simplification. A rich person whose wealth is diminishing (C_1 big) probably does not benefit in the same way from (a fixed) C_2 as a poor person (C_1 small) whose situation is improving.

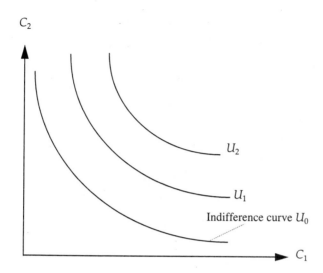

Figure 4.5 Indifference curves

Through the assumptions regarding the utility function, the form of the indifference curves in the C_1/C_2 space is also defined. An indifference curve connects the points of the same utility level. The C_1/C_2 diagram in Figure 4.5 shows these levels, with utility increasing towards the upper right in the diagram.

Utility does not change along an indifference curve, that is, $dU = 0$. Therefore, the slope can be calculated with the total differential of equation (4.3) (with the provisional assumption that $\rho = 0$):

$$\frac{dC_2}{dC_1} = -\frac{\partial U/\partial C_1}{\partial U/\partial C_2} \tag{4.4}$$

On an indifference curve, there are points with different consumption proportions C_2/C_1. Moving along the curve, proportion C_2/C_1 as well as slope dC_2/dC_1 change. The change in the slope of the curve is different depending on the utility function, that is, the form of the indifference curve. The two extreme cases in the Figure 4.6 illustrate this connection.

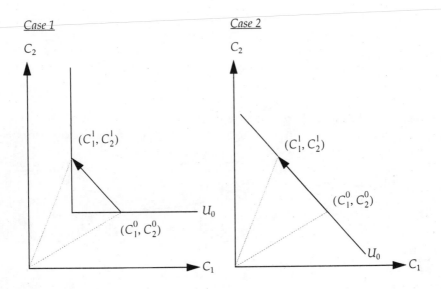

Figure 4.6 Extreme cases of indifference curves

Case 1

The change in consumption proportions from C_1^0/C_2^0 to C_1^1/C_2^1 brings a change of slope from 0 to $-\infty$.

Case 2

The change in consumption proportions from C_1^0/C_2^0 to C_1^1/C_2^1 does not have any effect on the slope.

Elasticity γ, which measures a percentage change in the slope of the curve in connection with a percentage change in the consumption proportion, is a measure for the curvature of the indifference curve.

Mathematically expressed γ is equal to:

$$\gamma = -\frac{d(dC_2/dC_1)/(dC_2/dC_1)}{d(C_2/C_1)/(C_2/C_1)} \tag{4.5}$$

As in the rest of the literature, a minus sign here precedes the expression, so that the value of the elasticity is greater than zero. The frequently quoted elasticity of intertemporal substitution is the inverse value of γ. It indicates how strongly a change in the slope of the indifference curve influences the consumption proportion.

On the intersection of a relatively sharp indifference curve and a budget constraint (thus defining an optimum point), the (optimum) proportion C_2/C_1 will shift only slightly because of a small change in the slope of the budget constraint – the elasticity of intertemporal substitution is relatively small. This kind of utility function, then, expresses the wish for a relatively even distribution or smoothing of consumption over time.

With the help of a mathematical derivation, it can be shown that if the two points in time 1 and 2 converge towards each other, then the marginal value of expression (4.5), for the moment in time t, has the following value:

$$\gamma = -\frac{U''(C_t) \cdot C_t}{U'(C_t)} \tag{4.6}$$

Here $U'(C)$ is the first and $U''(C)$ the second derivative of the utility function with respect to consumption. In non-dynamic literature, the fact that the parameter γ also expresses the risk aversion of the households is used.

4.3 KEYNES–RAMSEY RULE

a) Logarithmic Utility Function

The logarithmic utility function $U(C) = \log C$ represents a particularly comfortable form of a utility function with decreasing marginal utility. In the two-period model, we assume this kind of logarithmic utility function for the representative household and now also take the positive discount rate ($\rho > 0$) into consideration, according to:

$$U(C_1, C_2) = \log C_1 + \frac{1}{1+\rho}\log C_2 \tag{4.7}$$

In this way we arrive at the slope of the indifference curve from totally differentiating this equation with $dU = 0$ as:

$$\frac{dC_2}{dC_1} = -(1+\rho) \cdot \frac{C_2}{C_1} \tag{4.8}$$

In Figure 4.7, the tangential point of the utility indifference curve and the budget constraint shows the optimum distribution of consumption between the two periods. In the optimum, therefore, the slope of the indifference curve corresponds exactly to the slope of the budget constraint $(dC_2/dC_1 = -(1 + r))$.

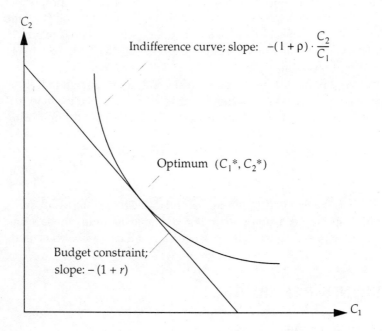

Figure 4.7 shows:
- C_2 (vertical axis)
- Indifference curve; slope: $-(1 + \rho) \cdot \dfrac{C_2}{C_1}$
- Optimum $(C_1{}^*, C_2{}^*)$
- Budget constraint; slope: $-(1 + r)$
- C_1 (horizontal axis)

Figure 4.7 Optimum consumption proportion in the two-period model

In the optimum, the following is true for the two-period model:

$$\frac{C_2}{C_1} = \frac{1 + r}{1 + \rho} \qquad (4.9)$$

The elasticity of intertemporal substitution is not contained in this expression, since it assumes a value of exactly one with a logarithmic utility function (see Subsection c).

b) Discrete and Continuous Growth Rates

The well-known Taylor theorem says that a function can at any differentiable point be expressed by a polynomial. For function e^x the Taylor polynomial is:

$$e^x = 1 + x + \frac{x^2}{2!} + \frac{x^3}{3!} + \dots$$

The growth rates which are relevant in growth theory are mostly very small ($x \ll 1$). This makes it possible to ignore terms of a higher order in the above equation; the result is the approximation:

$$1 + x \cong e^x$$

The smaller the considered time periods become, the better is the approximation to the real value of the function. This is why the transition described here is sometimes also called 'transition to small period length'.

Assuming that $g_C = \Delta C/C = (C_2 - C_1)/C_1 = C_2/C_1 - 1$, then it follows that $C_2/C_1 = 1 + g_C$. Taking logarithms of equation (4.9) then yields:

$$\ln(1 + g_C) = \ln(1 + r) - \ln(1 + \rho)$$

and with the shown approximation, we arrive at the following for the time-continuous growth rate:

$$g_C = r - \rho \tag{4.10}$$

According to this expression, consumption growth is possible when the market interest rate is bigger than the discount rate. The expression corresponds to the simplest form of the Keynes–Ramsey rule, the one with a logarithmic utility function, as well as population growth and a depreciation rate of zero.

c) CES Utility Function

The 'CES function' (constant elasticity of substitution) is often used in theory and empirics. In the dynamical context, the elasticity referred to is the elasticity of intertemporal substitution (which is why it is sometimes called the 'CIES function'). In the two-period approach, the utility function has the following form:

$$U = C_1^{1-\gamma} + \left(\frac{1}{1+\rho}\right) \cdot C_2^{1-\gamma} \tag{4.11}$$

Totally differentiating (4.11) gives the result:

$$dU = (1-\gamma) \cdot (C_1)^{-\gamma} \cdot dC_1 + \frac{1-\gamma}{1+\rho} \cdot (C_2)^{-\gamma} \cdot dC_2 = 0$$

which now allows us to calculate the slope of the indifference curve:

$$\frac{dC_2}{dC_1} = -(1+\rho) \cdot \left(\frac{C_1}{C_2}\right)^{-\gamma} = -(1+\rho) \cdot \left(\frac{C_2}{C_1}\right)^{\gamma}$$

In the optimum, the above expression has to be equal to the slope of the budget constraint ($dC_2/dC_1 = -(1+r)$), so that after transforming we arrive at:

$$\frac{C_2}{C_1} = \left(\frac{1+r}{1+\rho}\right)^{1/\gamma}$$

It must be noted that the exponent $1/\gamma$ corresponds precisely to the elasticity of intertemporal substitution. After transforming discrete growth rates into time-continuous growth rates as in Subsection b), we have:

$$g_C = \frac{1}{\gamma}(r-\rho) \tag{4.12}$$

In this general form of the utility function, consumption growth depends explicitly on the elasticity of intertemporal substitution. The smaller the elasticity, which means that the wish to smooth consumption over time is bigger, the smaller the growth rate that can be reached.

d) Determination of the Interest Rate

The last component for the derivation of the optimum growth path is the investment decision of the enterprises. According to the usual optimisation, all projects are realised that have a return (marginal product of capital *MPK*) which is higher than the interest rate of the required investment capital *r* (= marginal costs of the capital). In the steady state, the return of an additional investment, that is, the marginal product of capital *MPK*, corresponds to the interest rate *r*.

The per capita production function $f(k)$ can also be used instead of the aggregate production function $F(K,L)$ in calculating *MPK*:

$$r = MPK = \frac{dy}{dk} = f'(k)$$

If in (4.10) we substitute $f'(k)$ for r, with a logarithmic utility function we arrive at:

$$g_C = f'(k) - \rho \tag{4.13}$$

and with a CES utility function at:

$$g_C = \frac{1}{\gamma}(f'(k) - \rho) \tag{4.14}$$

In this chapter, depreciation and population growth have not yet been considered. But in order to determine the per capita income in the long-term steady-state growth, the necessary depreciation $\delta \cdot k$ and the investments $g_L \cdot k$ because of population growth have to be subtracted from absolute output $f(k)$:

$$y = f(k) - \delta k - g_L k \qquad \text{or} \qquad \frac{dy}{dk} = f'(k) - \delta - g_L$$

In order to distinguish dy/dk from $f'(k)$, one can designate the first expression as 'net marginal product of capital'. Capital intensity augments only if the profit of an investment is higher than the necessary replacement investments and the extra investments caused by population growth.

For per capita consumption growth, respecting g_L and δ, we arrive with a logarithmic utility function at:

$$g_c = f'(k) - \rho - \delta - g_L \tag{4.15}$$

and with the CES utility function at:

$$g_c = \frac{1}{\gamma}(f'(k) - \rho - \delta - g_L) \tag{4.16}$$

This is the general form of the Keynes–Ramsey rule. Depending on the applied model the equation is simplified by making certain assumptions, for example, neglecting depreciation.

4.4 RAMSEY–CASS–KOOPMANS MODEL

The 'Ramsey–Cass–Koopmans model', often quoted in the literature, is based on intertemporal optimisation as in Section 4.3, as well as on a neo-classical production function in the Solow tradition. Under these assumptions, the golden rule (see Section 3.4) can be modified.

In the long-term steady state without technical progress, per capita consumption amounts to (see equation 3.21):

$$c^* = f(k^*) - (\delta + g_L)k^*$$

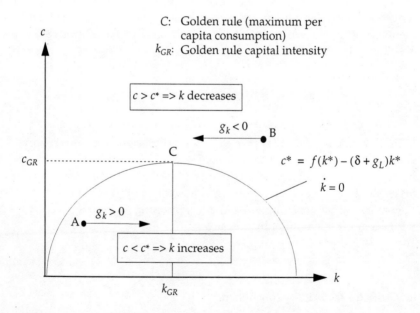

Figure 4.8 k-growth dependent on c

The connection between c and the growth of capital intensity g_k can be represented in a c/k-diagram. All possible steady-state combinations of c and k are represented in Figure 4.9 by the c^*-function, that is, on this curve we have $\dot{k} = s \cdot f(k) - (\delta + g_L) \cdot k = 0$. Maximum consumption in a steady state is reached at point C, at which the (non-modified) golden rule $f'(k^*) = \delta + g_L$ is valid.

If per capita consumption lies over c^*, then the remaining savings $f(k) - c$ do not suffice to finance the investments made necessary by population growth and depreciation. Consequently k will decrease (see point B in Figure 4.8). On the other hand, k will grow if the effective consumption c is smaller than c^* (see point A in Figure 4.8).

The central statement of the Keynes–Ramsey rule is, that consumption growth g_c depends on capital intensity k (see equation 4.16). In the c/k-diagram of Figure 4.9, there is just one single k, marked by k_{KR} (k_{KR}: Keynes–Ramsey capital intensity), that holds per capita consumption c constant, that is, $g_c = 0$. With $k = k_{KR}$ the following is true:

$$f'(k_{KR}) = \delta + g_L + \rho \tag{4.17}$$

This equation corresponds to the modified golden rule, where the discount rate of the households is taken into consideration

With $g_c \neq 0$, the two conditions $k > k_{KR}$ and $k < k_{KR}$ are to be distinguished:

$$k > k_{KR} \Rightarrow g_c < 0 \text{ because } f'(k) < \delta + g_L + \rho \tag{4.18}$$

and

$$k < k_{KR} \Rightarrow g_c > 0 \text{ because } f'(k) > \delta + g_L + \rho \tag{4.19}$$

Box 4.1: Intertemporal Optimisation with an Infinite Horizon

For simplicity, in the main text a two-period framework is assumed for the derivation of the intertemporal optimum. The same result is found with the help of the optimisation with an infinite horizon. For example in the Ramsey–Cass–Koopmans model, we can determine an optimum and infinitely long time path for consumption c (the 'control variable') with the help of the so-called control theory, from which the optimum path of the capital coefficient k (of the 'state variable') results at the same time. An optimal path shows the maximum possible utility for households over time. For this, while taking the discount rate into consideration, the utilities per time period are integrated over the infinitely long time horizon. Here the logarithmic per capita utility function is used for the representation; we then have $u = \log c$ at any moment in time. Total utility $U(0)$ then is determined as follows at moment 0:

$$U(0) = \int_0^{\infty} \log(c(t))dt \cdot e^{-\rho t}$$

The utility maximisation occurs under the restriction that only what is not consumed or used for depreciation can be used for accumulation. Here we apply the simple per capita production function $y = f(k)$; so we have:

$$\dot{k}_t = f(k(t))-c_t-(\delta + g_L)k(t)$$

Additionally, a so-called transversality condition has to be introduced as a restriction. For growth models of this kind, this condition requires that no positive wealth remains at the endpoint of the optimisation, since this would be a waste. In the case of the infinite horizon, the condition is that the value of the capital stock must converge towards zero in the long term. In order to solve the optimisation problem from the viewpoint of the social planner, a costate variable λ is introduced, which represents the opportunity costs of capital formation. In this way, running costs and future benefits of the capital accumulation can be determined; here, contrary to K, λ can quickly jump to another value. The following Hamilton function including the utility function and the restriction for capital accumulation is used to solve the maximisation problem:

$$H(t) = \log(c)dt \cdot e^{-\rho t} + \lambda[f(k)-c-(\delta + g_L)k]$$

In the optimum, the value of H is at its maximum. The first order conditions for an optimum are found, according to the 'maximum'-principle, by differentiating the Hamilton-function with respect to the control and to the state variable. These derivations are applied as follows:

$$H_c = e^{-\rho t} \cdot (1/c)-\lambda = 0 \qquad H_k = \lambda \cdot (f'(k)-\delta - g_L) = -\dot{\lambda}$$

By dissolving the first order conditions, we arrive at:

$$\frac{\dot{c}}{c} = g_c = f'(k)-\delta - g_L - \rho$$

that is, the Keynes–Ramsey rule, which corresponds to the expression in the main text. Detailed explanations as regards dynamic optimisation can be found, for example, in Chiang (1992). The procedure using Hamiltonians is more general than the one in the main text as here the parameter λ is allowed to vary over time and this cannot be expressed with the two-period approach of the main text.

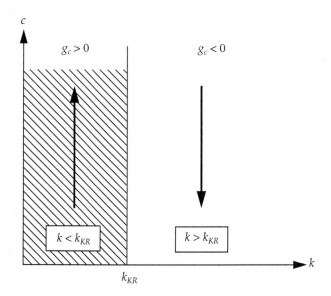

Figure 4.9 g_c *dependent on* k

From a combination of Figures 4.8 and 4.9, the complete phase diagram of the Ramsey–Cass–Koopmans model in Figure 4.10 results. In an economy, the two variables, capital intensity and per capita consumption, develop according to the shaded arrows. These result from a combination of the arrows in Figures 4.8 and 4.9.

Whether a steady state can be reached or not depends on the chosen point of departure. We can see that the starting points A and B do lead to the desired consumption in O; however, with a choice of points A′, A″, B′ or B″ the path converges either towards a consumption or a capital intensity of zero. Obviously this is not an optimum development.

The capital intensity k_{GR}, which is the target of the golden rule, can be realised in the short term; however, this point cannot be a steady state (see arrow starting from B′). The k_{KR}, which is the optimum according to the modified golden rule, is smaller than k_{GR}, since in the context of the Solow model, the golden rule neglects the discount rate ρ. The optimum path AOB is the so-called saddle path; accordingly the model has the characteristic of the so-called saddle path stability; for more details see Barro and Sala-i-Martin (1995, p. 73). Interpreting the result one can assign economic policy a specific role: the government should aim to lead the economy on to the stable saddle path.

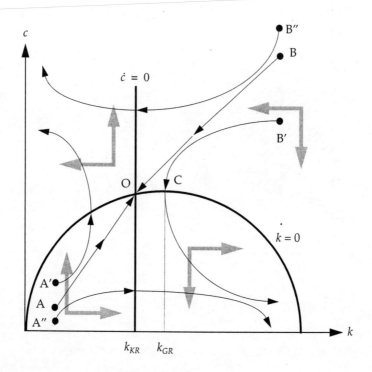

Figure 4.10 Ramsey–Cass–Koopmans model

SELECTED READING

- BARRO, R.J. and X. SALA-I-MARTIN (1995), *Economic Growth*, New York: McGraw-Hill.
- CHIANG, A. (1992), *Elements of Dynamic Optimization*, New York: McGraw-Hill.
- RAMSEY, F. P. (1928), 'A Mathematical Theory of Saving', *Economic Journal*, **38**, 543–59.

5. Positive Spillovers

5.1 ADDITIONAL ELEMENTS IN GROWTH THEORY

In the neo-classical growth theory, the long-term growth rate of an economy is given exogenously. Only the growth rate during the transitional dynamics towards the steady state and the capital intensity in the long-term steady state are determined endogenously. A theory on economic growth, however, should in fact be capable of predicting long-term development of income.

For an adequate enlargement of the theory, it makes sense to have another, closer look at the basic assumptions of the neo-classical growth model. Here the assumptions of a constant savings rate, of a decreasing marginal product of capital and of constant returns to scale in the aggregate production function are of first importance.

Interest-dependent saving is indicated with a view to the demand of the microfoundation of macroeconomics. This, however, does not help in explaining the long term. On the contrary: because the marginal product of capital decreases steadily over time, ceteris paribus the interest returns fall as well. Therefore, with interest-dependent saving, after a certain time the households will give up saving altogether. From that moment on, no further investments are possible and the growth process stops. If we compare the interest-dependent savings rate with the constant savings rate assumed by Solow, it becomes probable, assuming realistic parameter values, that the 'growth train' stops even earlier with an interest-dependent savings rate.

However, the Keynes–Ramsey rule, which was derived in the context of interest-dependent saving, lays the basis for determining the theoretical context. According to this rule, steady-state growth depends on the difference between the marginal product of capital and a constant value, this value being the sum of the discount rate, the depreciation rate and population growth.

Now the 'shortcoming' for the stalling of growth in the neo-classical growth model can be given: it is the assumption of the decreasing marginal product of the accumulated capital. If the marginal product of capital stayed above the value defined in the Keynes–Ramsey rule, a (positive) steady-state growth rate could be reached. Only in this case, interest returns are offered to the households, which leads to savings being made in the long term, too. But as soon as the interest returns are no longer greater than the sum of discount rate, depreciation rate and population growth, according to the Keynes–Ramsey rule, the capital intensity can no longer be augmented.

In the model with a constant savings rate, it is also the marginal product of capital that decides the long-term development of income. As can be clearly seen in the neo-classical model, in the long term, no growth can be made if the marginal product falls over time. However, if the marginal product stays constant and on an adequate level, a long-term endogenous path is achieved even with a constant savings rate. Here, however, the discount rate resulting from the individual optimisation will not appear in the calculation of the steady-state growth rate.

Neo-classical growth theory's third assumption of constant returns to scale in the aggregate production function is not the decisive obstacle for explaining growth endogenously. It must, however, be said that in certain models of endogenous growth, depending on the kind of production factors we are looking at, increasing returns to scale in the aggregate production function can arise (see Section 5.4).

5.2 CONSTANT RETURNS TO CAPITAL

In order to represent the influence of constant returns to capital (more precisely: constant marginal product of capital) simply, we shall first return to the constant savings rate and then study the same effect with interest-dependent savings. In the Solow model with a fixed savings rate and the usual Cobb–Douglas production function, the growth of the capital intensity is equal to (see equation 3.10):

$$g_k = s \cdot A(t) \cdot k(t)^{\alpha - 1} - (\delta + g_L) \tag{5.1}$$

Since α is less than one in the neo-classical growth theory, the term $A(t) \cdot k(t)^{\alpha - 1}$ decreases over time with an increasing capital intensity if the state of technology stays constant ($\dot{A} = 0$). The two terms on the right-hand side of (5.1) will then arrive at the same size at a certain moment, so that the growth rate of the capital intensity will be zero. Graphically expressed, an intersection point between the two geometrical loci which represent the two terms has to arise (see Figure 3.4).

If, however, the marginal product of capital, which has been multiplied by the savings rate s is constant or approaches a constant which lies above

$(\delta + g_L)$, then the capital intensity grows endlessly over time. The following two simple production functions allow for unlimited growth:

$$Y(t) = D \cdot K(t) \tag{5.2}$$

$$Y(t) = D \cdot K(t) + F(K(t), L(t)) \tag{5.3}$$

According to production function (5.2), the marginal product of capital is constant and takes the value D. From now on, the variable D will often be used as a scale variable instead of the parameter A, since in certain following models, technical knowledge A will be included for simplicity as knowledge capital under the general term capital with variable K or a similar expression. D can be introduced either as constant or as a function of certain other variables, depending on the model. In the literature, however, the original A is often used and a model with a function according to (5.2) is called an 'AK model' (see Rebelo 1991).

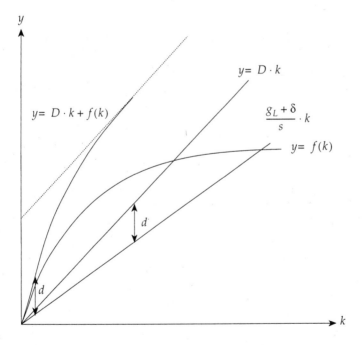

Figure 5.1 Unlimited growth I (constant savings rate)

Function F in (5.3) has the usual neo-classical properties, that is, it produces a decreasing marginal product of capital. Therefore, production function (5.3) also exhibits a decreasing marginal product of capital; however, in the course of time, marginal productivity converges towards D. In per capita notation, the two production functions shown in Figure 5.1 are:

$$y(t) = D \cdot k(t) \tag{5.4}$$

$$y(t) = D \cdot k(t) + f(k(t)) \tag{5.5}$$

Since no point of intersection between the two geometrical loci arises, that is, distance d never equals zero in Figure 5.1, the growth of the capital intensity and, in connection with it, the growth of the per capita income are unlimited in these two cases. Growth depends upon different model parameters; in other words, we now succeed in endogenously explaining growth rate by theory.

Following Section 3.3 the growth rate of capital intensity can also be represented directly as in Figure 5.2; in this way, unlimited growth is even more clearly visualised. The long-term growth of capital intensity with a constant savings rate shown in Figure 5.2 is found for equation (5.4), by introducing the marginal productivity D instead of $A(t) \cdot k(t)^{\alpha-1}$ in (5.1). The same is true for the production function (5.3), since here the marginal productivity converges towards D in the long term. The growth rate is:

$$g_k = s \cdot D - (\delta + g_L) \tag{5.6}$$

This growth can be calculated directly from (5.4); an economy then always finds itself on the steady-state growth path. For (5.3), the calculated growth occurs only after a phase of adjustment in the long term; it arises as in the Ramsey–Cass–Koopmans model.

With the interest-dependent savings rate, it is also the constant marginal product of capital which renders a long-term positive growth possible in the model. If we apply the simple production function (5.2) again, then, according to the Keynes–Ramsey rule (see Section 4.3), we shall arrive at the following result for steady-state growth rate g:

$$g = D - (\delta + g_L + \rho) \tag{5.7}$$

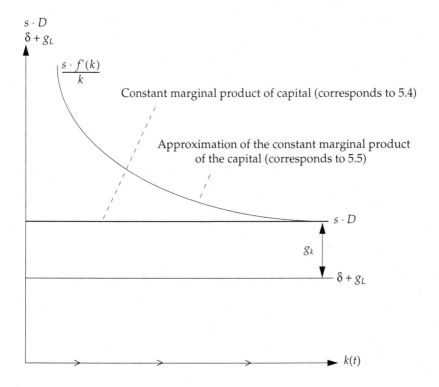

Figure 5.2 Unlimited growth II (constant savings rate)

As mentioned in the text above, the growth rate is positive when the marginal product of capital assumes (or approaches) a constant D, which is bigger than the sum of depreciation rate, population growth and discount rate.

Theory must now elucidate the question whether the assumption of marginal products of capital which are constant in the long term is realistic. In other words: does the attainable product of capital stay constant even if more and more capital is accumulated in the course of time? The answers to this question can be found if:

- the term 'capital' is looked at more precisely
- positive 'spillovers' are introduced into the theory.

❏ With regard to 'capital' it is only privately invested physical capital that is decisive for growth, but in general all forms of capital or capital-like stocks which show a productive value for an economy can be understood as production factors. Apart from physical capital, that is, machines, equipment and buildings, the other most important forms of capital are human capital, knowledge capital as well as the capital which is offered by the government, that is, public infrastructure.

Depending on the question posed, several or all of these capital components have to be taken into consideration for an adequate representation of the aggregate production restriction. Under very general conditions, the accumulation of an individual component in the course of time leads to an increase in the productivity of the other components. In this way, the incentive for accumulating these other components is heightened.

❏ With regard to positive 'spillovers'; Various economic activities lead as a 'side product'– that is, without direct compensation through the market – to augmentations of certain capital inputs such as, for instance, public knowledge or human capital. These impacts are positive external effects and are called positive spillovers (see chapter title) in growth literature.

Through the interdependence caused by spillovers, a cumulative process occurs, which, as a whole, influences growth in an economy positively. In the following paragraph, the spillover mechanisms in the growth process will be presented separately according to the knowledge, public services and human capital factors.

As a consequence of these two elements, the assumption of the constant marginal product of 'capital' as a whole becomes very plausible in the long run, as will be seen in the following models. What follows from this is that all components with a capital character accumulate sufficiently strongly in the course of time, to cause an ongoing growth. In the models, the growth rate is determined as an endogenous variable; it is dependent on production technology, preferences and economic policy.

5.3 DIFFERENT KINDS OF SPILLOVERS

a) Knowledge as Input and Output of the Production Process

In explaining endogenous growth processes, knowledge or knowledge capital has a special meaning. Therefore, a microeconomic foundation for model-endogenous representation of knowledge as input and as output of productive processes is required first.

Every enterprise activity needs a knowledge base, which consists of the knowledge necessary for production or the 'know-how'. Apart from the employees' increasing experience, this basic knowledge can also be extended through external sources such as industry-specific magazines, market previews and so forth. Knowledge is a productive input and should be included in the production function as such. The extent of necessary firm-specific knowledge, however, varies greatly between different industries, countries and periods.

In reality, the total knowledge is not given from outside, as it is in the neo-classical growth model, but augments through certain activities of individuals and enterprises, which act under market conditions, whereby a considerable part of the productive value of new information normally benefits the authors of a corresponding activity. Under market conditions, enterprises and individuals will be willing to extend their knowledge if the resulting benefits can at least cover the costs arising.

For instance, when investing in research as a knowledge-increasing activity, the investors receive new information directly. In research, in particular, indirect results can also be expected, for example, when it becomes known, after a research achievement, which paths did not lead to a result. Indirect results arise because it becomes clear which information sources were especially fruitful. This additional information can also be regarded as additional knowledge for the next research activity; it renders the following research more productive. An important hypothesis of the new growth theory states: usable knowledge capital is also produced as a 'side product' of a great number of private and government activities.

The significance of such learning effects is massively increased if we also consider the transfer of knowledge or knowledge diffusion. Through different channels, a certain share of the new information which was created under market conditions also falls to others. This means that the circle of those who benefit from new information can be very large. This positive influence of some on the activities of others constitutes, in the realm of knowledge, the mechanism of positive spillovers. In the exchange of knowledge, the decisive element is that knowledge, in contrast to private goods, can be used by many persons and enterprises simultaneously.

In business life and in research, positive spillovers in the form of knowledge transfer occur in many different ways. It is the market, above all, which accelerates knowledge exchange. This applies because the marketing of ideas in the shape of products leads to an acceleration of the information exchange among the participants of the market. As soon as a product appears on the market, all interested circles can look at all the aspects of the product and learn many things which can then be used productively by competing enterprises in their own production. In concrete cases, we should investigate which activities are especially learning intensive and how big is the circle of information spread. Furthermore, depending on their nature, different kinds of information are transferred with varying degrees of ease or difficulty.

In the terminology of public finance, the characteristics of the knowledge factor which are important for an endogenous growth can be determined as follows:

- The knowledge factor has the property of non-rivalry.
- The knowledge factor has the property of partial non-excludability.

Knowledge exhibits the properties of public goods, which are complete non-rivalry and non-excludability. Simultaneous use of knowledge by all interested circles is possible because of its property of non-rivalry. The property of partial non-excludability becomes decisive when one looks at the incentives for the creation of new knowledge. If, for example, excludability is given only minimally or not at all, then the incentives for a private supply of corresponding output are too small. The individuals will try to benefit from the services of others by free riding. From the point of view of welfare theory, the supply level reached through private initiative is too small in such cases. Here, a possible supply by the government must be evaluated.

If, however, excludability is partially given, the incentives for knowledge accumulation under market conditions are intact and at the same time, the productive effect of knowledge formation is multiplied by the diffusion of non-excludable knowledge.

If we consider an entire economy, it follows that the knowledge level augments continually with an increasing investment activity. As well as the physical capital, knowledge capital simultaneously accumulates on all levels. Because of this effect, the stock of knowledge which is publicly available and can therefore be used productively by all increases in the course of time. Institutional and organisational knowledge as well as technical knowledge can be subsummarised under the heading 'knowledge'.

The interdependence between productive activity, increase in the stock of knowledge and resulting increase in productivity corresponds to the idea of 'learning by doing' which was introduced into the newer economic literature by Arrow (1962). Arrow postulated a positive connection between the accumulation of physical capital and the public knowledge stock. Private net investments increase directly the available stock of private physical capital and indirectly – through learning effects in production, that is, through spillovers – the publicly available knowledge capital (see also Section 6.1).

b) Public Services

In fields of little excludability of services – as already mentioned – the incentives for private supply are low. Many of these goods and services are therefore provided by the government. Public services – for example, in the fields of basic research and infrastructure, but also in a larger sense in the field of legal security – clearly have a productive value for private enterprise. In the case of the supply by the government, the situation is different in that financing can rely on the tax monopoly of the state.

Normally, the tax revenues increase with a growing economy. The following mechanism, then, plays the decisive role during the growth process: an increasing productivity on the part of the private sector makes increasing tax revenues possible; this normally leads to an increase or improvement in the supply of productive public services, which again positively influences private activities. In other words and in connection with knowledge diffusion, it can be said that, via tax revenues and government supply, productive activities by private enterprises produce positive spillovers, which have a positive influence on growth. Contrary to knowledge transfer, however, this kind of spillover only functions because of a particular institution, the government's tax sovereignty.

For this kind of growth, it is necessary that the government should efficiently transpose the tax revenues into productive services for the private enterprise, and that the tax system should not limit the incentives for creating private profits too strongly. The interdependence between private capital and public services will be discussed more extensively in Section 6.2.

c) Human Capital

In a growing economy, the possibilities of making investments in education and, in that way, augmenting the stock of human capital, increase. In the field of education, learning effects and positive spillovers are also very plausible. It is reasonable that learning is easier the higher the individual knowledge stock already is. Learning is also more efficient the better the instructors in the education field are trained.

This means that individual education yields not only an internal profit but also benefits for others. These benefits are valid inside the education sector, but also have effects on the other sectors of an economy. Building on this fact, it can be assumed in a simple growth model that the marginal product of human capital is constant in the long run and so makes endogenous growth possible (see Section 6.3).

d) Accumulation in an Overview

Figure 5.3 shows an overview of the connection between the accumulation of different factors and income.

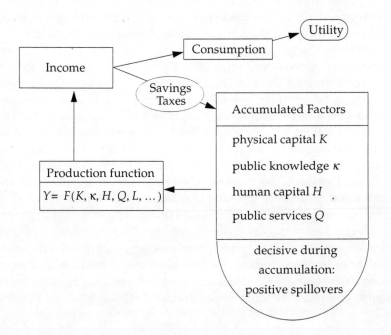

Figure 5.3 Accumulation and income

5.4 CONSTANT AND INCREASING RETURNS TO SCALE

The possibility of explaining long-term growth endogenously is often seen to be connected with the existence of increasing returns to scale in the aggregate production function. Even if these are often used in the new growth theory, they *are not* a necessary condition for endogenous growth.

Increasing returns to scale result when one bases the consideration on the following reflection. A general production function is:

$$Y = A \cdot \tilde{X} \tag{5.8}$$

Here A represents the level of the knowledge as in the preceding chapters, and $\tilde{X}$ captures production factors such as labour and capital. The difference between these two arguments in this production function lies in the excludability and the rivalry. Variable A is primarily, as discussed above, non-rival, while the other inputs such as normal private goods are in complete rivalry.

For the rival inputs together, the so-called 'replication argument' is plausible: if the input amounts in labour and capital are ceteris paribus doubled, the output also doubles; the degree of homogeneity is exactly equal to one. When expressing this same fact algebraically with the multiplying factor a, we arrive at:

$$a \cdot Y = A \cdot a \cdot \tilde{X} \tag{5.9}$$

An expansion of the knowledge is not necessary for the shown increase of Y, since the additional rival inputs can use the existing non-rival A just as well as the already existing rival inputs.

Let us assume now that the knowledge input can be voluntarily expanded by the market participants. If knowledge is additionally multiplied by factor a, then the following is true:

$$a \cdot Y < a \cdot A \cdot a \cdot \tilde{X} = a^2 \cdot A \cdot \tilde{X} \tag{5.10}$$

In this way it can be seen that with active knowledge increase, this production function shows increasing returns to scale; here the degree of homogeneity is greater than one. It also becomes clear that – if the production of additional knowledge is not cost free – then the rival inputs cannot be paid for with their marginal product.

Box 5.1: Empirical Determination of Knowledge Diffusion

The diffusion of knowledge is a process which is mostly invisible. There are no data or statistics which give information on knowledge diffusion. However, there are a few procedures which allow an approach to the phenomena in reality. We differentiate between direct and indirect procedures.

A direct procedure consists in determining the advance knowledge research results are based on. A study by Jaffe, Trajtenberg and Henderson (1993) concentrates on patents, which contain a large amount of new knowledge by definition. Patents have to quote existing patents, the knowledge of which was used for the finding of the results to be newly patented. In this way it can be determined, over the analysis of the citations, how the information spreads in time and space in the research field. As a result, for the case of the USA, the authors find that the diffusion of knowledge is of great importance. The diffusion does, however, happen in regionally limited spaces. It is shown in this examination as well that the more time that has passed since the patenting, the further the information has spread.

Indirectly, the diffusion of knowledge can be determined by the fact that certain enterprises or industries become more productive through the business activities of other enterprises or industries. It should, however, be noted that apart from the knowledge diffusion, other effects also play a role here. The following procedure was proposed by Coe and Helpman (1995) for the case of international knowledge diffusion. A knowledge capital stock can be constructed for each country by counting the investments in research and development and by assuming a depreciation rate for the knowledge stock which is augmented by R&D. With the help of the regression analysis, we can then examine how much the total factor productivity (TFP) of a country depends on the knowledge capital within the country (S^d) and how strongly it depends on the foreign knowledge capital (S^f). Here the total factor productivity was calculated with the help of an auxiliary calculation based on a simple neo-classical production function.

For a pool sample with data from the period between 1971 and 1990 from 22 countries, the following estimation result was found:

$$\text{TFP} = \text{const} + \underset{(0.010)}{0.095} \log S^d + \underset{(0.017)}{0.082} \log S^f$$

Standard error in brackets, R^2 (corrected) 0.47

According to this estimation both knowledge stocks have the expected significant influence on total factor productivity.

This simple estimation was further refined by the authors, by, for example, differentiating between G7 countries and other countries, or by multiplying foreign countries' influences with the import share of goods. The result of these calculations was that the G7 countries can benefit more from their own research efforts than the economically less important countries. It was also found that about a quarter of the profit from research expenses in G7 countries goes to foreign firms. However, according to the results, for smaller countries, the effect of the foreign knowledge stock can be greater than that of their own knowledge stock.

However, increasing returns to scale are not a necessary condition for the new growth theory. Only the condition of non-decreasing marginal products of the factors which can be accumulated under market conditions, which we generally summarise under the term 'capital', is necessary. Whether this means constant or increasing returns to scale depends on the role given to the remaining factors, such as labour, land or energy, in the production function.

This can be shown as follows. If we combine all factors with capital characteristics to form the variable $\tilde{K}$, then the simplest general and already familiar production function is:

$$Y = D \cdot \tilde{K} \tag{5.11}$$

This production function has constant returns to scale if D is interpreted as a constant, which makes the variables Y and $\tilde{K}$ comparable to each other. Then the doubling of a capital input leads exactly to a doubling of the output. This production function does not need to be seen as incomplete, since the factor labour can be contained as human capital in the general term 'capital'. The 'raw' labour force given by nature is not considered separately; only the human capital contained in the labour force has a productive nature (see Section 6.3).

The presented production function has increasing returns to scale if D includes factors such as land and 'raw' labour force and so forth (factors which cannot be accumulated under market conditions), because then a proportional increase in all inputs leads to an over proportional increase in the output. For example, if

$$D = L^{\phi} \tag{5.12}$$

then the doubling of all inputs leads to a more than double increase in the output, under the condition that $\phi > 0$.

An additional observation must be made on the subject of market forms which are possible in the presence of positive spillovers and factor compensations which lie below the marginal product. Positive spillovers are positive externalities, that is, the agents of the spillover-producing activities are not compensated for the spillovers from the market. In other words, according to the new growth theory, the growth process is possible mostly because there is a market failure. This is true for knowledge diffusion and the spreading of human capital above all.

A similar case applies for public infrastructure. Here the idea is that as many (members of the state) as possible benefit from the services, in other words, that the external benefits should be as great as possible. In this case, the goal is optimising the public input according to welfare analysis.

The market form of perfect competition can be kept, in a simplified form, in the new theory according to the neo-classical growth model, if knowledge production results exclusively from externalities of the current business activities, for example, from investment in physical capital. With the additional assumption that the individual market participant is relatively unimportant in comparison to the total market, constant or increasing, but not decreasing average costs can be assumed on the level of the individual enterprise. This means that maximisation of profit is feasible under normal conditions. An individual small enterprise can feel only marginally that its own activity increases the stock of total public knowledge over positive spillovers and that this helps render the future business activities more productive. On the aggregate economic level, however, positive spillovers lead to an increase in knowledge capital which can be generally felt, and consequently to sinking average costs. Long-term sinking of costs on an aggregated level, then, is the decisive stimulant for growth.

The market form of imperfect competition should be introduced when activities (such as research and development) are not compensated directly over the market. In this case, a certain monopoly power is necessary to the enterprises, in order for them to be able to pay for these activities out of the profit.

5.5 INGREDIENTS OF NEW GROWTH THEORY

The 'new growth theory' is a research programme in the neo-classical tradition, which was initiated by authors such as Romer (1986 and 1989), Lucas (1988), Barro (1990), Grossman and Helpman (1991) and Rebelo (1991) towards the end of the 1980s. What the models of the new growth theory have in common is that the long-term growth rate of an economy is explained endogenously.

Positive spillovers, which strengthen the growth process as learning effects, are an important building block for the microeconomic foundation of the theory. Spillovers are technological externalities, since they enlarge the production possibilities of others without market compensation.

In different models, varying capital components are in the foreground, while others are left out, depending on the field of application. Even with a limited choice in the kind of capital, it is true that the marginal value of capital used in the model must, all in all, be constant in the long term for endogenous growth. If one inserts this marginal product into the Keynes–Ramsey rule, the economic growth can be calculated directly. Table 5.1 is useful for a review of the above theories.

Table 5.1 An overview of the different models

Theories	Factor input relation	Savings rate	Long-term growth
Harrod/Domar	fixed	fixed	exogenous
Neoclassics/ Solow	flexible	fixed	exogenous
Ramsey/Cass/ Koopmans	flexible	depending on interest rate	exogenous
New growth theory	flexible	depending on interest rate	endogenous

The rest of the process now consists in introducing, one after the other, the different theories with positive spillovers and an endogenous growth path. With each model one single cause of long-term growth will be more closely observed. It is understood, however, that for transposition into reality, all causes together decide the long-term growth path.

In Chapter 6, the factors knowledge capital, public services and human capital will be introduced, with their contribution to the growth process. Then in Chapter 7, probably the most important field containing positive knowledge diffusion, the research sector, will be integrated into the growth theory. Further applications concern growth in open economies and the issue of sustainable growth.

SELECTED READING

- ARROW, K.J. (1962), 'The Economic Implications of Learning by Doing', *Review of Economic Studies*, **29** (1), 155–73.
- BARRO, R.J. (1990), 'Government Spending in a Simple Model of Endogenous Growth', *Journal of Political Economy*, **98** (5), S103–S125.
- COE, S. and E. HELPMAN (1995), 'International R&D Spillovers', *European Economic Review*, **39** (5), 859–87.
- GROSSMAN, G. and E. HELPMAN (1991), *Innovation and Growth in the Global Economy*, Cambridge Mass.: MIT Press.
- JAFFE, A., M. TRAJTENBERG and R. HENDERSON (1995), 'Geographic Localization of Knowledge Spillovers as Evidenced by Patent Citations', *Quarterly Journal of Economics*, **108**, 577–98.
- LUCAS, R.E. (1988), 'On the Mechanics of Economic Development', *Journal of Monetary Economics*, **22** (1), 3–42.
- REBELO, S. (1991), 'Long Run Policy Analysis and Long Run Growth', *Journal of Political Economy*, **99**, 500–21.
- ROMER, P.M. (1986), 'Increasing Returns and Long-run Growth', *Journal of Political Economy*, **94** (5), 1002–37.
- ROMER, P.M. (1989), 'Capital Accumulation in the Theory of Long Run Growth, in R. Barro (ed.), *Modern Business Cycle Theory*, Cambridge Mass.: Harvard University Press.

6. Endogenous Growth with Different Capital Stocks

In Chapter 5, the meaning of positive spillovers or 'learning by doing' for the growth process was emphasised. Spillovers constitute the theoretical foundation of a constant marginal product of capital, which is of central importance for endogenous growth. Through spillovers, public knowledge capital is formed, public services are increased, and human capital grows, which promotes growth in general. Disaggregating the capital stock into more than one component in models of endogenous growth therefore suggests itself. The basic idea of spillovers can only be adequately illustrated in a model with different capital stocks.

In the concrete theories about endogenous growth, it must be defined how spillovers can function. As regards the knowledge factor, the questions must now be asked: which activities generate learning effects and who can profit from these effects? The original idea of Arrow (1962) referred to the learning from investment activities which he observed in the airframe industry.

The concept of spillovers can also be applied to other industries and fields. Depending on the application, the circle of beneficiaries of spillovers must be drawn wider than one industry, so that it can, for instance, encompass all economic agents in one country, or even in other countries.

The following three sections show the most important kinds of models of the new growth theory. Different kinds of capital are analysed with their influence on long-term growth, namely knowledge capital, public services, and human capital. The extension of positive knowledge spillovers to the field of research and development, of first importance for growth, will follow in the next chapter.

6.1 KNOWLEDGE SPILLOVERS FROM PRIVATE INVESTMENTS

In the first class of theories about endogenous growth, physical and knowledge capital are simultaneously integrated into the macroeconomic production function. If we first consider the production function of enterprise i and, following neo-classical tradition, introduce the term A for total factor productivity, the output Y of firm i is dependent on inputs K and L according to:

$$Y_i(t) = A(t) \cdot F[K_i(t), L_i(t)] \tag{6.1}$$

If the concept of 'learning by doing' is applied to investment in physical capital, the knowledge capital of an industry or an economy at time t depends on the sum of all past net investments of the enterprises considered. If investments increase knowledge capital proportionally, knowledge or experience κ at time t is:

$$\kappa(t) = \sum_{T=0}^{t} I(T) \tag{6.2}$$

Furthermore, the intensity η by which experience influences total factor productivity must be defined. A general expression is:

$$A(t) = \kappa(t)^\eta \qquad \text{with } \eta < 1 \tag{6.3}$$

Each firm's knowledge is a public good so that the knowledge stock for all firms is equal to total knowledge. Using a Cobb–Douglas form and inserting (6.3) in (6.1) we obtain for the individual firm:

$$Y_i(t) = K_i(t)^\alpha \cdot L_i(t)^{1-\alpha} \cdot \kappa(t)^\eta \tag{6.4}$$

The aggregate production function then becomes:

$$Y(t) = K(t)^\alpha \cdot L(t)^{1-\alpha} \cdot \kappa(t)^\eta \tag{6.5}$$

In per capita terms, (6.5) is as follows:

$$y(t) = k(t)^\alpha \cdot \kappa(t)^\eta$$

For further analysis, it is useful to express the knowledge stock in units of capital intensity k. In the assumed proportional relation, the entire knowledge as a sum of past investments equals the entire capital stock, that is,

$$\kappa(t) = K(t)$$

Following (6.3), total factor productivity in per capita terms is:

$$\kappa(t)^\eta = K(t)^\eta = k(t)^\eta \cdot L(t)^\eta$$

For the per capita income, this results in:

$$y(t) = k(t)^{\alpha + \eta} \cdot L(t)^\eta$$

The existence of spillovers leads to a difference between the private marginal product and the social marginal product of capital. It is postulated that the individual firm is small in proportion to the total market and therefore cannot noticeably influence total knowledge capital. Then, private firms take into consideration only the returns on the additional private capital stock. In individual optimisation, the returns which result from higher knowledge capital are neglected. The private marginal product of capital MPK_P is calculated by taking the derivative of Y_i with respect to K_i in (6.4) while κ is exogenous for the individual firm. Using $\kappa = K$ and per capita terms, MPK_P becomes:

$$MPK_P = \alpha \cdot k(t)^{-(1-\alpha-\eta)} \cdot L(t)^\eta \qquad (6.6)$$

On the aggregate level, however, the accumulation of knowledge cannot be neglected. In the social marginal product of capital, denoted by MPK_S, the increase in public knowledge entailed by investments is therefore also contained. Again using $\kappa = K$ and taking the derivative of Y with respect to K in (6.5), MPK_S is given by the following expression:

$$MPK_S = (\alpha + \eta) \cdot k(t)^{-(1-\alpha-\eta)} \cdot L(t)^\eta \qquad (6.7)$$

Private marginal product and interest rate become identical in market conditions of perfect competition. Inserting the private marginal product into the Keynes–Ramsey rule (see Section 4.3) yields the growth rate for this model. Assuming a logarithmic utility function and setting the depreciation and the population growth rate equal to zero leads to:

$$g(t) = \alpha \cdot k(t)^{-(1-\alpha-\eta)} \cdot L(t)^\eta - \rho \qquad (6.8)$$

Thus three different cases can be discussed:

- $\alpha + \eta < 1$: As in the neo-classical model, the growth process stalls since the entire capital (physical and knowledge capital) shows a decreasing marginal product. Even the fact of increasing returns to scale in the production function does not alter this.

- $\alpha + \eta = 1$: The marginal product of capital is constant. From this model, the constant growth rate results:

$$g(t) = \alpha \cdot L(t)^{\eta} - \rho \qquad\qquad (6.9)$$

- $\alpha + \eta > 1$: The marginal product of capital increases with increasing k. Here the rate of growth also increases steadily. This is clearly unrealistic and will therefore not be considered further.

In expression (6.9), L is a scale variable which influences the rate of growth. This does not, however, coincide with reality, since highly populated countries do not on average grow faster than others. In a refined analysis, it is human capital which must be focused on as a scale variable connected with labour (see Section 6.3).

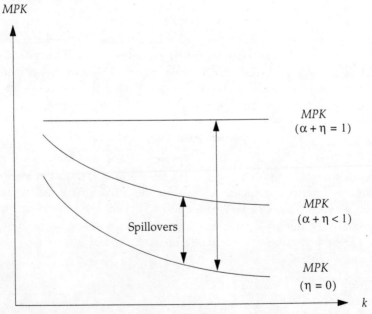

Figure 6.1 The marginal product of capital

The marginal product of capital without spillovers as well as the two cases with spillovers are shown in Figure 6.1. The marginal product of capital and the long-term growth rate are constant only if the two parameters add up to one (that is, $\alpha + \eta = 1$).

The difference between private and social marginal product of capital can also be shown as in Figure 6.2, where the marginal product of capital and the growth rate are represented on both axes. Using a logarithmic utility function, the Keynes–Ramsey rule results in a straight line with the value on the vertical axis being the discount rate. In the case of constant endogenous growth, the marginal product of capital is constant.

As can be deducted from Figure 6.2 for the case of $\alpha + \eta = 1$, the economic 'optimal' growth (g_s) in the presence of positive externalities is greater than the one which is reached under market conditions (g_p). This statement might have to be modified later, when negative externalities of the investments (for example, pollution) are considered as well (see Chapter 11).

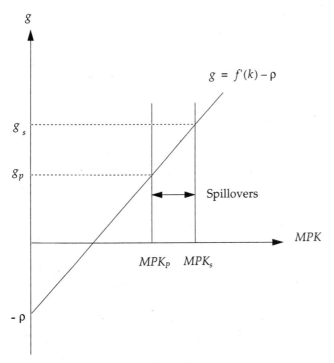

Figure 6.2 Market equilibrium and social optimum

Box 6.1: Empirics on Investment and Growth

The connection between the investment share and long-term growth has already been pointed out in the first chapter (see Figure 1.3). DeLong and Summers (1991) is an empirical study on this theme. Based on the history of economics, the influence of investment is first described qualitatively in this investigation. Then, the authors turn to quantitative analysis. They study the influence of equipment investments (i_e), non equipment investments (i_s), population growth (g_L) and a 'gap'-variable (y_{gap}) on the growth of different economies. Investments are measured as investment shares, that is, as shares of total income. The 'gap' variable measures the income distance between a given country and the USA during the starting period.

For the percentage growth rate of income per worker (g) in the period between 1960 and 1985 for a cross-section of 25 highly developed countries, the following estimated value was found:

$$g = 0.337\, i_e - 0.015\, i_s - 0.002\, g_L + 0.030\, y_{gap}$$
$$(0.054) \quad (0.033) \quad (0.146) \quad (0.009)$$

Standard errors in brackets, R^2 0.662

The result shows that equipment investments have an important and significant influence on economic growth. According to the estimate, an additional percentage point of investment in equipment brings a third of a percentage point of additional growth.

On the other hand, the influence of non equipment investments on long-term economic development is not significant in this study. Nor does population growth have a significant influence on growth in this sample. What does, however, seem important for the explanation of g is the specific difference in income level between a country and the USA, which mirrors a kind of convergence towards the leader of the post-war era. The authors also undertook these same estimates for other periods and other countries. The important and significant influence of equipment investments on growth always remains valid. However, the quality of the estimates declines considerably in further samples.

The questionable causality of the influence presents an important objection to this result. According to the accelerator theory of investments, the causality runs in the opposite direction, from growth rate to investments. As has been expressed in Section 6.1 based on new growth theory, growth rate and investment share are determined simultaneously. This happens depending on parameters and factors of the production and the utility function. In Chapters 6, 7 and 8, further such factors will be introduced into the theory.

Furthermore, the study is not quite satisfactory because the variables seem rather randomly chosen and have not been taken from a closed macroeconomic model. It is not quite clear, therefore, in what measure the authors wish to test empirically the neo-classical growth model and to what extent the new growth theory.

In the presented model, it has been possible to use the market form of perfect competition as in the neo-classical theory. This was possible because the production of knowledge arises as a pure 'side-product' of economic activities.

The next two sections deal with similar spillovers where the assumption of competitive markets can be continued. In the case of research and development (Chapter 7), however, this will no longer be possible.

6.2 PRODUCTIVE PUBLIC SERVICES

It is the goal of public basic research to elevate the general level of knowledge of all interested circles of an economy. The additionally created knowledge is at the economy's disposal as a non-rival input. Other public services, however, often do not have the character of public goods. Mostly, there is partial or total rivalry and/or excludability; in many cases, the government actually offers completely private goods.

All kinds of public services with a productive character are of importance for long-term economic development. In this context, the following are decisive factors:

- which productive value the public services have for the private economy and
- the fact that, normally, financing by the government can profit from a growing economy through increased tax revenues.

a) Steady-state Growth

The growth impact of public services is shown in the following simple model (see Barro 1990). It is assumed that public services are financed through a proportional income tax. Public services in their turn are to be freely available to all enterprises and individuals. The basic mechanism for endogenous growth consists of a continual increase in public services, which is made possible by increasing tax revenues.

Private investors optimise the private marginal product. In their calculations, however, they do not pay attention to the fact that, through the tax revenues, intensified private activities lead to increased public services in the future.

Notation:

- Q public services
- τ proportional income tax
- D constant parameter for the productivity level.

The aggregate production function is:

$$Y(t) = D \cdot F(K(t), Q(t)) \tag{6.10}$$

As a simplification, labour is contained as human capital in K (see Section 6.3). In the long term, which is relevant here, it is supposed that the government budget is balanced at any given moment:

$$Q(t) = \tau \cdot D \cdot F(K(t), Q(t)) \tag{6.11}$$

If the aggregate production function is divided by the population, we have the following expression for the per capita output:

$$y(t) = D \cdot f(k(t), q(t)) \qquad \text{1. variant} \tag{6.12}$$

Here Q was implicitly interpreted as a private good (in contrast to a public good) which is publicly provided, because q represents the public service per capita. If all can benefit equally from public services without rivalry (as in the case of public goods), then the per capita production function is written as follows:

$$y(t) = D \cdot f(k(t), Q(t)) \qquad \text{2. variant} \tag{6.13}$$

In various cases, the productivity of public services is dependent on how frequently they are used (problem of congestion). To simplify, we can take the capital stock as a measure for the use, that is, the greater the private capital stock (for example, number of factories) and the greater the claim to public goods (for example, roads) the smaller the productivity of these goods (for example, because of traffic jams). Then the formula for the production function is:

$$y(t) = D \cdot f[k(t), Q(t)/K(t)] \qquad \text{3. variant} \tag{6.14}$$

The last two model variants are interesting in comparison with the first, especially when the welfare effects of taxation are studied. From the point of view of welfare, normally, lump-sum taxes are judged as positive (not with respect to distribution), because they are non-distorting. But in the case of congestion, a tax which is proportional to aggregate output can be more pertinent. Such taxation ideally functions as a user fee that internalises the congestion distortion (see Barro and Sala-i-Martin 1995).

To simplify matters, we shall now argue using the first variant (Q as publicly provided private goods). Furthermore, it is useful to illustrate the relation between public capital and private capital. From (6.11) follows:

$$\frac{q(t)}{k(t)} = \tau \cdot D \cdot f[q(t)/k(t), 1] \tag{6.15}$$

The model is sufficiently described for the following application through this stipulation, the production function and the Keynes–Ramsey rule. It is easier to apply the Cobb–Douglas form to the production function. With Q as public services having the character of private goods, the per capita output is:

$$y(t) = D \cdot (k(t))^\alpha \cdot (q(t))^{1-\alpha} \tag{6.16}$$

and the disposable per capita income y_v is:

$$y_v(t) = (1-\tau) \cdot D \cdot (k(t))^\alpha \cdot (q(t))^{1-\alpha} \tag{6.17}$$

In this case, the privately available marginal product of capital is:

$$MPK_P = \frac{dy_v}{dk} = (1-\tau) \cdot \alpha \cdot D\left(\frac{q(t)}{k(t)}\right)^{1-\alpha}$$

By inserting MPK_P into the Keynes–Ramsey rule (see Section 4.3), the growth rate for this model is obtained. Assuming a logarithmic utility function and setting the depreciation and the population growth rate equal to zero leads to:

$$g = (1-\tau) \cdot \alpha \cdot D\left(\frac{q(t)}{k(t)}\right)^{1-\alpha} - \rho \tag{6.18}$$

In Figure 6.3, this expression is represented by the curve QQ. The condition for a balanced budget yields:

$$\text{revenues} = \tau \cdot y(t) = q(t) = \text{government expenditures}$$

Using the Cobb–Douglas production function it follows that:

$$\tau = \frac{q(t)}{y(t)} = \frac{q(t)}{D(k(t))^{\alpha}(q(t))^{1-\alpha}} = \left(\frac{q(t)}{k(t)}\right)^{\alpha} \cdot D^{-1}$$

The relation between public and private capital is thus:

$$\left(\frac{q(t)}{k(t)}\right)^{*} = (\tau \cdot D)^{1/\alpha} \tag{6.19}$$

The budget restriction of the government is represented by the straight line BB in Figure 6.3.

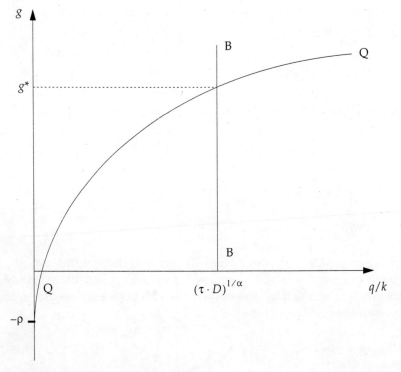

Figure 6.3 *Growth with public services*

By inserting (6.19) into (6.18) the growth rate, corresponding to the point of intersection in the figure, is expressed algebraically as:

$$g^* = \alpha \cdot D^{1/\alpha} \cdot (1 - \tau) \cdot \tau^{(1-\alpha)/\alpha} - \rho \qquad (6.20)$$

This is the steady-state growth rate of the introduced model, which is obviously doubly dependent on the tax rate τ, once positively and once negatively. As a next step, therefore, the level of the tax rate which leads to maximum growth of income can be calculated. Here it must again be noted that in the case of negative externalities of economic activities on the environment, this is not identical to maximum welfare (see Chapter 11).

b) Optimal Tax Rate

First, the effect of tax rate elevation will be explained in Figure 6.4 with the help of comparative dynamics (comparison between two steady-state development paths):

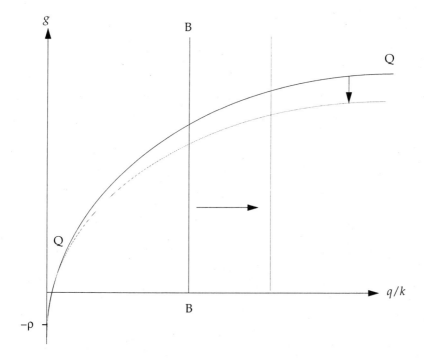

Figure 6.4 Effect of a tax rate increase

- A higher tax rate lowers the available income and the privately avail-able marginal product of capital. This leads to a rotation of the QQ-curve downwards (income effect).

- An increased tax rate raises the quantity of productive public ser-vices, so that the BB-curve shifts towards the right-hand side (spend-ing effect).

Whether the growth rate increases or decreases with a higher tax rate depends on the relative strength of these two effects.

For the calculation of the maximum growth rate, the steady-state growth rate g^*, illustrated in equation (6.20), can be differentiated with respect to the tax rate. In order to find the maximum, the following expres-sion is to be set equal to zero. This calculation will be left to the reader. A graphic figure and a simplified calculation will be presented here instead.

In Figure 6.5, the connection between the growth rate and the tax rate is represented graphically. The graph corresponds to the equation (6.20) with parameter values $\alpha = 0.7, D = 2$ and $\rho = 0.1$. As can be seen, in this case the maximum growth rate is reached with a value $\tau = 0.3$. According to this illustration, even negative growth rates are possible with very high as well as very low tax rates.

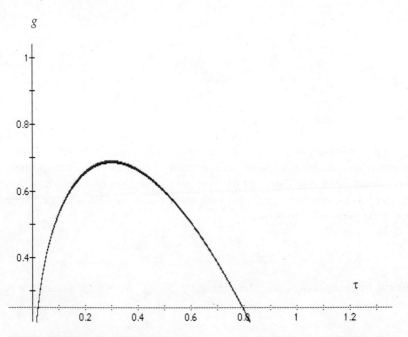

Figure 6.5 Tax rate and growth

c) Calculation of the Optimal Tax Rate

For the calculation of the optimal tax rate, it can be argued that an optimal size of the public sector leads to maximum growth. With tax income the government buys a sum of goods Y, which is then at the disposal of the private sector as services Q.

Since we are in a one-sector model here, Q and Y are the same goods as regards their production; that is, the production of a unit Y costs exactly the same as the production of a unit Q. In order to find the optimum, the supply of Q is therefore increased until the marginal product of Q ($= dY/dQ = dy/dq$) equals exactly one.

Here, the way in which Y depends on Q, or y on q, has to be taken into consideration. If k (short term) and D are given, then the relation shown in Figure 6.6 is valid at any given moment according to production function (6.16).

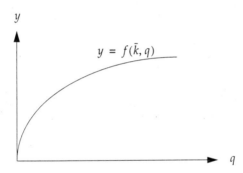

Figure 6.6 Output and public services

In the optimum, the marginal product of Q is independent of the chosen moment in time and herewith independent of the size of K equal to one. For an algebraic calculation of the optimal tax rate, we take the logarithm of the production function (6.16) with steady-state capital stock and take the total differential to yield:

$$\frac{dy}{y} = (1-\alpha)\frac{dq}{q} \tag{6.21}$$

In the optimum and using the expression (6.21), the marginal product is given as:

$$\frac{dy}{dq} = 1 = (1-\alpha)\frac{y}{q}$$

Therefore, the optimal tax rate τ^* is:

$$\tau^* = \frac{q}{y} = (1 - \alpha) \tag{6.22}$$

This result corresponds to the graphic representation in Figure 6.5, because $1 - \alpha$ in the chosen example equals 0.3 exactly.

6.3 HUMAN CAPITAL

Based on theoretical deliberation and on empirical information, there seems to be no doubt that human capital has positive effects on income level and economic growth. In Figure 6.7, the simple relationship between education (measured by the proportion of the population with secondary school education) and growth in an international cross-section is represented.

The illustration shows that, on average, the connection is positive. Some countries are quite far removed from the average correlation. However, human capital as measured by education levels – as employed in the illustration – represents an extremely imprecise procedure, which contains no qualitative component.

In the following simple model, human capital is inserted into the aggregate production function (see Lucas 1988). In the used production function, human capital H (which can be accumulated) replaces the variable for 'raw' labour L of the neo-classical model. For simplicity, the factor L is left out in this paragraph; this can be justified by the fact that the productive contribution of L alone is negligible, or that H and L are accepted as perfect substitutes. In the case of perfect substitutes, H is the scale variable which multiplies L and so enlarges the labour force, that is, makes it more productive. If human capital is transferable (in any form) then there is no upper limit to the accumulation of factor H.

Again, it seems appropriate to represent the intertemporal optimisation for investments in education as a two-period model. Basically, it must be assumed that human capital is utilised either for the running production of final goods or for education. Accordingly, a two-sector model has to be constructed which represents a final goods production and an education sector in the simplest way.

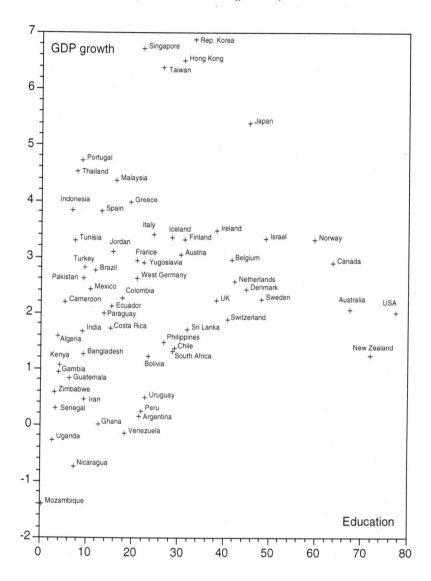

Note: Average per capita GDP growth: real, per annum and in %; school education: average % proportion of the total population with secondary or higher schooling attained, 1960–1985.

Source: Summers/Heston, Penn World Table 5.6; Barro-Lee data, World Bank.

Figure 6.7 Average growth rates, 1960-1990, and school education

It is assumed that the individual's available time is divided into a part u for goods production and a part $(1 - u)$ for education processes $(0 < u < 1)$. Here, the trade-off exists that a smaller u enlarges the future amount of human capital, but limits the running consumption possibilities. The aggregate Cobb–Douglas production function for the goods sector in production (without time indices) with the variable u for the part of H in production is:

$$Y = A \cdot K^{\alpha}(u \cdot H)^{1-\alpha} \tag{6.23}$$

The term $u \cdot H$ can be interpreted as effective labour supply which contains a qualitative component (H) and a quantitative component (u). In addition, a connection between in- and outputs and therewith a 'production function' has to be established for the second sector (education), as well. Input is the running human capital, output is the additional human capital which will be available in the future (see equation 6.24).

Again, positive spillovers are assumed in order to reach an endogenous growth path, this time in the education field. It is postulated that learning becomes easier proportionally to the sum of human capital used in education. Here the individual human capital of the students is considered as well as that of the instructors and co-students. By the assumption of learning effects, a constant marginal value can be assumed for human capital in the education sector, in the same way that it is assumed for physical capital in Section 6.1. Put differently, a constant input of H in the first period leads to a constant intertemporal growth of H – independent of how much human capital is already accumulated.

In the two-period representation, the change in human capital is given by the following functional context $(t = 1,2)$. μ is the productivity in the education sector and $(1 - u)$ the share of time which the individual invests in education in the first period:

$$\Delta H = H_2 - H_1 = \mu \cdot (1 - u) \cdot H_1 \tag{6.24}$$

This expression makes it clear (through division by H_1 on both sides) that with a constant time share $(1 - u)$ in education, a constant growth rate of human capital of the value of μ can be reached. On a steady-state growth path parameter, u is on a constant level. This level is determined by the optimising individuals who discount future consumption possibilities with rate ρ.

In the optimum, education is requested until the costs of education (= lost salary income) are equal to the discounted return on the additional human capital. Therefore the question of how the payment of the human capital and the prices of consumer goods will develop over time is important for optimisation. The prices of consumer goods are assumed to be constant in this model as in the neo-classical growth model, because the consumer goods are used as numéraire here.

The following discussion shows that the payment per unit of human capital remains constant as well. In the optimum, enterprises in the goods sector demand human capital so that payment for a unit of human capital w_H equals marginal product $dy/d(uH)$:

$$w_H = \frac{dy}{d(uH)} = (1-\alpha)AK^{\alpha}(uH)^{(1-\alpha)-1} = (1-\alpha)\frac{Y}{uH}$$

The human capital share of income, then, is:

$$\frac{w_H \cdot u \cdot H}{Y} = (1-\alpha) \tag{6.25}$$

On the steady-state growth path H and Y grow at the same rate, u is constant in long-term equilibrium according to the steady-state definition and α is a fixed parameter. From this it follows that the salary per human capital unit w_H is constant on the steady-state growth path. Individual welfare increases as a result of the fact that individuals own increasing quantities of human capital.

With constant prices and salaries on the steady-state growth path, total profit from human capital is proportional to the profit from consumption, that is, for two periods and with a logarithmic utility function for utility $\tilde{U}$ from the human capital in both periods:

$$\tilde{U} = \log H_1 + \left(\frac{1}{1+\rho}\right)\log H_2$$

As in the calculation of the Keynes–Ramsey rule, an expression for the indifference curves results, this time for the utility from the human capital in the two periods (see Section 4.3):

$$\frac{dH_2/dH_1}{H_2/H_1} = -(1+\rho) \tag{6.26}$$

The indifference curve is shown in Figure 6.8. The restriction for utility maximising is given by the production possibility frontier for education. The households can dedicate a part of their time to education. This brings an increase in human capital ΔH, so that the total sum of human capital in the second period is $H_2 = H_1 + \Delta H$. If no human capital at all is used for education, then $H_2 = H_1$; if all human capital is used for education, then $H_2 = H_1 + \mu \cdot H_1 = (1 + \mu) \cdot H_1$.

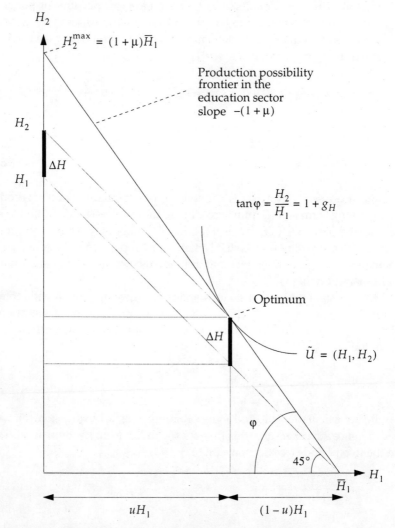

Figure 6.8 Optimum demand for education in the two-period model

In Figure 6.8, the amount of human capital which is used for education is represented from point $\overline{H}_1$ towards the left. The H available in the second period can then be determined by a straight line with a slope:

$$\frac{dH_2}{dH_1} = -(1 + \mu)$$

The negative sign results only from the fact that the use of human capital in education is measured from the right-hand side; the parameter for the returns in education is $(1 + \mu)$ and not μ, because the H used in the education is available again in the second period.

For the calculation of the optimum, the slope of the production possibility frontier is inserted into the expression of the indifference curve. This results in:

$$\frac{H_2}{H_1} = \frac{1+\mu}{1+\rho} \Leftrightarrow g = \frac{H_2 - H_1}{H_1} = \frac{1+\mu}{1+\rho} - 1 \qquad (6.27)$$

The represented relation of human capital increases in the optimum with higher efficiency in education and decreases with an increasing discount rate. From equation (6.24) it is known that:

$$\frac{H_2}{H_1} = 1 + \mu(1 - u)$$

If this expression is inserted into equation (6.27), the optimum u^* can be calculated as:

$$u^* = \frac{(1+\mu) \cdot \rho}{(1+\rho) \cdot \mu} \qquad (6.28)$$

A discount rate of 0 yields $u^* = 0$, that is, $H_2^{max} = (1+\mu) \cdot H_1$ would be available to the households in the second period. From a positive discount rate and the logarithmic utility function, however, another optimum results, as represented in the illustration.

Here the household keeps uH_1 for the production in the first period, and places $(1-\mu)H_1$ as an investment in education. This raises the human capital by ΔH, so that there is $H_2 = H_1 + \Delta H$ in the second period.

Box 6.2: Human Capital Model with an Infinite Horizon

The steady-state growth rate in the model under Section 6.3 can also be calculated with the help of an optimisation over an infinite number of discrete periods. For this, a logarithmic utility function ($U = \log C$) and the production function (6.23) of the main text have to be presupposed, with A being equal to one. The utility to be maximised of households U at time t is the discounted sum of the utilities of each single period:

$$U = \sum_{t=1}^{\infty} (1 + \rho)^{-t} \cdot \log C(t)$$

For every t the accumulation restrictions for the physical capital K and the human capital H are:

$$Y(t) = K(t)^{\alpha} \cdot (u(t) \cdot H(t))^{1-\alpha} = K(t+1) - K(t) + C(t)$$

$$H(t+1) - H(t) = H(t) \cdot \mu \cdot (1 - u(t))$$

Now the restriction for K to C and the restriction for H to u are dissolved. From the two new expressions (through insertion of the second into the first) we get:

$$C(t) = K(t)^{\alpha} \cdot \left(H(t) - \frac{H(t+1)}{\mu} + \frac{H(t)}{\mu} \right)^{1-\alpha} - K(t+1) + K(t)$$

This expression for consumption C is inserted into the above utility function. The first-order conditions are found by taking the differential of this enlarged utility function first for every t with respect to $K(t+1)$ and then for every t with respect to $H(t+1)$. The resulting expressions are to be set to zero. After a simple transformation, differentiating with respect to $K(t+1)$ results in the Keynes–Ramsey rule of this model (see Section 4.3). Differentiating of U with respect to $H(t+1)$ gives:

$$\frac{\partial U}{\partial H(t+1)} = (1+\rho)^{-t} \cdot \frac{1}{C(t)} (1-\alpha) K(t)^{\alpha} (u(t)H(t))^{-\alpha} \cdot \left(-\frac{1}{\mu} \right)$$

$$+ (1+\rho)^{-(t+1)} \cdot \frac{1}{C(t+1)} (1-\alpha) K(t+1)^{\alpha}$$

$$(u(t+1)H(t+1))^{-\alpha} \left(1 + \frac{1}{\mu} \right) = 0$$

Rearranging terms results in:

$$\left(\frac{K(t+1)}{K(t)} \right)^{\alpha} \cdot \frac{1+\mu}{1+\rho} = \frac{C(t+1)}{C(t)} \left(\frac{H(t+1)}{H(t)} \right)^{\alpha} \left(\frac{u(t+1)}{u(t)} \right)^{\alpha}$$

On the steady-state growth path, u is constant and the variables K, C, and H grow at the same constant rate g. For this expression, after insertion and rearranging, that means:

$$g = \frac{1+\mu}{1+\rho} - 1$$

The transition to the time-continuous representation results in the growth rate of expression (6.29) from the main text.

The transition from time-discrete form to time-continuous form can also be made for (6.27) (see Subsection 4.3 b). For the steady-state growth rate, this results in:

$$g_H = \mu - \rho = g_Y = g \qquad (6.29)$$

Using the logarithmic utility function, the growth rate equals the difference between the productivity parameter of the education sector and the discount rate. Measures which render the education sector more efficient directly increase economic growth. The negative influence of the discount rate in this model with investments in education is exactly analogous to the models with other kinds of investments.

As in Chapter 4 with the assumption of the CES utility function, the elasticity of the intertemporal substitution can be inserted. Economic growth is then determined by:

$$g = \frac{1}{\gamma}(\mu - \rho) \qquad (6.30)$$

$1/\gamma$ being, as in Chapter 4, the elasticity of the intertemporal substitution. In the most widely known essay about human capital in the context of the new growth theory (Lucas 1988), an additional externality of human capital in the Y-production is used, which, however, is not necessary to obtain an endogenous growth path. For international comparisons, this additional externality can, however, be useful; this will be explained in the following section.

6.4 AGGREGATE PRODUCTION FUNCTION AND CAPITAL FLOWS

According to the neo-classical growth model, international differences in capital intensity are accompanied by differences in the return on capital. In a perfect international capital market, this should lead to capital transfers from capital-rich to capital-poor countries.

In reality, however, relatively insignificant capital flows are to be observed, although there are great differences in the capital endowments of the different economies. Two hypotheses can be put forward as explanation:

Box 6.3: Empirical Cross-section Results on Growth

Following the theoretically discussed assessments of this chapter, it is elucidating to represent the empirically determined influence of further factors on growth. Barro and Lee (1993) is a study with many estimation results from a wide international cross-section of countries. The following variables were inserted as potentially growth relevant: the per capita income of the beginning at the period (y_s), the education level of the men (h_m), the education level of the women (h_w), the average life expectancy (l), the investment share (i), the part of governmental consumption of total income (c_q), the deviation of the official exchange rate of a currency from the black market rate (p) and the number of revolutions (r).

In the study, pooled data from two time periods were used: for the period 1965–75, 85 countries were taken into consideration; for the period 1975–85, 95 countries. The following estimation result was found for the growth rate of the real income per capita (g):

$$g = -0.026 \log (y_s) + 0.013\, h_m - 0.008\, h_w + 0.073 \log (l) + 0.120\, i$$
$$\quad (0.003) \qquad\qquad (0.004) \qquad (0.005) \qquad (0.013) \qquad (0.020)$$

$$-0.170\, (c_q) - 0.028 \log (1 + p) - 0.017\, r$$
$$(0.026) \qquad (0.005) \qquad\qquad (0.008)$$

SUR est. method, standard errors in brackets, R^2 0.58

Also in this specification, a conditional convergence over the significant influence of y_s results (see Box 3.2), the origin of which is not further specified in the study. The education level of men measured by the secondary school rate has the expected positive influence on growth, while the same indicator shows the 'wrong' sign in the case of women (although not at a significant level). This could be a consequence of the insufficient representation of human capital through the chosen school indicator or of the high correlation between the two school rates (multicollinearity). The parameter of life expectancy, which is important for incentives to form human capital, shows the right sign – as does the investment share. Contrary to Section 6.2, for the government sector, the consumption part, rather than the potentially growth-promoting investive part, was inserted. According to the study's assessment, the negative influence of variable c_q shows the growth-restraining effect of an oversized governmental apparatus. It must, however, be observed that in the private sector, an extension of consumption at the expense of investments also restrains growth; so the phenomenon is not government specific. The variable p as an indicator of market distortions in an economy and the slightly 'wobbly' variable r as indicator for the political stability show the expected negative influence on the growth rate.

This estimation as well as the others do not coincide in all points with the expectations stemming from growth theory. The difficulties of comparison of international data, the lack of robustness of the results, and the not completely theoretically based choice of parameters are the weak points of this study. Further empirical work will therefore be necessary in order to strengthen the empirical basis for growth theory in the future.

- Investors have a preference for investments in their own country.
- The neo-classical production function does not describe the true situation adequately.

The first hypothesis is plausible if the differences in return between the home economy and other countries are not too great (risk premiums on investments in foreign countries). As regards the new growth theory, the second point is especially interesting; we shall therefore continue the specifications of this discussion. Based on the neo-classical model and with the example of the two countries USA and India (see Lucas 1990), a useful form of the aggregate production function, which takes up the elements of Sections 6.1–3 again, will now be sought.

The neo-classical production function in the Cobb–Douglas form and in per capita terms is given as:

$$y = A \cdot k^{\alpha} \qquad\qquad \alpha < 1 \qquad\qquad (6.31)$$

With perfect competition, the (net) marginal product of capital equals the interest rate, and so:

$$r = A \cdot \alpha \cdot k^{\alpha - 1} \qquad\qquad (6.32)$$

Since capital intensity is difficult to measure for many countries, it is replaced by the (measurable) per capita income over the production function. Dissolving the equation (6.31) to k and inserting it into (6.32) results in:

$$r = \alpha \cdot A^{1/\alpha} \cdot y^{\frac{\alpha - 1}{\alpha}} \qquad\qquad (6.33)$$

According to this production function (assumptions: $\alpha_I = \alpha_U$ and $A_I = A_U$), the quotient of interest rates between two countries, India (I) and USA (U), would be:

$$\frac{r_I}{r_U} = \left(\frac{y_I}{y_U}\right)^{\frac{\alpha - 1}{\alpha}} \qquad\qquad (6.34)$$

Using the statistic, the relation of the per capita incomes of both countries corresponds to a factor of about 1 : 15. With a capital share α of 0.4 for both countries, this production function results in the fact that the quotient of capital returns between the two countries is the factor 58! Even with a strong preference for investments in their own country, probably few Americans would invest in America in such a case.

As a next step, the human capital factor will therefore be considered. In the same per capita terms, the aggregate production function with human capital is:

$$y = A \cdot k^{\alpha} \cdot h^{1-\alpha} \tag{6.35}$$

A higher endowment with human capital therefore increases the capital return. The relation of returns is:

$$\frac{r_I}{r_U} = \left(\frac{y_I}{y_U} \cdot \frac{h_U}{h_I}\right)^{\frac{\alpha-1}{\alpha}} \tag{6.36}$$

Based on empirical studies, it is estimated that the average human capital endowment per capita in the USA is about five times as high as in India. This would mean that the marginal product of capital would now be only five times greater in India than in the USA. This, however, still seems unrealistically high.

We shall now discuss parameter A, which can represent different economic factors. On the one hand, it encompasses public outputs such as the legal system, security and infrastructure. On the other hand, it represents technical, organisational and institutional knowledge which is country specific. Without citing empirical findings, it seems evident that the difference in returns can be substantially decreased by these factors.

In the aforementioned article by Lucas (1990), an additional variant is evaluated independently of A, namely positive spillovers of the human capital in the field of goods production (in addition to the spillovers in the educational field). The economic hypothesis is that labour forces are more productive the better is the average education of their business partners and collaborators. A corresponding aggregate production function is:

$$y = A \cdot k^{\alpha} \cdot h^{1-\alpha} \cdot h^{\xi} \tag{6.37}$$

where the last factor retains the positive spillovers of human capital in goods production. Based on comparisons with empirical studies, Lucas comes to the conclusion that the externalities of the human capital can also explain why the returns on capital in India and in the USA do not diverge so strongly in reality.

The externalities of human capital as well as differences in A result in salaries being much higher in the USA than in India, so that from the viewpoint of factor mobility, it is above all the labour force which has an economic incentive to change geographical place.

SELECTED READING

- ARROW, K.J. (1962), 'The Economic Implications of Learning by Doing', *Review of Economic Studies*, **29** (1), 155–73.
- BARRO, R.J. (1990), 'Government Spending in a Simple Model of Endogenous Growth', *Journal of Political Economy*, **98** (5), S103–S125.
- BARRO, R.J. (1991), 'Economic Growth in a Cross Section of Countries', *Quarterly Journal of Economics*, **106** (2), 407–43.
- BARRO, R.J. and J. LEE (1993), 'Losers and Winners in Economic Growth', *NBER Working Paper*, no. 4341.
- BARRO, R.J. and X. SALA-I-MARTIN (1992), 'Public Finance in Models of Economic Growth', *Review of Economic Studies*, **59** (4), 645–61.
- BARRO, R.J. and X. SALA-I-MARTIN (1995), *Economic Growth*, New York: McGraw–Hill.
- BRETSCHGER, L. and H. SCHMIDT (1999), 'Converging on the Learning Curve: Theory and Application to German Regional Data', *Weltwirtschaftliches Archiv/Review of World Economics*, **135** (2).
- DELONG, J.B. and L.H. SUMMERS (1991), 'Equipment Investment and Economic Growth', *Quarterly Journal of Economics*, **106** (2), 445–502.
- LEVINE, R. and D. RENELT (1992), 'A Sensitivity Analysis of Cross-country Growth Regressions', *American Economic Review*, **82** (4), 942–63.
- LUCAS, R.E. (1988), 'On the Mechanics of Economic Development', *Journal of Monetary Economics*, **22** (1), 3–42.
- LUCAS, R.E. (1990), 'Why Doesn't Capital Flow from Rich to Poor Countries', *American Economic Review, Papers and Proceedings*, **80** (2), 92–6.
- UZAWA, H. (1965), 'Optimum Technical Change in an Aggregative Model of Economic Growth', *International Economic Review*, **6**, 18–31.

7. Research and Development

7.1 CHARACTERISTICS OF RESEARCH

In developed economies, 2–3 percent of the gross domestic product are used for activities which belong to the category of research and development (R&D). Through R&D, it becomes possible to achieve so-called 'technical progress', which plays an important role in the growth process. It is commonly believed that technical progress is the most important factor in explaining the big differences between the economies of the 18th century and the wealthy economies of today. The following forms of technical progress can be distinguished:

- product innovations
  - new products
  - qualitatively better products
- process innovations
  - new (intermediate) inputs
  - new input combinations.

New products in the field of consumption lead to a wider product variety. It is realistic to assume a natural preference of the households for variety ('taste for variety'). So the utility of the consumers rises with increasing innovation, because of an expansion of the range of goods supplied from which one can choose. This supply is composed of old and new products. If the product quality of existing goods improves through innovation, then it becomes probable that the older products will be requested only rarely or not at all, and will disappear from the market.

In the field of production, the invention of new input factors is able to change the production process. New inputs are so-called intermediate goods as they have to be invented and produced before they are themselves used for production. The number of intermediate products which are needed to produce consumer goods is often related to the number of firms producing these goods. The bigger the number of enterprises which are involved in producing a product, the greater the division of labour the economy experiences. Ever since Adam Smith at least, an increasing division of labour is understood to be an essential driving force for long-term economic development, as innovations lead to greater specialisation of the individual enterprise in specific activities. On the other hand, process innovations can also alter the production functions of the enterprises, that is, the factor input combinations and by this the factor productivity.

Like other investments, innovative activities can be described and explained by economic theory. They arise from intentional decisions made by profit-maximising agents under normal market conditions. The accuracy of the information about the research results is an important determinant for rational decisions on factor input in research. Put differently, the possibilities of predicting these results depend on the decision situation in which the investing persons find themselves. As regards the amount and quality of the information which is available for decisions, the following situations are possible:

- strong uncertainty
- uncertainty
- situation of risk
- certainty.

With strong uncertainty about the result of the research investments, neither the possible results of research nor their probability are known. In this case, the enterprises will most probably spend a percentage of the total sales or profits which is traditionally given to research. In the case of uncertainty, the possible results of research are known, but their probabilities are unknown. In these cases, specific decision rules may be applied. But in comparison with other fields of the economy, a strict optimisation of the factor input in research is possible only when the probabilities of the possible results also become known, which corresponds to the situation of risk. In neo-classical tradition, this is the most appropriate case for modelling R&D. Complete certainty, however, is a characteristic which contradicts the nature of research and innovation. In all fields of research, there exist two basic types of innovations:

- continuous innovations, which produce continuous progress in knowledge
- radical innovations, which produce big jumps in knowledge increase.

A further possibility is to distinguish between drastic innovations, where the innovating firm is not constrained by potential competition from previous incumbents, and non drastic innovations, where potential competition still exists. In the following models, only continuous non drastic innovations will be considered. For the particular consequences of other types of innovations, see, for example, Aghion and Howitt (1998).

7.2 INNOVATIONS UNDER MONOPOLISTIC COMPETITION

Only under the condition that the goods included in the model can be differentiated from each other can there be a theoretical consideration of product innovations. This is why, in this chapter, for a part of the considered economy, the transition is made from the assumption of homogeneous goods of the neo-classical growth model to the assumption of differentiated goods.

In the models of the new growth theory, differentiated goods are used as:

- consumption goods
- intermediate goods used for the production of consumption goods (see Section 7.3)
- components (services) for the production of capital goods (see Section 7.4).

The case of consumption goods is not considered further in the following text; it is equivalent to the second case, which is described extensively in the following section. Differentiated goods are heterogeneous by assumption and can therefore not be perfectly substituted among each other. This creates a limited market power for the individual firms which produce differentiated goods. Every enterprise is confronted with a decreasing demand curve for its product. In this case, it can set the price higher than the marginal costs without losing the whole demand, as would be the case under perfect competition. If additional profit remains for the firm, after covering the fixed costs, then other firms find it worth entering into this market.

Market entries by other firms reduce the market share of the enterprises which are already established, or put differently, the demand for the products of an individual firm decreases. Their profit also declines correspondingly, until in the steady state net profit (gross profit minus fixed costs) is no longer made, and entrance into the market is of no interest to potential new suppliers. This market form is based on a contribution by Chamberlin (1933) and is generally called monopolistic competition.

Figure 7.1 shows the situation of monopolistic competition; for simplicity, the demand curve in the graphic representation is assumed as linear. The positive net profit in time 1 is assumed to vanish as a consequence of market entries which lead the price and quantity of the considered firm to a point without net profits in time 2. With new rivals competing in the market, the demand curve shifts to the left for the individual enterprise.

Notation:

- x_1^D demand for goods of an enterprise before the entry of rivals
- x_2^D demand for goods of an enterprise in the steady state (no net profit)
- AC average costs
- MC marginal costs
- MR marginal revenue
- p_x price of the differentiated good

The consequence of a steady state of monopolistic competition is that the profit of the individual supplier is exactly enough to cover the fixed costs, that is, $AC = x^D$ with the usual optimality condition $MC = MR$ (but $p_x \neq MC$).

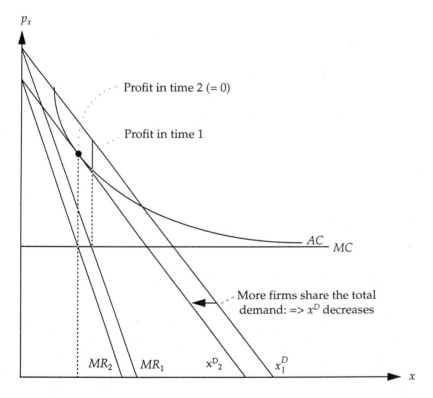

Figure 7.1 Monopolistic competition

It should be noticed that this result is based on the following model assumptions:

- Every supplier has (limited) monopoly power.
- The production costs are composed of fixed costs and constant marginal costs.

The existence of fixed costs in monopolistic competition can be based on a microeconomic foundation, which is plausible in the dynamic perspective and effective for modelling in the new growth theory. According to Romer (1990), the fixed costs for enterprises consist of the need to generate or to buy the know-how for the production before starting the production of a differentiated good. Further argumentation is based on the following assumptions:

- The fixed costs consist of the know-how for the production of a new differentiated good.
- The know-how is offered by a research sector, which has other production conditions than the rest of the economy.
- The know-how is contained in a so-called product 'design'.

In monopolistic competition the size of the market or demand for all differentiated goods has a central meaning: the greater the total demand for goods, the bigger the number of suppliers of differentiated goods operating profitably. In this way, a growing total market leads to an increasing utility (because of the taste for variety) and/or to a higher division of labour and so to a higher productivity in the production of consumption goods.

7.3 A TWO-SECTOR MODEL WITH ENDOGENOUS GROWTH

The following model is the simplest version of a growth model with differentiated goods. It follows the basic idea of Romer (1990) and simplifies the production structure according to the Grossman and Helpman model (1991, Chapter 3). However, the differentiated goods are intermediate goods and not consumption goods as with Grossman and Helpman.

In this model, product innovations are evident in new intermediate goods. These are used in the production of consumption goods which are demanded by the households. Labour is supplied as a primary production factor. For the marginal product to be constant in research, positive spillovers from research to public knowledge are assumed.

Figure 7.2 shows how the economy is divided into two sectors in the model: the first sector is the research sector, the second comprises all other activities.

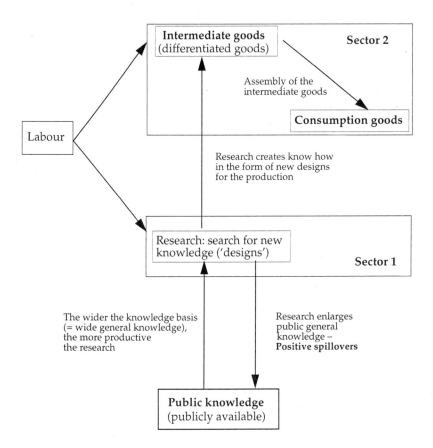

Figure 7.2 Two-sector model with research and development

In sector 1, new designs are developed, which enable the production of new intermediate goods in sector 2. Research activity, however, not only makes the development of new designs directly possible, it also indirectly enlarges public knowledge, which then is again available as a free input in research activity. In other words, research brings an internal profit, which is contained in the design, and an external benefit, which falls to the total research sector (compare also Subsection 5.3a).

In sector 2, differentiated goods, which are used as intermediate products, are produced by using labour and the designs from sector 1. In contrast to the following Section 7.4, it is assumed that the intermediate products can be assembled to generate a consumption good without further input. In this way, the fields of intermediate product production and assembly can be treated as one and the same sector.

For the modelling of sector 2, the assumptions as regards production and demand structure of the monopolistic competition are decisive. How the differentiated intermediate products for the production of consumption goods are to be used has to be clearly determined in the model. In recent literature, the use of the 'CES' function has become widespread, and is thus an obvious choice for a starting point in this textbook growth model.

Here a slightly changed notation expresses the difference in the production of consumption goods in this model as compared to neo-classical theory. Since the consumption goods are now composed of various components, they will here be described as 'high-tech'-consumption goods.

Notation:

- $x_1...x_n$ n different intermediate goods
- p_x price of an intermediate good
- Y^H high-tech consumption goods (superscript H for high-tech)
- β fixed parameter of the CES function.

In Figure 7.3, the construction of a high-tech good in the case of two intermediate products is shown graphically. As is usual in production theory an isoquant results, where the intermediate products represent the inputs and the high-tech consumption good the output. The analytical representation corresponds to the simple CES function.

If n intermediate products are used for the production of the quantity of consumption goods Y^H, then the corresponding CES function is as follows:

$$Y^H = \left[\sum_{J=1}^{n} (x_J)^\beta \right]^{1/\beta} \tag{7.1}$$

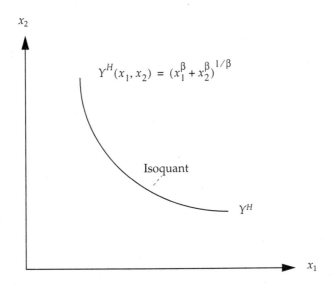

$$Y^H(x_1, x_2) = (x_1^\beta + x_2^\beta)^{1/\beta}$$

Isoquant

Y^H

Figure 7.3 Isoquant of a CES function

In order to simplify the analysis, it is now assumed that all the intermediate goods show the same production structure, i.e. all intermediate good firms have identical cost functions. Since the individual intermediate goods enter symmetrically into equation (7.1), the produced amounts are then of the same size for all intermediate products, that is, $x_1 = x_2 = \dots = x_n = x$.

With this assumption, which is called 'symmetrical equilibrium' in the literature, equation (7.1) can be simplified to:

$$Y^H = [n \cdot x^\beta]^{1/\beta} = x \cdot n^{1/\beta} \tag{7.2}$$

The insertion of the shown CES production function has various consequences:

- Any two intermediate goods are equally good substitutes for each other. Moreover, the possibility of substitution is independent of the production level, that is, the elasticity of substitution is constant.

- According to the CES form, the elasticity of substitution between two intermediate goods ε is (compare Box 7.1):

$$\varepsilon = \frac{1}{1-\beta}$$

- The elasticity of substitution corresponds to the price elasticity of demand for the individual firm, if all other prices and the total consumption expenditures are constant (see Box 7.2). The use of this price elasticity is realistic if the individual enterprise is small in comparison to the total market (Chamberlin's 'large-group case'). In this case, an individual enterprise has no influence on the other participants in the market. This is assumed in the following.

- With a constant price elasticity of demand for a differentiated good, the optimum price of an intermediate product is calculated, according to microeconomic theory, by a constant mark-up over the marginal costs MC. In this way, the profit per intermediate good enterprise can be calculated. The following then results from the usual profit maximisation (Amoroso–Robinson condition):

$$MC = p_x \cdot \left(1 - \frac{1}{|\varepsilon|}\right) = p_x \cdot (1 - (1 - \beta)) = \beta \cdot p_x \tag{7.3}$$

- The enterprises' optimum mark-up factor over the marginal costs is therefore $1/\beta$ in this model. For this mark-up to be bigger than one and a positive profit to result, $0 < \beta < 1$ must be true. With this, it is contemporaneously assumed that $\varepsilon > 1$.

In this model, the profit per intermediate good is found by using the optimum mark-up factor. The incentives for investments in the development of new designs are set over this profit. The profit per intermediate good enterprise π_j can be calculated by multiplying the difference between the average return and the marginal costs, by the amount of the sold intermediate good:

$$\pi_j = (p_x - MC) \cdot x = (1 - \beta) \cdot p_x \cdot x$$

The entire input of resources X for the production of the consumption goods, for example, the total input in intermediate goods, equals the number of different designs n, multiplied by the amount of intermediate products supplied per enterprise x, that is, $X = n \cdot x$. The sum of firms' profits of the n symmetrical intermediate goods enterprises gives the aggregate profit π:

Box 7.1: Elasticity of Substitution in the R&D Model

That the elasticity of substitution really is equal to ε in the chosen CES form can be verified as follows. If we describe any x-good with the index j, the production function (7.1) can be written as:

$$(Y^H)^\beta = x_j^\beta + \dots$$

Differentiation of this expression with respect to the quantity of the jth x-good leads to:

$$\beta(Y^H)^{\beta-1} \cdot \frac{\partial Y^H}{\partial x_j} = \beta x_j^{\beta-1}$$

Then the same process is applied for good i. Now we form the relation between the expression for the jth good and the ith good according to:

$$\frac{\partial Y^H/\partial x_i}{\partial Y^H/\partial x_j} = \left(\frac{x_i}{x_j}\right)^{\beta-1}$$

On the left-hand side in the numerator stands the marginal product of the ith good, in the denominator that of the jth good. The relation between these marginal products corresponds to the quotient of prices of x-goods i and j, so that:

$$\frac{\partial Y^H/\partial x_i}{\partial Y^H/\partial x_j} = \frac{p_{xi}}{p_{xj}}$$

The relative demand for the two goods can be derived out of the two above expressions as follows:

$$\frac{x_i}{x_j} = \left(\frac{p_{xi}}{p_{xj}}\right)^{-\frac{1}{1-\beta}} = \left(\frac{p_{xi}}{p_{xj}}\right)^{-\varepsilon}$$

Taking logarithms and differentiating, result in:

$$\varepsilon = -\frac{d(x_i/x_j)}{d(p_{xi}/p_{xj})} \cdot \frac{p_{xi}/p_{xj}}{x_i/x_j}$$

So it can be seen directly that the substitution elasticity is equal to ε.

$$\pi = n \cdot \pi_j = (1-\beta) \cdot p_x \cdot x \cdot n = (1-\beta) \cdot p_x \cdot X \tag{7.4}$$

In order to show the gains from diversification in the production of consumption goods, the output in consumption goods Y^H is to be expressed as a function of the total input X:

$$Y^H = x \cdot n^{1/\beta} = X \cdot n^{(1-\beta)/\beta} \tag{7.5}$$

From this it follows that:

$$\frac{Y^H}{X} = n^{(1-\beta)/\beta} \tag{7.6}$$

Equation (7.6) shows that productivity, in the production of consumption goods, increases with an increasing number of intermediate goods. For even with a constant input of X, the amount of output can be increased with an increasing n. This is the model representation of the advantage, which results from the increasing division of labour in an economy. Here, only parameter β determines the gain from diversification in this specification. This point will be reconsidered in Section 7.5.

In order to calculate the steady-state growth rate, we must defined the way in which the primary labour factor will be allocated to the two sectors of the economy under conditions of a market economy. For, the more labour is engaged in the research sector, the more designs are produced and the bigger becomes the growth rate of general knowledge.

Permanent input of labour in the research sector leads, through the diversification effect (equation 7.6), to a higher output in consumption goods with the same input (higher productivity). Research activity becomes continuously more productive in time, through positive spillovers and the growing amount of knowledge in the research sector. With a certain intensity of spillovers, a constant labour input in the research laboratory makes possible a constant growth rate in produced designs.

In the model, employment in the research sector is equal to the fixed labour supply minus the employment in sector 2. So on the one hand, in order to find the steady state, a labour market restriction has to be formulated. On the other hand, the greater the chances of profit to be attained with designs, the more attractive research activity is to the investing party. However, this can be calculated only under the condition that a capital market is additionally taken into consideration. In a market economy, this market equalises the returns on different investments.

Box 7.2: Price Elasticity in the R&D Model

For many suppliers of intermediate goods ('large-group case') ε, according to the following derivation, is not only the substitution elasticity (see Box 7.1), but at the same time the price elasticity of demand for a differentiated x-good.

Using the CES form, the demand for intermediate good number j can be derived as follows. The costs of the Y^H-production (c_Y) depend upon the weighted prices of the x-goods; they are like a CES price index, which corresponds to the chosen CES production function (7.1).

This index, which will not be derived any more precisely here (in advanced textbooks of microeconomic theory such a derivation can be found), is:

$$c_Y = \left[\sum_{J=1}^{n} (p_{xJ})^{1-\varepsilon} \right]^{\frac{1}{1-\varepsilon}}$$

Dividing by the amount of consumption goods, one arrives at the per-unit costs of a Y^H-good (c_Y/Y^H). According to Shepard's Lemma, which is often used in microeconomics, differentiating per-unit costs with respect to the price of the jth intermediate product (which is to say with respect to the factor price) results in the sought-after demand for the jth x-good per consumption good. Multiplication of both sides by Y^H leads to:

$$x_j = \frac{(p_{xj})^{-\varepsilon}}{\sum_{J=1}^{n} (p_{xJ})^{1-\varepsilon}} \cdot p_Y \cdot Y^H$$

From the perspective of the individual enterprise, the prices of the other suppliers (that is, the sum in the nominator of the expression), the price index p_y, as well as sum Y^H are constant, when n is large. The price elasticity of the demand for good number j can then be calculated by taking logarithms and differentiating the expression, while keeping the named parameters constant. This results in:

$$\frac{dx_j/x_j}{dp_{xj}/p_{xj}} = -\varepsilon$$

Thus, with the simplifying assumptions of the chosen formulation, the same parameter ε can be used for both important elasticities in this model.

The supply on the capital market is determined by the households' propensity for saving, which acts according to the assumptions regarding the intertemporal optimisation. In the present model, the simultaneous equilibrium of labour market and capital market results in the steady-state growth rate. In the following, for a clearer overview, the time indices will always be left out when there is no ambiguity.

Notation:

- a_x input factor for labour in the intermediate goods sector
- a_g input factor for labour in research
- L fixed labour supply
- L_x labour demand in the intermediate goods sector
- L_g labour demand in the research sector
- w labour wage
- g_n growth rate of the designs
- κ public knowledge
- z market value of a design.

Let us first consider the labour market. The primary labour factor can be employed either for the production of intermediate goods or for research. According to the assumption, the assembly of intermediate goods into consumption goods does not use any additional resources and therefore uses no labour.

The entire demand for labour is therefore composed of the demands of the two sectors and amounts to $L_g + L_x$. The labour demand of the research sector L_g can be derived from the production conditions for new designs, which will now be determined.

To simplify matters, we shall now again look at two periods out of a sequence of many periods. The economy starts with a number of designs defined in the past. In the period considered first, additional new designs are developed, which are also used for the production of intermediate goods in the second, following period. The transition from the second period to the third and then to the fourth and so forth happen analogously.

The production function for the development of Δn new product designs for the second period, which arise in addition to the ones which already exist in period 1 (n_1) is:

$$n_2 - n_1 = \Delta n = \frac{1}{a_g} \cdot L_g \cdot \kappa_1 \tag{7.7}$$

The reciprocal of the input factor is nothing other than the productivity of labour in the research laboratory, which is to be multiplied by the labour input of L_g. κ_1 stands for the positive influence of public knowledge on research activity. The greater the knowledge is, the more productive research becomes and the greater will be the amount of newly developed designs.

For simplicity, the models of endogenous growth with R&D assume that the new development of a design increases knowledge in a relation of one to one. The assumption of these proportional spillovers of R&D leads to the standardisation $\kappa(t) = n(t)$. So the growth rate of the number of designs or of knowledge is, according to (7.7):

$$\frac{\Delta n}{n} = g_n = \frac{1}{a_g} \cdot L_g \tag{7.8}$$

The labour demand of the research sector results by reformulating (7.8) as:

$$L_g = a_g \cdot g_n \tag{7.9}$$

The labour demand of the intermediate goods sector is:

$$L_x = a_x \cdot n \cdot x = a_x \cdot X \tag{7.10}$$

For simplicity, the input coefficient for the production of differentiated goods is standardised to one, that is, $a_x = 1$. Since only one primary input is considered, this assumption does not limit the quality of the results. In order to simplify the amount X as well, an additional 'modelling trick', which will also simplify the capital market, can be introduced.

The trick consists in choosing a numéraire in the model in such a way that the calculating effort becomes as small as possible. Money, which would normally play the role of numéraire or calculating unit, does not exist in this model. In the models with a monetary sector, all prices are expressed in currency units. In this model without money, however, the prices are standardised in such a way that the value of the entire consumption expenditures always assumes the value of one. In other words: if the quantity of consumed high-tech goods in a growing economy augments continuously, the prices of these high-tech goods fall in such a way that the value of the consumption expenditures (the quantity multiplied by the prices) is always one. The advantages of this rather unusual procedure should soon become clear.

The entire consumption expenditures for high-tech goods correspond to the expenditures of buying intermediate products, since no additional costs arise in the assembly of the intermediate goods. So the value, which is found by multiplying the price of an intermediate good by the number of intermediate products and the amount of an intermediate good is one, that is, the following is true:

$$1 = p_x \cdot n \cdot x = p_x \cdot X \qquad \text{or} \quad X = 1/p_x \qquad (7.11)$$

So with the consumption expenditures standardised to one and the input coefficient for the production of differentiated goods standardised to one, the labour demand of the intermediate product is simply $1/p_x$.

An equilibrium arises on the labour market when the fixed labour supply L is equal to the sum of the labour demands of the two sectors, that is:

$$L = a_g \cdot g_n + \frac{1}{p_x} \qquad (7.12)$$

The prices of the intermediate products p_x can be substituted according to (7.3) by $p_x = (1/\beta) \cdot MC$. Since, under the simplifying circumstances, the marginal costs MC correspond to the labour wage w, (7.12) can be transformed into:

$$a_g \cdot g_n + \frac{\beta}{w} = L \quad \text{or} \quad g_n = \frac{L}{a_g} - \frac{\beta}{a_g \cdot w} \qquad (7.13)$$

Under this condition, an equilibrium reigns on the labour market. In Figure 7.4 (see below), the labour market steady state (7.13) is represented by the straight line LL, which represents the resource restriction in the form of a budget constraint in this model. In the X/g-diagram chosen here, the expression has the following form:

$$X = L - a_g \cdot g_n \qquad (7.14)$$

The second step in solving the model consists in formulating the capital market equilibrium. The investing parties compare the returns on research with the interest on other assets, which in this model are assumed as risk free and comprising a certain market interest rate. The research returns depend on the value which a design possesses in the future. In the chosen two-period approach, the returns of a research investment are equal to the sum of the profit made under monopolistic competition in the second period and the market value which the design has at the end of the second period. In R&D, in the case of free market access, this market value is equal to the production costs of a design. That is why, at the end of the second period, the value of a design corresponds to the production costs in the steady state.

In both periods, the production costs of a design are determined on the basis of equation (7.7) by multiplying the input coefficient by the labour wage, and dividing by the 'free' input of public knowledge. With free market access into research, this quotient is equal to the market value of the design z according to:

$$z(t) = \frac{a_g \cdot w(t)}{\kappa(t)} = \frac{a_g \cdot w(t)}{n(t)} \qquad\qquad t = 1,2 \qquad\qquad (7.15)$$

The research returns of the second period are discounted with the market interest rate, since this interest return is created on the alternative asset. The Keynes–Ramsey rule (see Section 4.3) sets the interest rate in relation to the discount rate of the households. With a logarithmic utility function and without special attention to population growth or depreciation, the consumption growth, according to this rule, is equal to the difference between the interest rate (marginal product of capital) and the discount rate.

In the Keynes–Ramsey rule, the growth of the nominal consumption expenditures can replace the real consumption growth. The growth of the nominal consumption expenditures is then equal to the difference between the nominal interest rate and the discount rate.

Now since, by assumption, the entire nominal consumption expenditures are constant in this model, then for the result of the intertemporal optimisation this means that at every moment in time, the nominal interest rate corresponds to the discount rate, that is:

$$r = \rho \qquad\qquad (7.16)$$

r being the nominal interest rate. Thus, the future research returns in this model are discounted with the rate ρ. In the two-period model, the capital market is in equilibrium, provided that the discounted research returns of the second period correspond to the development costs of a new design in the first period ($= z$), that is:

$$(1 + \rho)^{-1} \cdot (\pi_2 + z_2) = z_1$$

or by inserting for z:

$$(1 + \rho)^{-1} \cdot \left(\pi_2 + \frac{a_g \cdot w_2}{n_2}\right) = \frac{a_g \cdot w_1}{n_1} \qquad (7.17)$$

The term which is added to π_2 in the brackets on the left-hand side shows that the returns of the investments in research apart from the profit under monopolistic competition π also consist of the market value of the design at the end of the second period.

Finally, before solving the capital market and the entire model, we shall discuss the development of the wages, that is w_1 and w_2. In the human capital model in Section 6.3, the wage rate was constant and the growth of individual wealth was achieved through an augmentation of per capita human capital. In this model, growth of individual wealth is achieved through an increase in the number of intermediate goods and an increasing labour division. The wage rate is constant in this model too, since a stable solution of the model is obtained only in this way. This result, which relies on certain assumptions about the formation of expectations and the market equilibrium, is further discussed in Grossman and Helpman (1991, Chapter 3).

If we set $w_1 = w_2 = w$ and express the profit according to equation (7.4) (while respecting the standardisation of consumption expenditures to a value of one) in terms of the variables of the model as $(1 - \beta)/n$, the following results for the steady state of the capital market:

$$(1 + \rho)^{-1} \cdot \frac{(1 - \beta) + a_g \cdot w}{n_2} = \frac{a_g \cdot w}{n_1} \qquad (7.18)$$

Here, as in Chapter 4, it makes sense to write this expression in the time-continuous form by 'transition to small period length'. After dividing both sides by $a_g \cdot w$ and multiplying by n_2 and a Taylor approximation (see Section 4.3 b), the growth rate of the designs becomes:

$$g_n = \frac{1 - \beta}{a_g \cdot w} - \rho \qquad (7.19)$$

Box 7.3: Capital Market in Time-continuous Representation

Instead of the representation in two periods, the steady state of the capital market can also be derived in the time-continuous formulation, which is used by Grossman and Helpman (1991). Again, the market value of a design will be defined by the variable z. In an equilibrium of the capital market, the returns on the research investments must be equal to the returns of the alternative asset, which is a bond yielding the fixed rate r. As with securities, it must be taken into consideration for the design that its market value can fall or rise. Therefore, at a given moment, the returns consist of the profit which can be made at that moment as well as the change in value of the design, which we define as $\dot{z}$ according to the aforeused notation. If π is the profit under monopolistic competition, then the following is true in the steady state of the capital market:

$$\pi + \dot{z} = r \cdot z$$

The returns of the design are on the left-hand side; on the right-hand side are the returns when the same amount z is invested in the bond. With the standardisation of the nominal consumption expenditures to a value of one at every moment in time, $r = \rho$ is true according to the Keynes–Ramsey rule (see main text). Furthermore, the expression can be divided by z, which results in:

$$\frac{\pi}{z} + \frac{\dot{z}}{z} = \rho$$

Profit π is $(1 - \beta)/n$ (consider equation (7.4) and the standardisation of the consumption expenditures to a value of one) and just as in the main text the value of a design is equal to the production costs:

$$z = \frac{a_g \cdot w}{n}$$

The following consideration is to be added for the percentage change of z. The households have to observe an intertemporal budget constraint. In the time-continuous model, they optimise over an infinite time horizon. The constraint means that the expenditures discounted over all times must correspond to the profits discounted over all times plus the value of the entire wealth. The wealth consists of the value of all designs plus the capitalised value of all wage payments. Since the expenditures are standardised to a value of one according to the assumption, the present value of the expenditures converges towards a fixed value; so the value of the total wealth $n \cdot z$ also has an upper bound, and converges towards a constant. In the long-term steady state then, the percentage quantitative increase of designs g_n corresponds to the percentage decrease of the design value $\dot{z}/z$, that is, $g_n = -\dot{z}/z$. If profit, value of the design and (negative) growth rate are introduced into the steady state of the capital market, then we arrive at:

$$g_n = \frac{1 - \beta}{a_g \cdot w} - \rho$$

which is analogous to (7.19) in the main text.

This is the basic condition for a steady state on the capital market, which in Figure 7.4 is represented by straight line $\pi\pi$. Equation (7.19) shows that investments in designs increase with the increasing patience of the households, the lowering of the prices in the research laboratory, and the increasing of the mark-up over the marginal costs in the monopolistic competition. In the X/g-diagram, this steady state has the form

$$X = (g_n + \rho) \cdot \left(\frac{a_g \cdot \beta}{1 - \beta} \right) \qquad (7.20)$$

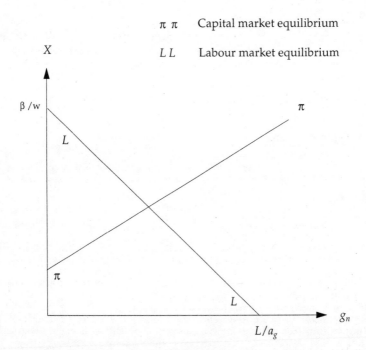

$\pi\,\pi$ Capital market equilibrium

$L\,L$ Labour market equilibrium

Figure 7.4 Steady-state growth with R&D

The steady-state growth rate arises out of the simultaneous dissolution of the labour market and the capital market, which in Figure 7.4 corresponds to the point of intersection of the two geometrical loci.

If (7.13) is solved for w and the result is inserted into (7.19), we arrive at the following result for steady-state growth g_n:

$$g_n = \frac{(1-\beta) \cdot L}{a_g} - \beta \cdot \rho \qquad (7.21)$$

The growth of the number of designs also determines the growth of the amount of consumption goods. Expression (7.5) can be transformed into the following by using $X = 1/p_x = \beta/w$:

$$Y^H = \frac{\beta}{w} \cdot n^{(1-\beta)/\beta} \qquad (7.22)$$

Of the parameters β, w and n, only n changes over time, according to the calculated growth rate. Taking logarithms and differentiating with respect to time leads to:

$$g_Y = \frac{1-\beta}{\beta} \cdot g_n \qquad (7.23)$$

With (7.21) it follows that:

$$g_Y = \frac{(1-\beta)^2 \cdot L}{\beta \cdot a_g} - (1-\beta) \cdot \rho \qquad (7.24)$$

Since $0 < \beta < 1$, the equation (7.24) implies that in this model the growth of the economy, measured in units of consumption goods, augments with:

- the increase in size of the basis of primary resources (labour L) $(dg_Y/dL > 0)$;
- the increase in productivity of labour in the research laboratory, that is, the decrease of a_g $(dg_Y/da_g < 0)$;
- the greater patience of the consumers, that is, the decrease in the discount rate ρ $(dg_Y/d\rho < 0)$;
- the augmentation of the profits from the diversification, that is, the increase in the mark-up $1/\beta$ $(dg_Y/d\beta < 0)$.

Based on the equations for the capital and the labour market, these influences can be reconstituted by shifting the corresponding curves in Figure 7.4.

A necessary enlargement of this approach regards the disaggregation of the labour factor into different skills, that is, into high-skilled and low-skilled labour. Since research and development is especially intensive in the demand for high-skilled labour, the derived expression $(dY^H)/(dL) > 0$ is especially true for the available sum of high-skilled labour.

The connection between the sum of low-skilled labour and the economic growth depends upon how easily the two qualification levels of labour can be substituted in the production. If substitutability is very high, the connection between the sum of labour and growth is valid for both qualification levels.

With a substitutability which is not as good, an increase in unskilled labour can make the growth path of an economy fall, because with a decrease in high-skilled labour in research, designs will become more expensive in comparison with consumption goods. The critical threshold for the value of the substitution elasticity depends on the specification of the chosen growth model. Further discussions of this theme can be found in Grossman and Helpman (1991, Chapter 5).

7.4 DIFFERENTIATED CAPITAL COMPONENTS (ROMER MODEL)

The same elements as in the model in Section 7.3 are contained in the model by Romer (1990), especially the production innovations under monopolistic competition and a research sector, which creates product designs. However, in contrast to the above, the assembly of the intermediate goods into a consumption good is no longer free of charge. In the Romer model, the intermediate goods are differentiated capital components which are used for the production of consumption goods in combination with the input of labour. Put differently, the capital stock of the economy is disaggregated into distinct types of producer durables. Labour is disaggregated into skilled and unskilled labour. The sum of skilled labour is given exogenously, that is, it does not grow as in the human capital model in Section 6.3. In order to accentuate the difference from freely multipliable human capital, skilled labour will here be defined by the variable T.

Notation:

- T skilled labour
- L unskilled labour
- Y^H consumption (final) goods
- x_j differentiated capital components (producer durables)

- a_g input factor for skilled labour in research
- T_Y employment of T in the final goods sector
- T_g employment of T in the research sector
- w_T wage rate for skilled labour
- g_n growth rate of the designs
- z price (market value) of a design.

In contrast to the above model, three sectors must now be modelled. A special final goods sector for consumption goods is now added to the research sector and the intermediate goods sector. With the input of differentiated capital services and skilled as well as unskilled labour, this sector produces consumption goods. In order for the model to be simply solvable, we use a Cobb–Douglas function as in the paper by Romer (1990) for the production of the consumption goods.

The three sectors will now be formally represented in turn. Thereafter, a simple method for solving the system for the steady-state growth rate will follow; the method will be different from the solution path shown in the above model.

The consumption goods sector produces final goods Y^H with the input of unskilled labour, skilled labour, and n differentiated capital components, that is, producer durables. This occurs with the following production function:

$$Y^H = T_Y^\alpha \cdot L^\beta \cdot \sum_{j=1}^{n} x_j^{1-\alpha-\beta} \qquad (7.25)$$

The aggregation of the intermediate goods, this time to an enlarged capital input, again occurs over the already introduced CES function. Here also, perfect symmetry between the differentiated goods is assumed. The final goods Y^H are consumed by the households and so create a direct utility. Therefore, in the long-term steady state, the output growth of consumption goods is to be optimised, taking intertemporal consumption preferences into consideration. Here the households perform the optimisation according to the Keynes–Ramsey rule as usual (see Section 4.3).

As in the above model, the intermediate goods enterprises buy designs with the know-how for production of the differentiated intermediate goods or capital inputs from the research sector. Monopolistic competition reigns on the market for differentiated goods. The demand for intermediate goods results from the optimisation of the firms of the final goods sector. Marginal product (*MPK*) of the jth capital input in the production of consumption goods is found out by differentiating (7.25) with respect to x_j:

$$MPK_{x_j} = (1 - \alpha - \beta) \cdot T_Y^\alpha \cdot L^\beta \cdot x_j^{-\alpha-\beta} \qquad (7.26)$$

The other marginal products can be calculated analogously. In the steady state, the marginal product of the jth intermediate good is equal to the price of this intermediate good, and all x-goods have the same price p_x. Thus, the revenues of the jth intermediate good enterprise are:

$$p_x \cdot x_j = (1 - \alpha - \beta) \cdot T_Y^\alpha \cdot L^\beta \cdot x_j^{1-\alpha-\beta} \qquad (7.27)$$

To simplify matters, it is assumed that as inputs for the production of x-goods, x-goods are also used; then, according to the assumption, $\zeta \cdot x$ has to be put in for the production of the amount x of intermediate goods, for which a market interest rate r has to be paid. Therefore, the variable costs which arise in the production of intermediate goods are equal to $r \cdot \zeta \cdot x$, and the profit of intermediate good enterprise number j is:

$$\pi_j = p_x \cdot x_j - r \cdot \zeta \cdot x_j$$

$$= (1 - \alpha - \beta) \cdot T_Y^\alpha \cdot L^\beta \cdot x_j^{1-\alpha-\beta} - r \cdot \zeta \cdot x_j \qquad (7.28)$$

The CES formulation for differentiated capital input leads analogously to the model in (7.3) to an optimum mark-up for intermediate goods of $(1 - \alpha - \beta)^{-1}$. Now the profit is as follows:

$$\pi_j = (\alpha + \beta) \cdot p_x \cdot x_j$$

$$= (\alpha + \beta) \cdot (1 - \alpha - \beta) \cdot T_Y^\alpha \cdot L^\beta \cdot x_j^{1-\alpha-\beta} \qquad (7.29)$$

In the third and last sector of the economy, research is undertaken with the help of skilled labour and based on general knowledge. If a research firm develops a new design, it can, as in the above model, make it impossible for others to use it by patenting. The other firms that are active in the research field still benefit from the new discovery, since the know-how contained in the design enlarges the publicly accessible knowledge.

The production of new designs occurs as in the above model (see expressions 7.7 and 7.8), with the only difference that skilled labour is now used as input. With the renewed standardisation to proportional knowledge spillovers, that is $\kappa(t) = n(t)$, the growth rate of the designs is now:

$$\frac{\Delta n}{n} = g_n = \frac{1}{a_g} \cdot T_g \tag{7.30}$$

Steady-state growth is derived as follows. The growth of the designs and therefore of the amounts of consumption goods depends on the employment of skilled labour in the research laboratory. Because of the restriction of a fixed supply of skilled labour, this employment is equal to the total supply minus the employment in the final goods sector, which is now to be determined.

In equilibrium, the wage for skilled labour must be the same in both sectors. If all intermediate goods are used symmetrically, then the marginal product and therefore the wage rate of factor T in the final goods sector is:

$$w_T = \alpha \cdot T_Y^{\alpha - 1} \cdot L^{\beta} \cdot n \cdot x^{1 - \alpha - \beta} \tag{7.31}$$

In this model, as in the neo-classical theory, the consumption goods serve as numéraire, which is why the price of the final good is equal to one. In the research laboratory, in which Δn new designs are developed at any given moment, the value marginal product of skilled labour with a given level of knowledge is:

$$w_T = z \cdot n \cdot \frac{1}{a_g} \tag{7.32}$$

By equating both expressions, we have:

$$\alpha \cdot T_Y^{\alpha - 1} \cdot L^{\beta} \cdot x^{1 - \alpha - \beta} = z \cdot \frac{1}{a_g} \tag{7.33}$$

The price of the design z results from the reflection that in the steady-state at any moment, the profit of an intermediate goods firm π_j is equal to the interest returns on an investment of amount z in the asset which yields a fixed return r, that is, at every moment in time, the following is true for every design:

$$\pi_j = r \cdot z$$

So z is the quotient of profit and interest rate. Inserting the profit from expression (7.29) leads to the following equation:

$$z = \frac{\alpha + \beta}{r} \cdot (1 - \alpha - \beta) \cdot T_Y^{\alpha} \cdot L^{\beta} \cdot x^{1 - \alpha - \beta} \qquad (7.34)$$

Now this z is inserted into expression (7.33). The result is solved for T_Y, and so we have found the required employment of skilled labour in the final goods sector, according to:

$$T_Y = a_g \cdot \frac{\alpha}{(1 - \alpha - \beta)(\alpha + \beta)} \cdot r \qquad (7.35)$$

The employment in the research laboratory is given by the fixed supply T through $T_g = T - T_Y$. According to (7.30) and (7.35), the growth rate of the designs is derived through:

$$g_n = \frac{T_g}{a_g} = \frac{T}{a_g} - \frac{\alpha}{(1 - \alpha - \beta)(\alpha + \beta)} \cdot r \qquad (7.36)$$

With the parameters of the production function, expression (7.36) represents the supply effect and is represented by the straight line TT in Figure (7.5). According to the supply effect, the resulting growth rate is influenced by the model parameters as follows:

- positively by the total supply of skilled labour T
- positively by the productivity of skilled labour in research $1/a_g$
- negatively by the interest rate r.

In the chosen specification, the growth rate of the designs or knowledge is equal to the growth rate of consumption, that is, $g_n = g$. Therefore, the model can be closed, as shown in Figure (7.5), with the use of the Keynes–Ramsey rule. With a logarithmic utility function, according to Section 4.3, this rule is $g = r - \rho$.

As can be seen, the steady-state growth also depends negatively on the discount rate of the households in this model, through the Keynes–Ramsey rule. The amount of skilled labour and the productivity parameter of the research laboratory shift the TT curve in the diagram in a vertical direction. The steady-state growth is independent of the input amount of unskilled labour. This result is caused by the utilisation of the Cobb–Douglas production function in the final goods sector and is not a robust characteristic of this kind of growth model.

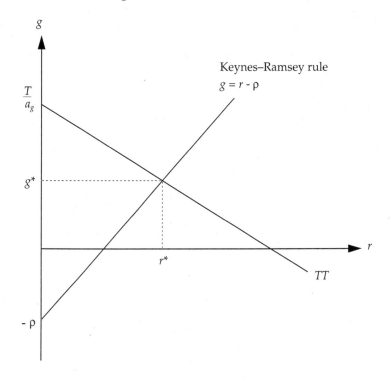

Figure 7.5 Steady-state growth in the Romer model

7.5 EXTENSIONS OF THE MODEL

a) Gains from Specialisation

In the model introduced in Section 7.3., the parameter β serves two purposes: it measures the gains from specialisation and it directly yields the optimal mark-up for firms operating under monopolistic competition. This setting has far-reaching consequences regarding policy recommendations. It leads to the conclusion that there is always too little research under market conditions compared to the social optimum, see Section 7.6 and Grossman and Helpman (1991, p. 71). Assuming the gains from specialisation to be very small compared to monopoly power, however, it might be the case that the incentives to invest in R&D are too high under free market conditions. A possible formulation for high-tech goods Y^H to express this distinction between gains from specialisation and monopoly power is proposed by Benassy (1998):

$$Y^H = n^{\zeta + 1 - 1/\beta} \cdot \left[\sum_{j=1}^{n} (x_j)^\beta \right]^{1/\beta} \qquad (7.37)$$

Assuming again a symmetrical equilibrium as in (7.2) and setting $X = n \cdot x$, we obtain for the output of high-tech goods:

$$Y^H = n^\zeta \cdot X \qquad (7.38)$$

which differs from (7.5), which was used until now. According to (7.37), the optimal mark-up for the intermediate goods firm is still $1/\beta$, as the change in the term outside the parenthesis has no effect on the substitution possibilities between intermediates x. However, expression (7.38) says that now the parameter ζ determines the gains from specialisation. The higher ζ, the larger the gains from using an increasing number of intermediates and the higher the growth rate with a given labour input into R&D.

In the specification (7.37), there is nothing to pin down the size of ζ with respect to β. Assuming very small gains from specialisation (low ζ), the case cannot be ruled out that incentives to invest in R&D are too high compared to the social optimum because of high monopoly profits which themselves cause a distortion; for a summary of all the distortions in the model and the consequences for policy, see Section 7.6.

b) Returns on Research

In the formulation of the research sector, it was assumed that every new design increases the stock of public knowledge proportionally. Knowledge is postulated to have constant returns in the research sector. The general idea behind this setting is that successful inventions increase the productivity of later research. Examples such as the discovery of calculus and the development of integrated circuits seem to support this mechanism. In other areas, however, it might be that new ideas are increasingly difficult to discover, that there might be something like a 'fishing-out' of a limited pool of total knowledge.

A more flexible specification for the research sector has been proposed by Jones (1995); in a slight change, compared to (7.8), it is:

$$\Delta n = \frac{1}{a_g} \cdot L_g \cdot n^{\phi} \tag{7.39}$$

If $\phi > 0$ we have the case where the productivity of research increases with the stock of knowledge; with $\phi < 0$ we have the scenario of 'fishing-out'. One can also refer to the first as 'standing on shoulders' and the second as 'standing on toes' in the research sector. Before, it was assumed that $\phi = 1$, whereas the case $0 < \phi < 1$ might be more realistic or at least more general. If this is assumed, the growth rate of designs becomes:

$$g_n = \frac{1}{a_g} \cdot L_g \cdot n^{\phi - 1} \tag{7.40}$$

In the long-term steady state, this growth rate is constant, so that by taking logarithms, differentiating (7.40) and setting to zero, one obtains for the long term:

$$g_n = \frac{g_L}{1 - \phi} \tag{7.41}$$

In this case, the long-term growth rate depends only on the population growth rate and a fixed technical parameter, which means that growth becomes invariant to economic policy (assuming g_L to be exogenous). As in the neo-classical growth model, policy can only influence the medium term, whereas the long term is given exogenously.

Several empirical observations seem to support this view. The number of scientists and engineers has increased significantly in the post-war period without obvious effects on productivity growth rates. In a similar manner, efforts in the education sector have been increased substantially in recent years while subsequent growth has not accelerated. Moreover, several empirical studies (see Boxes 3.1 and 3.2) find that the return to capital is decreasing over time, which could be applied to the case of knowledge capital. Finally, growth rates among countries differ substantially; however, this is not necessarily due to different R&D activities but to factors such as public infrastructure (see Chapter 6).

On the other hand, in contrast to the number of workers, the share of GDP allocated to R&D has not shown the same rates of increase but has been fairly constant over time. Moreover, the prediction of (7.41) would be that countries with a high population growth rate have a high income growth rate, but it is known that this does not apply (see, for example, Figure 9.2). Nevertheless, there are two important arguments in favour of decreasing returns to research. First, technology seems to become more and more complex, so that an increasing effort in research may become necessary to keep the rate of innovation on the same level. Second, as the number of goods rises, an innovation on any product might directly affect a smaller share of total economic activity, so that the total effect of spillovers becomes weaker over time.

When regarding the issues of returns to research in particular and knowledge-based growth in general, several measurement problems have to be observed. There are many research and education activities of firms which are not officially listed under the general heading R&D but which increase the knowledge of an economy as well. Moreover, the output of R&D can only be measured indirectly with certain proxy variables. It is especially difficult if innovations are aimed at improving the quality of products. Finally, it is not easy to find out what a correct measure for the depreciation rate of knowledge might be and what events can alter this depreciation rate.

c) Increasing Product Quality

The endogenous innovation model of Section 7.3 can be changed to a framework with a fixed number of differentiated goods but with an increasing quality of goods over time (see, for example, Grossman and Helpman 1991, Chapter 4). Research is undertaken to improve the quality of existing intermediate goods. Each type of good is said to have a 'quality ladder', along which improvements of a predetermined size can occur.

Innovations appear with a certain probability. This is technically expressed by assuming that each industry experiences sporadic technological breakthroughs, with the arrival of innovations being guided by independent Poisson processes.

A successful researcher obtains exclusive rights over the use of the improved good. But in this model set-up, only the leading-edge quality of each type of intermediates is sold in the market, whereas old goods are displaced as soon as a higher quality is available. Here, the full power of 'creative destruction' is brought into effect. When deciding on how much to invest in R&D, one therefore has to consider the size of the profit flow as well as the predicted duration of the flow. The smaller the expected duration, the smaller the anticipated payoff from R&D.

As in the expansion-in-varieties model of Section 7.3, the quality-ladder approach predicts faster growth when the resource base becomes larger (more inputs being available for research), when the productivity of inputs in the R&D rises, when households have a lower discount rate and when the gains from quality improvements are valued more highly. The main difference of the quality-ladder model from the expansion-in-varieties approach lies in the policy conclusion regarding the optimal research level and optimal growth rate of an economy (see Section 7.6).

d) Resource-saving Innovations

As regards production technique in the context of the new growth theory, the connection between primary factors and economic growth is one of the most interesting questions. In the models introduced, the primary factor is labour, which was introduced either in the aggregated form or disaggregated into two qualification levels. However, in an enlargement of the theory presented, other inputs such as raw material and energy will also have to be considered as primary factors (see Chapter 11).

In the model introduced in Section 7.3, a positive influence of the labour input on growth results. In this approach, a larger amount of labour causes the labour costs to fall; the additional labour forces are divided between both sectors. Economic growth increases because the input in the research sector rises.

The special characteristic of the chosen kind of modelling lies in the demand for research outputs. In the chosen CES specification for consumer goods, it is independent of the wage rate. In reality, however, research is often especially intensive when wage rates are high. This happens so that expensive labour can be used more efficiently, or can be reduced through increased technical knowledge. This is how the well-known phenomenon of economies which are actually still growing but generate only constant or even decreasing employment over time, arises. For the representation of this phenomenon, an additional channel, which creates a relationship between wage rates and research returns, must be planned in the model. A high wage rate becomes a great stimulant for research when the designs, that is, knowledge, represent a good substitute for labour. In the case of unskilled labour, the industrial robot has become a major substitute for workers. A model incorporating labour-saving technical progress is introduced in Bretschger (1999b).

Another point is the role of unskilled labour in view of costs in the research sector. The energy and natural environment factors can also be considered. These inputs show a similarity in that they are both used in moderation in the research laboratory. It is clearly skilled labour which is in most demand in research.

As already mentioned, the size of substitutability of the different inputs in production plays the decisive role in this context. Romer's approach in Section 7.4 is an exception, since the substitution elasticity is exactly equal to one with the chosen Cobb–Douglas production function. It is possible only in this way that the supply of unskilled labour does have no influence on the growth path in this model of a closed economy, because with this production function, substitution effect and output effect compensate each other exactly.

e) Market Structure

According to the assumption of the chosen models with R&D, there is perfect competition in the research sector. In both approaches, the market value or price of a design was set equal to the production costs for the production of the design; therefore a positive mark-up over marginal research costs is excluded. However, in the research sector, as in other sectors, monopolistic elements create too small an amount of produced output in comparison to perfect competition. Therefore, when monopoly or monopoly-like situations are observed in the research field, a fiercer competition situation leads to higher efficiency of the labour allocated to this sector. Therefore, a decrease in monopoly power in research increases the economic growth rate analogously to the positive influence on economic growth of the labour productivity of the research laboratory.

The connection between the intensity of competition in the production of differentiated goods and the growth rate is more difficult. In this model, greater competition intensity means smaller mark-ups on the marginal costs, and therefore lower profits per enterprise in the monopolistic competition. In the model presented here, economic growth shrinks with the increase in competition, because this reduces the stimulus for the production of designs.

For a more complete view of the reality of this assertion, two points should be added. First, it should be possible to differentiate monopoly because of innovations from monopoly based on the regulation of cartels, which have nothing to do with innovations. In reality, an improved protection of knowledge property rights intensifies the stimulus for investment in research. On the other hand, for example, regional arrangements among suppliers of standardised products with the goal of artificial geographical segmenting of markets is no contribution to dynamic development. Second, it can be observed that monopoly-like positions of enterprises in innovative sectors lead to possible scale effects in research. For example a big firm is much more likely than smaller firms to be able to entertain a diversified pool of a specifically educated labour force and in this way contribute a continual service in research.

7.6 CONSEQUENCES FOR ECONOMIC POLICY

There are several distortions in an economy which is represented by the dynamic R&D model of this chapter. First, in the sector of intermediate goods we have non-competitive pricing. If there were another sector of consumer goods with prices equal to marginal cost, there would be a static distortion. However, in the models studied so far, there is only one final goods sector. A specific effect of innovations is the destruction of profits of already existing producers. On the other hand, each new good increases the surplus for either consumers or producers (depending on the use of the new good as consumer good or intermediate good in production). With the symmetric CES specification used in Sections 7.3 and 7.4, the profit destruction effect just happens to offset the surplus effect. There is thus no specific role for economic policy in these respects.

The dynamic distortion in the R&D model which is effective comes from the knowledge spillovers in research. The existence of positive externalities in the research sector is a form of market failure. The social marginal product of research investments is higher than the private marginal product. In the simple CES specification of Sections 7.3 and 7.4, a correctly measured government subsidy of the activities with positive spillovers leads to the internalisation of the external effects and so to an increase in both growth and welfare.

Although choosing concrete projects which are worth subsidising is not easily realised in general, it is precisely this task which in reality cannot be omitted in government-financed basic research. Beyond that, it is above all the conditions for learning-intensive activities such as research and development which should be optimal in an economy. This sector should be supported as a whole. The decision on the concrete factor input then rests with the private investors, who must pay attention to the existing market stimulants because of their participation in the costs.

Various arguments in favour of further preferential treatment of individual research fields can be put forward. For instance, big indivisibility can arise in certain projects, that is, research can succeed only if it surpasses a critical size. It is also a strategic question for a country, whether its own enterprises should receive subsidies when the foreign competitors are also subsidised by the host government. Finally, the incompleteness of the capital markets or the importance of vertical binding (for example, the creation of employment in the intermediate goods sector) can be reasons for subsidies.

There are also good arguments against subsidies from the government. The information problem is greater for government actors since they are further away from the concrete problems than are the market participants. What is more, private lobbying activity can strongly influence decisions of government employees. It must also be said that, from experience, subsidies have a tendency to persist, that is, they remain in force even when the situation of the private enterprises no longer justifies them. Furthermore, private institutions such as professional associations or chambers of commerce can improve the exchange of information in a field or region in such a way that a part of the spillovers is already internalised. In addition, even in the field of research there is a danger of bureaucratisation in the presence of government engagement.

Under Subsection a) in the extensions of Section 7.5, the gains from specialisation were altered. If the gains from specialisation become small, it is possible that there is too much R&D under market conditions. The evaluation of the different effects of R&D is thus also an empirical matter. In the extension under c) with the quality of products increasing over time, the case of too large a research sector cannot be excluded either. However, it seems that the effect of positive knowledge spillovers is in many cases still the most dominant of all effects, so that the trade-off between the social benefit of research subsidies and the difficulties in political implementation as discussed above remains the central issue.

The advantages and disadvantages of government research subsidies are to be weighted according to the circumstances, so that a balanced basis for the concrete political decisions can be created. In conclusion, the reader is reminded that, in contrast to the neo-classical growth theory, in the context of the new growth theory, a larger growth rate is not automatically equated with an increased welfare, for higher growth rates require an additional economic resource input with corresponding opportunity costs.

SELECTED READING

- AGHION, P. and P. HOWITT (1998), *Endogenous Growth Theory*, Cambridge Mass.: MIT Press.

- BENASSY, J. (1998), 'Is There Always too Little Research in Endogenous Growth with Expanding Product Variety?', *European Economic Review,* **42** (1), 61–9.

- BRETSCHGER, L. (1999b), 'Labour Supply, Migration, and Long-term Development', manuscript, University of Zurich.

- CHAMBERLIN, E. (1933), *The Theory of Monopolistic Competition*, Cambridge Mass.: Harvard University Press.

- DIXIT, A. and J.E. STIGLITZ (1977), 'Monopolistic Competition and Optimum Product Diversity', *American Economic Review,* **67** (3), 297–308.

- GROSSMAN, G. and E. HELPMAN (1990), 'Comparative Advantage and Long-run Growth', *American Economic Review,* **80**, 796–815.

- GROSSMAN, G. and E. HELPMAN (1991), *Innovation and Growth in the Global Economy*, Cambridge Mass.: MIT Press.

- JONES, C. (1995), 'R&D-based Models of Economic Growth', *Journal of Political Economy,* **103**, 759–84.

- ROMER, P.M. (1990), 'Endogenous Technological Change', *Journal of Political Economy,* **98** (5), part II, S71–S102.

8. Open Economy

8.1 EXTENSIONS OF TRADE THEORY

a) Trade and Dynamics

The traditional theory of foreign trade is based on the neo-classical assumptions regarding the production function. Models with two countries, two goods and two input factors are the most widespread in textbooks. Here, the simple approaches are static, since inputs such as labour and land are assumed to be fixed. If capital is introduced as an input, middle-term adjustment processes, which lead the system to a new steady state after shocks, can be modelled according to the neo-classical growth model.

Another direction taken in studies is to look at the consequences of exogenous growth in the foreign trade position of a country. Here for both cases, that of growth on the demand side (greater consumption demand from foreign countries) and that of growth on the supply side (better production conditions in the domestic economy), an evaluation can be made about whether the trade streams are intensifying in the dynamic process or becoming less important.

In this kind of analysis, special attention is given to the fact that growth changes the terms of trade for an economy. Following a dynamic development, the relation between export and import prices for a country can worsen in such a way that the general wealth effect becomes negative as a whole (the case of 'immiserising growth'). Of course, this only happens under extremely unpropitious circumstances.

In principle, it is not always necessary to use multi-sector models for the explanation of foreign trade. In a direct application of the intertemporal optimisation according to the explanations in Chapter 4, exports and imports can also be explained in a one-sector model. Instead of different factor endowments, differing discount rates and/or growth possibilities can cause countries to trade with each other. It is propitious to wealth if certain countries create or increase their debts in foreign countries for the sake of a higher present-time consumption and pay back the debt in the future.

The goods exchanged between the countries are physically the same, but the moment of consumption can be optimised in the participating economies over this so-called 'intertemporal trade'. However, the benefits of intertemporal trade are guaranteed only if the agents have rational expectations and the paying back of the debts can be enforced by law or political power.

In the fields of trade theory mentioned so far, growth is exogenously given. On the other hand, different approaches were presented in Chapters 6 and 7 which lead to an endogenous explanation of economic growth. Therefore, the influence of foreign trade on the mentioned growth fields, and especially on the conditions for the accumulation of capital, can be examined in general. The influences in the inverse direction, that is, of accumulation on foreign trade, must likewise be introduced into the theory.

As was explained in Chapters 5–7, the endogenous explanation of the growth process is based on economies of scale, which increase in the course of time. Expressed in the example of research, this means that the more research already done in the past, the more productive research is; the greater the knowledge capital, the greater the advantage. The same is also true for the other capital components. Therefore, it is obviously of decisive importance for the international division of labour in what way the economies of scale of a country can be shared by the other countries, and inversely, in what way the individual country can participate in the economies of scale of the other countries.

Since the possibilities of exploitation of scale effects are broader in the international context, new growth chances arise out of the establishment of outward relationships. For example, in the international transmission of knowledge capital, such chances are to be expected. As already stated above, knowledge capital can arise as a side product of different kinds of investments, such as physical capital investments or R&D investments. The size of the geographical spread of the positive knowledge spillovers is therefore of importance in the field of knowledge diffusion (compare Box 5.1).

In the different models of Chapter 6, endogenous growth was also explained by the accumulation of other factors such as public services and human capital. Typically, the effect of public services is limited to the geographical region which belongs to the political unity. Human capital is internationally mobile only if skilled labour forces migrate over the country boundaries. In reality, this share of internationally mobile skilled labour is small in comparison to the total amount of skilled labour.

If economies of scale remain partly or totally limited to a country or region, distinct specialisation patterns arise in the interregional and international division of labour. Because a country or region can gain economies of scale in special industries which are non-, or barely, existent in other places. By considering the history of many regions, it can be shown how such specialisations, for example, in financial centres, heavy industry locations, high-tech regions and so on, arose through accumulated scale effects. Often it was a rather accidental fact that led to the beginning of such a development.

Another crucial point in the transition from autarky to free trade is the change induced by trade in the intersectoral factor allocation. After the opening of an economy, a country with comparative advantage in traditional production can specialise more in this field without giving up its other activities completely, because of the relative factor endowment. In contrast, countries with comparative advantage in research or in high-tech sectors will use more resources in these fields and will import more traditional goods.

In the following, we shall concentrate on the approach of Chapter 7 with endogenous research and development, since it is helpful to understand the opening of a dynamic economy to free trade. The different effects in the field of economies of scale and resource reallocation will be discussed in turn. One characteristic of this model is the production of differentiated intermediate products under monopolistic competition. Before concentrating on the dynamics, therefore, in the next subsection we shall introduce the consequences of this market form for the international goods trade.

b) Monopolistic Competition with Foreign Competitors

Basing our consideration on the model in Section 7.3, we will look at international trade with differentiated intermediate goods which are produced under monopolistic competition. Since trade with intermediate products takes place within a certain industry, it is commonly called 'intraindustrial' trade.

With regard to the domestic economy, in the international context it is true for intermediate products that each individual enterprise will specialise in a particular product. This is the only way to guarantee complete coverage of the fixed costs. In equilibrium with intraindustrial trade, all economies produce differentiated products, but one particular good is always produced only by one country. Those varieties that are not produced in a country can be imported from another country. In this way, the gains from diversification fall to all countries.

The argument of gains from trade with differentiated goods is based on the assumption that there is a greater variety of goods available in a country after starting foreign trade. This is generally expected but does not need to be true for every model of monopolistic competition. The number of enterprises which produce differentiated goods is an endogenous variable which will normally change after opening to foreign trade. In the model under Section 7.3, in all economies which participate in foreign trade, the productivity in the production of high-tech consumption goods rises when there is a greater variety of intermediate products.

With the applied CES form, the mark-up over the marginal costs stays constant even with the establishment of trade relations. This constant mark-up guarantees that in the case of an enlargement of the total market volume a greater number of enterprises exists, or put differently, can cover their fixed costs. In this way, in the CES formulation of monopolistic competition, the greater variety is guaranteed by free trade, because foreign trade always leads to an increase in the total demand.

In the applied model, the establishment of trade relations means a jump in the number of available intermediate products. Productivity rises in both countries because more of the high-tech consumption good Y^H can be produced everywhere. In this way, the utility of the households increases according to the parameters of the utility function. This can be checked with the following expression based on equation (7.6):

Notation:

- a autarky
- f free trade

$$\left(\frac{Y^H}{X}\right)_a = (n_a)^{(1-\beta)/\beta} < \left(\frac{Y^H}{X}\right)_f = (n_f)^{(1-\beta)/\beta} \qquad (8.1)$$

since $n_a < n_f$ and $0 < \beta < 1$.

With differentiated goods, it is undefined in the model which country produces which variety itself and which varieties are imported. In reality, it is usually enterprise-specific initiatives of the past which decide the concrete specialisation in particular intermediate goods.

As long as the production of intermediate products does not lead to 'pure' rents (rents which do not serve to cover fixed costs) – and this is the basic assumption of monopolistic competition – the allocation of production of specific intermediate goods to different countries does not matter with regard to welfare.

c) A Growth Model of the Open Economy

For trade with final goods, traditional trade theory takes – with the exception of intertemporal trade – at least two consumption goods sectors into consideration. In the widespread approach with two countries, two factors and two goods, each country exports a good according to its comparative advantage in the factor endowment. A model which can easily be applied for our purposes includes the following two goods or sectors:

- high-tech consumption goods, which are assembled from differentiated intermediate goods
- traditional consumption goods, which are produced under perfect competition with constant returns to scale.

The primary factors, such as labour, are allocated more in one or the other sector according to international division of labour. The first sector encompasses two activities: the production of intermediate products and the assembly of these intermediate products into a high-tech consumption good. Since, as can be seen in the model in Section 7.3, no primary factors are necessary for the assembly, this activity falls into the same sector as the intermediate goods.

In addition to the intraindustrial trade, an interindustrial trade can be examined in this model, because a cross-border exchange of traditional products for high-tech goods can be represented. As an addition to the discussions in Section 7.3, we disaggregate the labour factor into skilled and unskilled labour. The two-sector economy is enlarged by a third sector, which contains research, for the representation of dynamics. Here again, it is the task of research to develop new designs for intermediate products. This three-sector approach was introduced into the theory mainly by Grossman and Helpman (1991).

In this dynamic model, the growth rate is determined by the total amount of resources in the production of designs and the efficiency of these resources. It is therefore decisive how, in the research sector, the costs and the expected products of the investments change through the establishment or stepping up of foreign trade. The following channels can be examined:

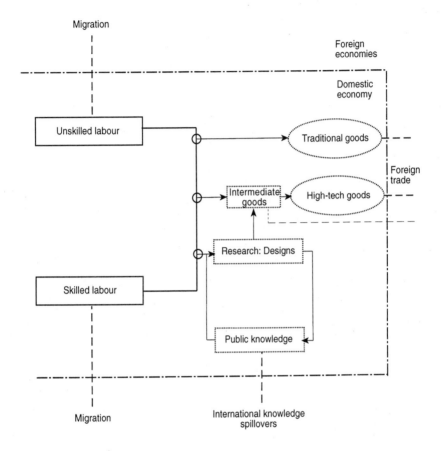

Figure 8.1 Foreign trade and growth with R&D

- international knowledge diffusion
- position of the country on world goods markets
- factor endowment (changed through migration of skilled and unskilled labour).

For this examination, the growth model from Chapter 7 can be formulated algebraically for two countries. From this follows the complete mathematical derivation of the influence of foreign trade on the growth path (see Grossman and Helpman 1991). Here, the results are represented in the simplified form of a survey. As a first step, Figure 8.1 shows the graphic representation of the production and the goods structure of the model as well as the different impacts of foreign trade on a country.

With the help of this structure, the listed effects of foreign trade will be discussed in the two sections on scale effects and resource reallocation effects.

8.2 SCALE EFFECTS OF FOREIGN TRADE

a) International Knowledge Diffusion

The long-term economic development of the economies represented by the model in Section 7.3 is determined by the accumulated knowledge. The stock of public knowledge increases, on the one hand, through investments in research and development of the domestic economy. On the other hand, knowledge from abroad also has an effect, which differs according to the intensity of the international knowledge diffusion.

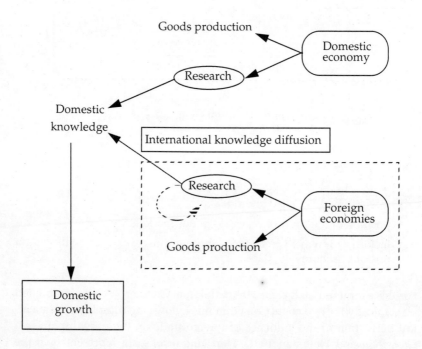

Figure 8.2 International knowledge diffusion

The transferability of knowledge over a country's borders depends, on the one hand, on the specific kind of knowledge and, on the other hand, on the available communication possibilities. As can be seen in Figure 8.2, international knowledge spillovers have the effect of an enlarged domestic labour input in the research laboratory. Spillovers over country borders make the level of public knowledge rise faster since foreign countries now contribute to its increase as well. Since in this way, there is more public knowledge available as free input in research and development at any moment in time, the output in designs and therefore also the economic growth increase. The fact that, under certain circumstances, foreign knowledge might not flow into the country, is represented in the figure by a separate, dotted arrow.

b) Position on World Goods Markets

The increasing internationalisation of the goods market is not without effect on the economic growth of the participating economies. The connection between openness in goods trade and growth rates in an international cross-section is represented in Figure 8.3. According to this representation, this connection, which is measured independently of further factors, is positive but not too close. There is, however, no statement connected to this measurement about the causality of the influence.

In the model in Chapter 7, every enterprise in the field of differentiated goods will specialise in producing a product variety which exists only once, after free trade has been established. This means that, for the research sector, foreign trade sets new incentives, since designs which already exist in another country – in contrast to autarky – have no market value. Trade in differentiated goods eliminates the duplicative research efforts in the development of new brands. All research efforts expand the world-wide knowledge basis, since all research efforts aim at a product which is new on the world market and redundancies are thus avoided. This is positive for the economies which participate in the world trade.

Additionally, in taking up free trade, the markets for the individual supplier of differentiated goods become larger. With increased production, the average costs fall according to the assumptions, and so because of the CES assumption, the profit per enterprise rises. This could lead to additional enterprises entering the market if another effect did not have the contrary impact: the number of competitors in foreign countries rises through the opening of the markets, which causes the profit per enterprise to fall. The question, therefore, is which effect dominates.

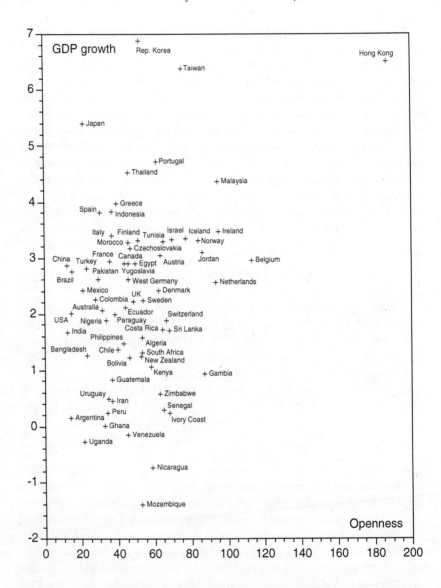

Note: Average GDP growth: real, per annum, per capita and in %; openness as the
         sum of exports and imports divided by GDP.
Source: Summers/Heston, Penn World Table 5.6.

Figure 8.3 Average growth rates, 1960–1990, and openness of the economy

The case of the pure scale effect (see title) can be seen especially clearly in this model. It can be understood best by imagining an establishment of trade between two identical economies. In these economies, the factor prices are already the same before starting free trade. With identical factor prices in the two countries, the fixed costs (= costs of the designs) and the marginal costs of the intermediate product producers are also the same. Since, with the CES assumption, the demand for all domestic and foreign intermediate products is symmetrical, the same amount of all intermediate products is demanded. Since, additionally, the mark-ups are identical, the profit per enterprise is already the same everywhere before the establishment of free trade.

In this case, the profit per firm does not change with the establishment of free trade, that is, the positive and the negative influence of free trade balance each other precisely. The mark-up over marginal costs stays constant by assumption. The stimulants for research and the attractiveness of design production do not change through the integration of the goods markets in connection with the competition effects.

As an enlargement of the model, one could assume that the mark-up factor becomes smaller in free trade. This would mean that the stronger competition on the goods markets which are free world-wide has a negative effect on growth. Another modification of the model would work against this negative effect: the fact, as seen in Chapter 7, that a decrease in the monopolisation in the research sector arises, which influences growth positively.

c) Changes in Resource Supplies

In the considered model, the migration of labour forces over the country borders has an effect on growth through the amount of available primary factors. After an immigration, for example, a greater number of primary factors, which can be used for diverse activities, exist in the considered country.

If the labour quantities in skilled and unskilled labour change with migration, the relative factor and goods prices will normally shift. In consequence the factors will be reallocated among the three sectors (see next section). However, if the quantities of both qualification levels increase proportionally, for example, each by one percent, a scale effect arises because of the factor migration.

According to Section 7.3, the aggregate labour factor L has the following influence on economic growth (see equation 7.15):

$$g_n = \frac{(1-\beta) \cdot L}{a_g} - \beta \cdot \rho \qquad\qquad (8.2)$$

So a proportional immigration of labour forces increases the domestic growth rate, while emigration causes the attained growth to fall. Even if after an immigration the production quantities of tradable goods do increase, an additional output still arises in the research laboratories; in the case of emigration, the corresponding development occurs in the inverse direction.

Besides the neglected qualification aspect of labour (following under 8.3), the position of the domestic economy on the world goods markets is not considered separately in this result. It can, however, be shown that the additional consideration of the goods markets does not change the statement as regards the scale effect. On the other hand, it has to be recalled that the applied model is not rich enough as regards labour-saving technical progress. Under the assumption that a great amount of labour reduces the stimulants for labour-saving technical progress, a counteracting force to the positive scale effect shown here arises.

8.3 REALLOCATION OF RESOURCES

a) Integration of Goods Markets

In reality, one should start from the principle that the relative factor input prices before the establishment of free trade are different internationally. Then foreign trade leads to a change in the factor prices. This also leads to a shift between the sectors of a part of the primary factors in every economy participating in the trade, that is, an intersectoral reallocation of resources results.

This reallocation changes the long-term economic development, because the endogenous growth path of the model in Chapter 7 is, apart from the pure scale effects (as the sum of available knowledge), decisively influenced by the sectoral structure of the economy. The more resources are allocated in the research field, the higher the attained growth rate becomes.

For growth, it is important how the costs of research change, and it is above all the wages of factors such as skilled labour, which is in intense demand in the research laboratory, which are of interest here. If, for example, the relative price of skilled labour falls, the costs of R&D decrease, which makes the investment stimulus rise. This makes the growth rate in the model increase.

Through the resource reallocation effect, an economy receives positive growth impulses if – under the assumption of perfect international knowledge diffusion – it intensifies its trade relations with a country which is extraordinarily rich in skilled labour. This kind of goods market integration can be analysed in the same way as an increase in skilled domestic labour, meaning a positive dynamic scale effect.

Consequences for the goods markets or the international division of labour also arise if the international knowledge diffusion is incomplete. If, in an extreme case, there is no international knowledge diffusion, then the scale effects in the research field are limited to the individual countries as is the case in autarky. If a country has a head start in research productivity, it can build this up progressively in the course of time. This means that it will attain an ever-growing share of the world market in the field of differentiated intermediate products. In the extreme case, the other countries with an initial delay in research productivity see themselves forced, after some time, to specialise completely in traditional goods.

Since the initial delay of certain countries and the advantage of others (divergence of the levels) increases steadily over time, the international division of labour is accentuated through foreign trade when there are locally limited scale effects. In certain circumstances, it can, however, be possible for a country to make up the delay in the research productivity or even to overtake other countries through additional investments limited in time. If such an overtaking succeeds, the international specialisation will thereafter automatically run in the opposite direction. In such a case, one talks of 'hysteresis', because the measure taken at a limited moment in time has permanent effects. This is true for the extreme case of non-existent international knowledge diffusion. As soon as the international knowledge diffusion becomes more intensive, the 'backward' countries are better placed for entering into research and for producing differentiated goods even without special support.

If, with free goods trade, international knowledge diffusion is not intensive enough, it can be, in the applied model, that a country with a large endowment of skilled labour concentrates on the production of differentiated intermediate goods. Even though traditional production decreases in this country, it is possible that, in the long-term steady state, research also suffers from this concentration on differentiated goods, which is negative for the growth rate. This case shows the importance of knowledge transmission in international relationships, which, in the context of trade theory, cannot be stressed enough.

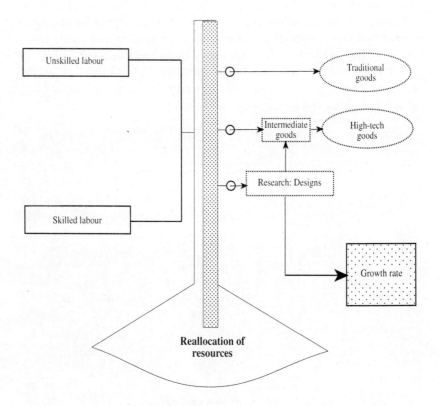

Figure 8.4 Reallocation through trade

With complete knowledge diffusion and not too different levels of factor endowment, all economies participating in free trade create innovations and receive positive spillovers. However, if the circle of considered countries is wide, one has to assume that certain economies do not, for different reasons, have this capability to produce innovations which are fit for world-wide competition. These countries can, however, specialise in copying foreign designs with certain imitation activities and then supply them at a cheaper price on the world markets. This is possible only under the condition that the patent protection of the leading countries cannot be totally enforced on the international level.

Using this idea, the applied model can be transformed into a model with product cycles, based on the assumption that, because of existing 'technology gaps', only certain countries (in the 'North' of the globe) execute innovative activities. In these 'North–South' models, the North invents new differentiated products which can be copied by the other countries (in the 'South' of the globe) after a certain period. As soon as it is possible, the production of these goods moves to the South, since, by assumption, the production costs are lower there.

b) Integration of Labour Markets

In Sections 7.3 and 8.2, the positive connection between the supply of aggregate labour and the growth rate was underlined. With a disaggregation of the labour factor, this statement is also true for high-skilled labour, since it is used intensively in the research laboratory. A migration structure which is mixed but concentrated on high qualifications can equally lead to an immigration, bringing improved chances of long-term development.

Somewhat different statements are true for low-skilled labour, since this type of labour is demanded mostly in the production of traditional goods. With a migration structure which is strongly concentrated on low-skilled labour, it can happen that, after an immigration, a country specialises increasingly in sectors with below average growth and, therefore, cannot benefit from the enlarged endowment with factors as regards growth.

The elasticities of substitution between high- and low-skilled labour in the represented sectors are decisive for the measure of sectoral redistribution after migration. Consider the case of immigration of unskilled labour: With a high elasticity of substitution there is an increasing probability that skilled labour is released from traditional production and is therefore additionally available for research. With a low elasticity of substitution, however, traditional production spreads in such a way, because of the same immigration, that employment of skilled labour in the other sectors decreases, which causes the growth rate to fall.

It can be shown that, in a closed economy and under the assumption of the Cobb–Douglas utility function, the critical value for the substitution elasticity (at which the direction of the effect changes) lies at a value of one. If international knowledge diffusion is perfect, the division of labour in the world results in such a way that it is again the value of one which is critical. If, on the contrary, international knowledge diffusion is so small that it becomes negligible, the critical value rises. In this case, the domestic market share on the world goods markets is also an important determinant, since it is decisive for the reactions on the goods markets after the migration. For the interpretation of these results, the statement that the new growth theory is based on the existence of positive externalities is of primary importance. This is the reason why the free market processes and the assumption of optimising agents do not lead to an optimum growth rate in the field of migration. Given this kind of market failure, the voluntary migration of the labour force is neither automatically positive nor automatically negative for the participating countries.

8.4 COMPETITIVENESS

In public discussion, the expression 'international competitiveness' is of absolutely primary importance. However, this frequently cited term has no direct equivalent in economic theory (built on neo-classical traditions). Some economists even strongly insist that it must be avoided at all costs in theory, since it is not clear-cut at all.

The problem of talking about competitiveness in economic theory lies first in the fact that the fixing of only one goal entity such as 'competitiveness' takes no restrictions whatsoever into consideration. Restrictions and the emphasis on trade-offs are, however, absolutely crucial to economic theory. The difficulty of theoretical transposition also involves three other main points:

- Competitiveness is based on relative positions.
- The expression 'competitiveness' has different meanings on different aggregation levels.
- Dynamics, up to now often neglected in theory, play an important role in competitiveness.

These three points will be discussed further in Subsections a) – c). A final assessment follows in Subsection d).

a) Relative Positions

Case studies on competitiveness oriented on economic actuality tend to concentrate on the success stories of individual enterprises or personalities. In contrast to this, every theoretical comprehension is necessarily connected with reductions and simplifications. Only a few differences among the actors, which lead to differences in the relative positions of the countries, industries or enterprises studied, can be taken into consideration at once.

The differences most frequently applied in trade theory up to now lie in the supply of production factors such as labour and capital as well as in the available technologies and raw materials, and increasingly also in the gains from scale effects and the international division of labour in product cycles. Through the application of growth theory, the palette of international differences can be enlarged by the important component of dynamics. Now, the long-term temporal development of determinants of foreign trade and of the relative positions in competition has become central to, rather than a fleeting impression of, these determinants.

b) Problems of Aggregation

For statements about competitiveness, the considered aggregation level is decisive. The success of an enterprise has repercussions for the activity of the other enterprises in the same location; the higher the degree of aggregation of the consideration, the more important the modelling of these repercussions becomes. In many older trade models, aggregate economies, sometimes with several sectors, are represented. Goods are internationally mobile, but factors are internationally completely immobile; comparative advantage alone decides the direction of foreign trade. Over the adjustments of relative prices, the success of certain enterprises or industries leads to higher costs for the others, since all producers compete for the same domestic resources.

In contrast to the early trade theories, it can no longer be ignored that capital and labour are in part internationally mobile and orient themselves by the absolute advantage in the case of direct investments and migration. Absolute advantages of countries arise for example from the availability of immobile factors and the political, institutional and social conditions particular to the individual country. On the aggregate level of economies, the comparative and the absolute advantages together determine competitiveness and international division of labour.

c) Dynamics

In the traditional trade model – with the emphasis on comparative advantage – competitiveness means that an economy adjusts itself quickly to the new situation after international shocks. The dynamic adjustment mechanisms on factor markets and goods markets determine on the reaching of full employment and the quality of the new long-term steady state. In individual economic perspective, the dynamics of enterprises and industries also play an important role; here it is above all the capability of adjustment to new trends and of the preparation of new solutions to problems which are of interest.

Therefore, the importance of dynamics and longer terms is stressed from the viewpoint both of comparative advantage and of single enterprises. The integration of long-term dynamics into newer growth theory is the consequence of this fact. Economies are competitive if, inside the international division of labour, they are able to establish an income development which is positive in the long term. Here it needs to be taken into consideration that this income must be measured correctly and that negative externalities such as harm done to human beings or to the natural environment by economic activities influence welfare negatively.

d) Conclusion

An enterprise is competitive if it can produce its goods at low costs (for example, because of technical advantages) and sell them successfully (for example, because of good marketing). A location (such as a region or a country) is competitive if the local enterprises exist successfully on a high technological level in the interregional and international competition, and if external enterprises are able to hold a strong position in this location. A high level of technology means high productivity of the employed factors such as labour and capital. High productivity allows the enterprises of a location to be competitive as regards prices and at the same time to pay good or above-average wages.

Not only the present level of productivity but – in view of the future – also its growth rate are important for judging competitiveness, since productivity is the result of long-term efforts. Seen from this perspective, the determining of an endogenous growth path under the model conditions of open economy is very close to what is called competitiveness in the present-day political debate.

This leads to the conclusion that the productivity of all employed factors in the total – the so-called total factor productivity – is a good measurement entity for the competitiveness of a location. In order to calculate this entity, however, the sums of the applied production factors must be statistically known (see Section 3.6).

In growth theory, the productivity of the enterprises of a location is influenced by the determinants which were discussed in the models in Chapters 6 and 7. In reality, additional factors can be important. It is imperative that the enterprises can find the required quantity and quality of the production factors which suit their production technique at their location. There are also the multiple interdependencies between markets which determine the productivity of the enterprises of a location.

For certain industries it is a noticeable advantage if the suppliers and customers are situated in close proximity. In addition, it is also helpful for certain enterprises if other enterprises in the same industry are located near by. On the one hand, this ensures that the regional labour market passes a critical measure so that the pool of labour forces is sufficiently rich. On the other hand, the diffusion of knowledge at a location is improved by the concentration of enterprises with similar activities. Finally, the political conditions are a decisive factor for the productivity of the employed factors at a location. Some of these are the quantity and quality of public services, institutional regulations as well as the quality and the reliability of the legal system.

SELECTED READING

- AGHION, P. and P. HOWITT (1998), *Endogenous Growth Theory*, Cambridge Mass.: MIT Press.
- BRETSCHGER, L. (1997): 'International Trade, Knowledge Diffusion, and Growth', *International Trade Journal*, **XI** (3), 327–48.
- BRETSCHGER, L. (1999a): 'Knowledge Diffusion and the Development of Regions', *Annals of Regional Science*, forthcoming.
- DIXIT, A. and V. NORMAN (1980), *Theory of International Trade*, Cambridge: Cambridge University Press.
- ETHIER, W.J. (1982), 'National and International Returns to Scale in the Modern Theory of International Trade', *American Economic Review*, **72** (3), 389–405.
- GROSSMAN, G. and E. HELPMAN (1991), *Innovation and Growth in the Global Economy*, Cambridge Mass.: MIT Press.
- HELPMAN, E. and P. KRUGMAN (1985), *Market Structure and Foreign Trade*, Cambridge Mass.: MIT Press.
- OBSTFELD, M. and K. ROGOFF (1996), *Foundations of International Macroeconomics*, Cambridge Mass.: MIT Press.
- RIVERA-BATIZ, L.A. and P.M. ROMER (1991), 'Economic Integration and Endogenous Growth', *Quarterly Journal of Economics*, **106** (2), 531–55.

9. Extensions

9.1 FINANCIAL MARKETS

In the growth models applied up to now, households have a limited number of possibilities to invest their savings. Those who convert these savings into investments also have few alternatives at their disposal. In the simplest neo-classical models, one is even 'forced' to save a fixed part of the income and to let the funds flow into physical capital investments.

In the context of intertemporal optimisation, the possibility for the households to choose between ongoing consumption and a risk-free investment in the form of bonds was introduced. In the presented models with education and research and development, the spectrum was enlarged by the possibility of investments in human capital and in research projects. The neo-classical growth model was already enlarged by a monetary sector in Section 3.9. In this section, we shall discuss what changes would occur if additional assets such as money or different investments with possibly more risk are also taken into consideration in newer growth theory.

a) Money as Additional Asset

In an economy, money has two principal functions: it causes the transaction costs of trading processes to fall and it is a form of value storage. For the introduction of money into a growth model, different possibilities are possible. Money plays a role in production, saving and financing, the three key fields of simple growth models. Following the monetarism debate, the question needs to be asked again in what way money and the entire financial sector are neutral as regards long-term real economic development.

The integration of money as a means of value storage is what lies closest. In this enlarged growth model, the savings of the households then flow either into money or physical capital; the latter contributes to regular income, as in all growth models. In static consideration, money as an asset absorbs means of saving and thus reduces the physical capital investments. In the neo-classical growth model, it is the steady-state per capita income which decreases (see Section 3.9); in the new growth theory it is the long-term growth rate.

In the dynamic perspective, the attractiveness of investing in money is determined by how flexibly goods prices and interest rates and thereby real interest rates react to changed monetary policy. The interest rates are important for the speculative demand for money and play a role because 'money' is often held in the form of short-term bonds.

Different simplified variants are possible as regards temporal adjustments of prices. Fast price adjustments (inflation) and sluggish nominal interest rates lead, after a money supply expansion, to a 'flight' into physical capital investments, since the costs of holding money increase. If the additionally released physical investments are productive, then long-term economic development is positively influenced. If, however, the additional investments only cause a speculative boom (for example on the market for real estate), then the positive growth effect is questionable.

Sluggish price adjustments cause portfolio imbalances, which can, under certain circumstances, lead to lower investments in physical capital (model type 'Keynes–Wicksell I'). However, sluggish price adjustments can also cause disequilibria on the goods market, which can lead to 'forced saving' (model type 'Keynes–Wicksell II'). Again, the latter case would be positive for the long-term economic development, while lower investments are negative for the long term.

b) Multiple Assets and Capital Markets

A great variety of possible investments exists in reality. The intertemporal allocation of the savings to investment projects occurs over the financial markets. The idea of a financial sector which is neutral as regards the real development is rejected by most economists. The financial markets seem to fulfil important economic functions. It is therefore logical to deduce that real economic consequences are bound to this. Otherwise, the immense expenditure on the financial markets would appear as a total waste of resources.

From the point of view of growth, how the accumulation of productive factors is influenced by the structure of the financial markets is decisive. The decisions on the financial markets influence the growth process by the sorts and amounts of financed investments. The more efficient and productive the design of the financial sector, the better are the conditions for an adequate growth.

Different possible problem fields arise here. For one thing, there is the question whether enough risk capital for the financing of risky research projects can be held ready on the financial markets. In the existing growth models with an integrated research sector, the differentiation of risk categories has still rarely been studied. In reality, there are also credit rationings which may hinder economic development, since the number and choice of the financed projects are no longer determined by the usual optimum conditions.

Distortions in the financing structure can also be a possible cause of hindrances of growth. These can arise, for example, because the managers do not have the same interests as the owners of a firm, or because the possibilities of financing are limited for small or medium-size firms. Another important factor for an optimum mediation function of the financial sector is the stability of the banking system.

c) A Simple Growth Model with Financial Intermediation

While, in the 1960s and 1970s, the effects of the integration of money into the diverse growth models was central to studies, it is above all the role of financial intermediation on which the interest has been concentrated in recent times and in the context of the new growth theory. By making the growth rate an endogenous variable, it can particularly be shown that the existence of a financial sector not only has level effects, as in the neo-classical model context, but can also influence the growth path itself.

The model presented below is based on the following assumptions (see also Pagano 1993). The production function is of the 'AK'-type, that is, it is postulated that the output is a linear function of a capital stock which here is broadly defined:

$$Y(t) = AK(t) \tag{9.1}$$

Here A corresponds to the total factor productivity. What is summarised under K is not only physical capital but also human capital, which does not consist of the 'raw' labour force but of the education level, which can be increased in time.

Furthermore, it will be assumed that there is no population growth and that the produced goods can be either consumed or invested. The capital depreciates at a rate δ. In this closed economy without a government, the capital market is in a steady state, if the gross investments I correspond to the savings S.

During the process of financial intermediation, a share $1 - \zeta$ of the savings is lost. ζ can be seen as a measure of the efficiency of the financial sector. So the following is true:

$$\zeta S(t) = I(t) \tag{9.2}$$

The growth rate of the income between t and $t + 1$ results out of equation (9.1):

$$g(t + 1) = \frac{Y(t + 1)}{Y(t)} - 1 = \frac{K(t + 1)}{K(t)} - 1 \tag{9.3}$$

Applying (9.1), transforming and omitting the time indices results in:

$$g = A \cdot \frac{I}{Y} - \delta = A \cdot \zeta \cdot s - \delta \tag{9.4}$$

where $s = S/Y$. So the growth rate is dependent on factor productivity A, the efficiency of the financial sector ζ and the savings rate. In the following section, each of these factors will be discussed in more detail.

The mediation of financial means of private households to enterprises is not free; on the contrary, especially in a world without specialised capital mediators, considerable transaction costs arise. These can be reduced by developing a financial sector in which intermediaries 'pool' the saved means and allocate them to different investment projects. Still, these transactions absorb a share ζ of every saved unit, which stay with the financial intermediaries as compensation for these services. So ζ is a direct measure of the efficiency of the capital mediation.

ζ is influenced by the market structure in the financial sector. A concentration of the market power can lead to monopoly rents and therefore to a decline in the efficiency as well as of the overall economic growth rate. Negative effects on ζ are to be expected of a heavy tax burden as well as of an inefficient regulation of the financial sector.

A key function of financial intermediation is the allocation of resources to those projects which have the greatest marginal product. The following are the reasons which, in reality, stand behind the positive influence of the efficiency on the factor productivity A shown in the above model.

Banks have better information and methods for judging alternative investment projects than private households. Therefore, there is normally a tendency, in an economy with an efficient financial sector, to choose the more productive projects.

Financial intermediaries make time transformation and risk transformation of assets possible. Apart from insurance markets, these functions are also taken over by banks and capital markets, and make it possible for individuals to spread non-insurable risks as well as to diversify unsystematic risks by forming portfolios. Additionally, the creation of, for example, shares of investment funds which can be sold to a broad public increases the liquidity of the savers with simultaneous investment of the 'pooled' means in longer-term, more productive projects. So, in the model, the functions of the financial sector named above lead to a higher growth rate over an increase in the factor productivity.

The third variable which can be influenced by the development of the financial markets is the savings rate. However, the direction of this effect is disputed in literature. It can, for instance, be shown that with a broad hedging of existential risks (health, unemployment and so on) over insurance markets, a decrease of 'cautionary saving' occurs so that the consumption share rises and the savings rate falls.

9.2 INTERDEPENDENCE BETWEEN BUSINESS CYCLE AND GROWTH

A time series for the aggregate income can be observed statistically, for example, for a specific country. In older macroeconomics, a division of such a time series into a long-term trend and cyclic deviations from this trend was usual. The explanation of the long-term trend was the content of growth theory, the fluctuations were the subject of business-cycle theory. However, statistical methods and economic reflections have shown that a strict division is difficult.

For there are influences on both sides: on the one hand, the long-term development can be influenced by the fluctuations and, on the other hand, the long-term trend can also influence the type and intensity of the fluctuations. Therefore, four possible influence channels of the business cycle in the longer term will be described briefly in the following.

a) Opportunity Cost Approach

According to the opportunity cost approach, activities which increase productivity are more important in recession than in an economic boom. The reason for this lies in an intertemporal substitution between the processes which are innovative and those which are directly productive. It is argued that the return on processes which are directly productive is lower in recession, since the demand for consumer goods is smaller. The opportunity costs (the reason for the title) of the not-directly-productive processes such as research and development or education are therefore lower in recessions than in an economic boom.

The presupposition of this approach is that there is a differentiation between the two kinds of investments, because the traditional investments in physical capital clearly act pro-cyclically in the medium-term development. According to the opportunity costs approach, the innovative investments – such as research, development and education processes – act in an anticyclical manner. This, however, is hard to prove on the basis of statistics. It also has to be noted that the 'learning-by-doing' effects, which are production increasing, act more strongly in phases of expansion than in recessions.

Even if it is true that recessions awaken healing forces for the long-term economic development, this does not necessarily have to be the direct result of the intertemporal substitution described above. The fact that recessions eliminate the enterprises which are the least productive, as well as the observation that disciplining effects (faster reorganisations because of the increased danger of bankruptcy) arise, act in the same direction.

b) Human Capital Approach

In contrast to the opportunity cost approach, it can be argued that recessions have a negative influence on the long-term economic development too. In this context, an important point seems to be that unemployed human capital depreciates faster than employed human capital. The more important 'on-the-job training' is for the total amount of human capital, the more weight this argument has.

Continuing education opportunities for the unemployed therefore fulfil two functions. On the one hand, the employment possibilities for skilled labour are greater than those for unskilled labour. On the other hand, human capital is central to long-term growth. Development is positively influenced by positive spillovers in the education sector and in the current production.

c) Vintage Models

The technical progress in the neo-classical model and in the model in Chapter 7 has been treated independently of capital input; this is the case of so-called 'disembodied technical progress'. Progress in the shape of a higher knowledge level then leads to an increase in productivity for all involved inputs. An example of this for the capital input is the improvements in computer software; these lead to an increased productivity for all computers, including those of a past vintage. But there is also technical progress which is tied to the introduction of new capital, for example the invention of new computer hardware.

In the context of the so-called 'new investment theory', the relevance of technical progress which is connected with the new capital, the 'embodied technical progress', was discussed in the 1960s. The connection consists mostly in the fact that, over the vintage structure of the capital stock, a relationship develops between the business cycle and middle-term economic development. Quality and quantity of the investments in a vintage influence the economy for as long as the corresponding vintage is used in the production.

As regards the long-term economic development, however, the integration of the technical progress in new machines is purely a level effect. It can be shown that a growth model with 'embodied technical progress' can be rewritten for the long term as a model with 'disembodied technical progress'. Furthermore, it must be stated that the long-term steady state is independent of the share of technical progress which is 'embodied' and which is 'disembodied'.

d) Regime-dependent Growth

In the context of the neo-Keynesian rationing models, disequilibrium situations on goods and labour markets are analysed. Economic activities – including investments – are regime dependent; this means that they depend on which disequilibrium reigns in which market. For example, an excess supply on the goods market influences the enterprise activities negatively, since not all the produced goods can be sold. An excess demand on the labour market also acts negatively on enterprise activity, since too little labour is available for the production ('dried out' labour market).

Here, one has to assume a regime sequence in an economy during the business cycle and certain savings and investment behaviour which are specific for a special regime. In this way, a dependence of the long-term economic development on the short-term cyclical fluctuations occurs. The basic models of the new growth theory could be broadened by these aspects in a further step.

9.3 MULTIPLE EQUILIBRIA, POVERTY TRAPS

In many poorly-developed economies, positive growth rates could not be reached in the past, at least not over a long period. Remaining in a situation which is marked by a low living standard is sometimes called a 'low-level trap' or 'poverty trap'. It is normal to look for the causes of the lack of growth in the unfavourable social and power structures of the country concerned. These factors, which have not been looked at very closely in macroeconomic growth theory up to now, surely play an important role. Within the context of macroeconomic growth theory, there are also explanation possibilities.

From the viewpoint of aggregate production functions, the existence of poverty traps means that the accumulation of growth-sustaining production factors does not occur proportionally. In a low income region there exists under bad conditions a stationary steady state, to which the economy always returns if it does not move away from it very clearly. Only after a certain development level does growth swing on to a path which allows an adjustment growth of neo-classical pattern, or a continuing growth in the sense of the new growth theory.

Based on the explanations in Chapter 3, the per capita income in a closed economy in a one-sector model is dependent on the capital intensity. The temporal change of capital intensity k is then determined by the difference between the per capita savings and the term with the enlarged depreciation of the per workplace capital (physical depreciation plus population growth), that is, the following is true after division by saving share s, which here, for simplicity, is assumed as constant, see equation (3.4):

$$\frac{\dot{k}}{s} = f(k) - k\left(\frac{\delta + g_L}{s}\right) \qquad (9.5)$$

From this expression, the following two explanations for the existence of poverty traps arise, which, in an adjusted form, can also be taken over for the interest-dependent savings rate.

a) Increasing Returns to Scale on a Low Income Level

On a low level, the aggregate production function can show increasing returns to scale, for example, because of indivisibilities in the social infrastructure expenditures. This causes the savings to be smaller than the amount necessary to increase the capital equipment per worker. Point k^{**} in Figure 9.1 is unstable, because an economy with a lower capital equipment cannot accumulate any capital; it relapses to zero, according to the expression for the temporal change of k. However, as soon as it succeeds in leaping over k^{**}, adjustment growth to a neo-classical steady state (k^*) or continuous growth as in the new growth theory is possible.

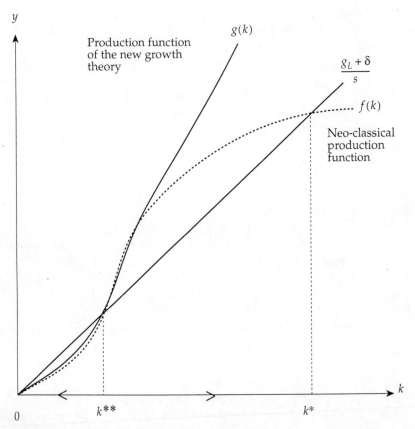

Figure 9.1 Increasing returns to scale on a low level

The idea of the so-called 'big push' is based on the poverty-trap approach: Since an economy with a low development level can only break out of the trap on its own with enormous difficulty, an impulse from outside could make the passing of the critical threshold much easier. This argument, among others, has often served as an explanation for economic aid for poorer countries.

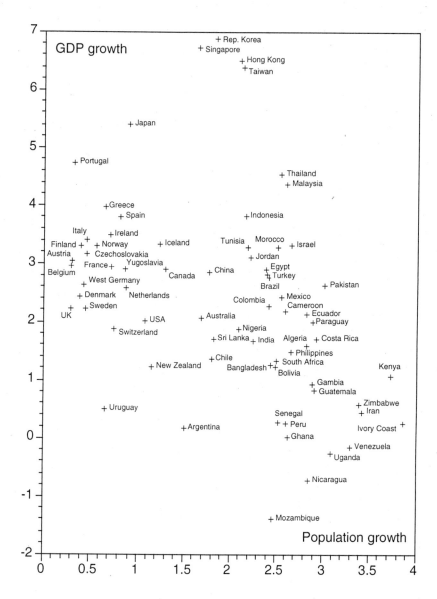

Note: Average GDP growth; real, per annum and in %; population growth: per annum and in %.

Source: Summers/Heston, Penn World Table 5.6.

Figure 9.2: Growth rates, 1960-1990, and population growth

b) Variable Savings and Population Growth Rate

As Figure 9.2 shows, it seems that it is not only in theory that population growth plays an important role for the economic development of a country, but also in reality.

It is plausible to assume that richer economies have a higher savings rate. It can also be shown empirically that population growth is smaller in more highly developed economies. In Figure 9.3, with the production function assumptions used above, this leads to a first steady state on a low level with k^{***}.

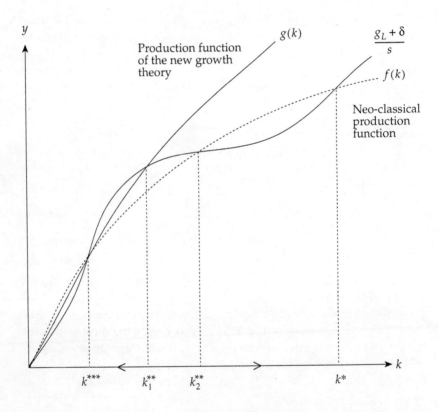

Figure 9.3: Increasing savings rate and decreasing population growth

The steady states with k^{**}, which are represented in Figure 9.3 according to each production function, are unstable as under Subsection a), while the considered economy on the right-hand side of k^{**} again either converges towards the neo-classical steady state or swings on to a continuing growth path.

Different possibilities of microeconomic foundation for the macroeconomic conditions of poverty traps exist. One variant concentrates on the costs of human capital formation and on population growth. This is based on the crucial position of the formation of human capital for long-term development.

On a high development level with a lot of human capital, the returns on human capital investments are relatively high. At the same time, the time-intensive education of children is tied to relatively high opportunity costs, since, in accordance with the accumulated human capital, wages are high. This leads to moderate population growth. Both circumstances together are positive conditions for continuous growth of per capita human capital and so for attaining continuous growth.

On a low development level, the case is precisely the reverse. The returns of human capital are lower and the greater uncertainties lead to higher discount rates for future incomes. Here the individual enlargement of a family brings economic advantages. These are conditions which normally lead to a stagnation of the per capita human capital of the population.

9.4 THEORY OF EVOLUTION

Besides the neo-classical theory and the new growth theory, an evolutionary approach to the explanation of the endogenous technological change and of the economic growth process has developed since the beginning of the 1980s. The following section will discuss briefly the most important building blocks of the evolutionary model and will show the main differences from traditional theory.

a) Macroeconomic Aspects

The central element of the evolutionary approach is technological change. Similar to a concept in the theory of science, a differentiation is made between a 'technological paradigm' and small gradual modifications in the reigning paradigm. The invention of the steam engine, of electricity, of the internal combustion engine or the semiconductor technique are examples of technological paradigms. Such revolutionary technological eruptions have global consequences and render substantial progress in productivity possible. Besides these technological 'leaps', there is also an improvement and modification of the existing technologies, which happens in a continuous process. This process is the result of the enterprises' search for new products, market niches and monopoly positions.

The smaller the returns on the improvement efforts of an existing technology result, the more resources will be dedicated to the development of a new technological paradigm. A technology change can then occur. The enterprises which still cling to the old technology, however, will try anything to prevent the menacing change of paradigm. The result of these efforts is called the 'sailing ship' effect: the development of the steamboat led to a series of substantial improvements in sailing boat technology, which saved the sailing ship from competition by the steamboat for quite some time.

Technological progress is seen as an evolutionary process, which results from the firms' search for ways of making a profit. The market functions as a selection mechanism which, according to the principle of 'survival of the fittest', rewards innovative and flexible firms with profits and eliminates unprofitable enterprises. The productivity progress resulting from this process makes it possible for an economy to stay on a stable growth path.

In certain circumstances, however, several alternative steady-state paths can exist for an economy, of which it is not necessarily the optimum path that has to be chosen. It can be shown that such situations can arise especially if several new key technologies compete and if there are also so-called network externalities. One talks of network externalities when the productivity of a technology rises with an increasing number of users. Examples of this are, for instance, enterprise systems of personal computers, the video systems VHS and Betamax, or the QWERTY-keyboard arrangement on typewriters. When such technologies compete on the markets, there is a tendency – because of increasing returns to scale (network externalities) – for one of the technologies to impose itself, to set the standards and to push the others out of the market.

As a great number of historical examples show, this technology is, however, not necessarily the 'best'. Often it is pure chance which, in an early phase of the technology competition, decides on the winners and the losers. The market result then is not predictable (even with ex-ante knowledge of the preferences of the buyers as well as the technological possibilities), and potential inefficiencies can arise. The chosen growth path is dependent on historical chance events, which is why such economic development is called 'path dependent'.

b) Microeconomic Aspects

The rejection of a few of the central microeconomic assumptions is what makes the main difference between the evolutionary explanation approach and the traditional model in the neo-classical tradition. The consequence of this, however, is a substantial increase in the difficulty of formal modelling.

The first critique is aimed at the possibility (postulated for the entrepreneurs) of maximising an explicit profit function. The fact that the development of innovations involves great uncertainties makes it, according to this viewpoint, impossible for an enterprise to determine in advance the possible exact profits and losses. This means that the firm neither moves in a world of total certainty nor does it know the probabilities of uncertain future events. Because of these great uncertainties, the assumption of rational expectations is sometimes also given up on an individual level and replaced by the concept of bounded or adaptive rationality. What happens on the enterprise side, then, is not profit maximisation any more but 'profit search'. That is, the enterprises find themselves in a constant process of searching for ways of making a profit. In this they have to adapt their actions to the changing conditions of the surroundings. The competitive selection process allows the survival of only those enterprises which can adapt the fastest to the new conditions. So it is the enterprises which have developed the most efficient behaviour patterns which will impose themselves. Therefore the 'fight for life' which occurs on competitive markets has many similarities with the biological evolutionary process.

Finally, the construct of the aggregate production function is often rejected in the theory of evolution, as development is seen as a disequilibrium process which is only in exceptional cases restricted by production capacities.

SELECTED READING

- NELSON, R.R. and S.G. WINTER (1982), *An Evolutionary Theory of Economic Change*, Cambridge Mass.: Harvard University Press.
- PAGANO, M. (1993), 'Financial Markets and Growth', *European Economic Review*, **37**, 613–22.

10. Sustainable Development

10.1 NATURAL ENVIRONMENT

The environment offers a great diversity of services to the human being:

- as a consumption good, for example, in the form of air to breathe, space for recovery and natural beauty;
- as a supplier of resources, for example water, sun, oil;
- as a recipient for waste, in the atmosphere, on the land, in the water and so on;
- as a geographical location for economic activities.

There is strong competition between these functions of the environment, which causes, in general, the 'environmental problems'. Negative external effects are often the consequence of using the environment, that is, individual activities are impaired or persons are injured, without payment being made for this over the market. Negative externalities occur either in production, when, for instance, buildings of a firm are damaged by acid rain, or they occur in consumption, when, for instance, the air becomes polluted, which harms individuals.

Natural resources, such as oil, largely determine the aggregate production possibilities in an economy as production factors. Here problems arise out of the fact that certain natural resources are exhaustible and others become exhaustible with overuse. When using these resources for production or consumption, several issues of efficiency and distribution have to be observed (see Figure 10.1).

The optimum use of natural resources as well as the internalisation of external effects are problems of economic efficiency. According to microeconomic principles, the social marginal product and/or marginal utility of the resources determine optimum prices and quantities. Another point, which is often stressed in connection with the environment, is the distribution aspect. In particular with regard to the prospects of future generations, appeals for 'fairness' are made from many sides to the present generation. Comparing opportunities between different generations means analysing the intergenerational distribution of welfare. Focusing on intragenerational distribution aspects, it must be noted that environmental policy proposals have little chance in the political process if they influence the income distribution of the present generation negatively. So the solution of the incumbent environmental problems has the two dimensions of economic efficiency and of distribution today as well as with regard to the future.

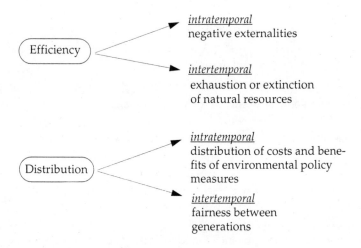

Figure 10.1 Dimensions of environmental problems

10.2 SUSTAINABILITY

a) From Limited to Sustainable Growth

In the course of the 1970s, the concept of 'limits to growth' dominated the discussion on the intersection point between growth theory and environmental economics. In view of the limits to natural resources and sinks, that is, of natural production means and the capacity of nature to absorb waste and pollution, many predicted an inevitable decrease in income for the distant future, at least in the case of continuation of growth of the economy after the same pattern.

In this debate on the limits of growth, various economic aspects did not attract enough attention from the viewpoint of economics. The following are three of the important points:

- In the judgement of economic theory, it is not the growth of economy itself which explains the increased pollution of the environment, but the wrong market signals which arise because of the negative externalities of certain market processes. Therefore, an internalisation of these external effects through policy instruments is an important contribution to the long-term compatibility of environment and economy.

- From the economic point of view, it is stressed that a strong enough substitution of environment-intensive activities by less environment-intensive activities leads to a solution of the impending problems and that technical progress can also help to overcome the scarcity of resources in nature.

- The models which were used in predicting the 'limits' are pure time-series models; they do not have a consistent theoretical basis. Furthermore, the results are easily altered with changing assumptions, for example, as regards the supply of raw materials. In economic theory, there is a preference for smaller models which are theoretically consistent and have easily intelligible paths.

As one of the consequences of this counterposition, the notion of 'sustainable growth' has lately established itself as a main goal in theoretical and political debate in the field of the environment and growth. The concept of sustainability was originally used in forestry. The management of a forest is sustainable if the forest stays intact in quantity and, as regards its diverse functions, in quality.

This same principle of sustainability can also be applied with regard to other renewable resources of nature. However, definition problems for sustainability arise when transferring this principle to the level of all environmental goods and bringing it together with economic growth:

- How far are substitutions between environmental goods permitted? For example, is it possible to compensate for worse air quality with better water quality in the world's seas?

- How far are substitutions between the stock of environmental goods and accumulated capital such as human capital permitted? Can knowledge on solar energy substitute for disappearing oil reserves?

- How far are substitutions between environmental goods and the factor knowledge permitted? Can a greater know-how in the field of wind energy substitute for smaller coal reserves?

- What do we assume the technological possibilities and preferences of future generations to be?

We shall first discuss the concept of sustainability on an aggregate economic level, followed in Chapter 11 by a separate presentation of each of the problems in the realisation of sustainable development.

b) Flow and Stock Concepts

Up to now, the following definition of sustainability of the so-called 'Brundtland report' is the most widespread: 'A development is sustainable, if it meets the needs of the present generation without compromising the ability of future generations to meet their own needs' (World Commission 1987, p. 43).

This definition is very broad. It contains concepts such as 'development' and entities such as 'needs' which need to be given preciser economic content with the help of growth theory and microeconomics. Specifically, in economic theory the entities, by the temporal development of which sustainability can be judged, are to be defined. Basically, there are two concepts for determining goal entities:

- the flow concept
- the stock concept.

Adopting the 'flow concept', the temporal course of flow variables such as income, consumption or utility is observed. According to this conception, development is sustainable, if the present growth rate of the observed flow entity can be sustained in the long term, or if an absolute decrease of the entity between the generations can never be observed. With flow entities it is the individual welfare or the per capita utility of the population which stands in the foreground.

According to the 'stock concept', sustainability is given if a stock entity, which has to be precisely defined, does not decrease in the course of time but stays at least constant. The following are examples of such goal entities for stocks:

- a capital aggregate which contains accumulated capital stocks such as physical capital and human capital as well as the natural capital stock
- an aggregate natural capital stock
- threshold values for certain natural resources such as forest stock
- the present stocks for certain natural resources.

Various arguments for a stock concept can be enumerated. First, there is uncertainty about the value of the elasticity of substitution between natural resources and accumulable capital. Second, there is an asymmetry between the different types of capital with respect to reversibility: once certain critical natural capital stocks are lost, they cannot be reintroduced. Put differently, a constant stock of certain natural resources can be necessary because natural threshold and irreversibility effects may severely limit the trade-offs that can be allowed between different resources without threatening sustainability. Third, the scale effects from the loss of critical natural capital are not known and, finally, consumers have an apparent 'loss aversion' that arises when certain natural resources are depleted.

In the context of stock concepts, 'weak' and 'strong' sustainability have become widely used terms. Weak sustainability means that any form of natural capital can be run down, provided that proceeds are reinvested in other forms of capital, for example, man-made capital. Strong sustainability, however, requires that the stock of natural capital should not decline. Here, a distinction must be made between the requirement to conserve every single natural resource and the requirement to conserve an aggregate natural capital stock which leaves room for certain substitution possibilities.

In order to put the theoretical principles of strong sustainability into practice, one can lay down two main rules for the use of renewable natural resources. First, the harvest rates should equal the regeneration rates. Second, the waste emission rates should equal the natural assimilative capacity of the ecosystem. For non-renewable natural resources, the problem is quite different. Any positive rate of exploitation will lead to the exhaustion of the finite stock. However, it should be noted that the effect of exhaustion of certain stocks on welfare is by no means obvious; at least it is not directly given for all natural resources. It might be that utility remains constant even with a decreasing stock of certain resources or that several (very special) resources do not have an impact on utility at all. In many cases, a 'quasi-sustainable' use of non-renewable resources can be achieved by limiting their rate of depletion to the rate of creation of renewable substitutes.

In partial fields, where irreversibilities or great uncertainty are of importance, a stock concept might be applied in the form of so-called 'minimum standards' for the state of nature. The usefulness of such standards can be emphasised with the following arguments:

- With a decreasing environmental quality, future economic costs of production and consumption might increase sharply.
- The option value for an intact environment rises with an increasing income, that is, a growing willingness to pay for the existence of the option of enjoying or using the natural environment exists.
- The abatement costs of environmental damage from the present situation up to a certain environment standard are relatively low but can bring a high potential benefit.

- More information on the damage to the environment is available in the future.

c) Synthesis

The arguments in favour of stock concepts or of strong sustainability given above should make us more cautious about depleting natural capital. But the issues raised do not add up to a complete justification for implementing stock concepts when aiming to achieve sustainability. The exclusive concentration on criteria for natural capital stocks is not adequate because it lacks consideration of the economic sector and especially neglects the requirement of intertemporal efficiency. Consequently, according to the anthropocentric approach of economic theory, it is the welfare of the human being which must stand at the centre of theoretical reflections. From the viewpoint of economics, a development is sustainable when the members of future generations find themselves in a situation as good as or better than that of the present generation, this being measured by the individual welfare. Seen from this anthropocentric viewpoint, the flow concept is therefore the appropriate tool for judging sustainability.

But to pursue the welfare targets in the long run, it needs to be observed that some important environmental fields are distinguished by the irreversibility of environmental damage as well as the great uncertainty about the effects of this damage. In these fields, a further decline in environmental qualities or decrease in environmental capital brings great risks. It is therefore necessary to conserve a specified stock of natural capital. With appropriate determination this stock can be interpreted as a 'safe' minimum standard. In the sense of an in-between goal, such a minimum standard is designed to guarantee that the goal of sustained long-term economic growth or sustained welfare increase, which is of primary importance, is reached. If, in these cases, stock-oriented environmental policies lead to the desired effects, then sustainability in the sense of the flow concept is attained at the same time. Regarding welfare, the greater the number of environmental fields with uncertain and irreversible effects, the more important it is to have minimum standards for natural resources gain as regards welfare. In addition, the stock concept becomes more significant when the uncertainty about the preferences of future generations is seen as an important social problem. Put differently, to take the special attributes of natural resources into account, it is appropriate to supplement the final goal of non-decreasing welfare between generations with an intermediate target concerning certain requirements for the state of the environment. The higher the probability of irreversibilities and the larger the uncertainties about aggregate costs of damage, the more safe minimum standards for certain natural capital stocks become a rational means to obtain sustainability.

In the context of growth theory, the problem of sustainability can be rendered clearer with the help of aggregate production functions and utility functions. This will be discussed below. Using this apparatus it can be seen that the development of the flow entities is not independent of the size of the stocks, since the stocks have an influence on production and consumption possibilities. But only in exceptional cases do both concepts lead to the same conclusions. One can also state that the flow concept corresponds to the stock concept only if we can find a very comprehensive measure of the term 'capital' in the model.

Basically, there are two opposite kinds of external effects which are important for the long-term development of welfare: positive externalities which, according to the new growth theory, support the accumulation stimulants in the long term, and negative externalities, which lead to many of the well-known environmental problems in production and consumption. The problems of limited renewable and non-renewable natural resources in production and consumption can be added to these non-market mechanisms. Here natural resources can represent the function of nature as a source of services as well as a dump for waste.

In the following applications, sustainability will be given when the welfare of individuals does not decrease in the long term. Thus sustainability will be analysed exclusively on the basis of the flow concept in the following theoretical representation. Using endogenous growth models, the formal treatment of uncertainty and irreversibilities would exceed the scope of this book.

d) Growth and Development

In the previous chapters, the emphasis was on the growth rates of income and consumption. The conclusions of the different models referred to welfare, that is, to optimum solutions for consumption and growth. In view of the problems introduced in this chapter, environmental variables have now to be added to the theory. In particular, the quality of the natural environment has to be included in the utility function that measures welfare. Moreover, environmental variables will be considered in the different production sectors.

When the term 'development' is used in general, it refers to rising aggregate consumption and output but also includes aspects such as environmental quality, social factors and the distribution of income. As stated above, the utility function now not only includes consumption possibilities but also environmental quality. Thus for dynamics, the final objective of the normative theory of sustainable growth is the long-term development of a broadly defined individual utility. But because of the far-reaching reduction in complexity to build growth models, only a relatively small number of variables can be considered in each new model. It corresponds to the methodology in economics not to analyse all aspects of development at once.

This is in contrast to the sometimes voiced statement that economists neglect the qualitative aspects of development in general. According to the view taken here, it is not meaningful to say that economics is about growth whereas other social sciences are concerned with development. What is true in this case is that economics concentrates on a few variables which govern development and tries to give an accurate prediction for these variables in the future. In the following, these variables include income and consumption as well as natural resources and the state of the environment. For simplicity, parameters for income distribution and social conditions will not be considered in the text. In principle, they could be added to the models if one allows for heterogeneous agents; for income inequality, see, for example, Aghion and Howitt (1998, Chapter 9).

10.3 DIFFERENT DEVELOPMENT PATHS

Three different types of balanced growth paths are introduced to characterise long-term development. The first corresponds to the outcome when all quantities and prices in the economy are determined on free markets irrespective of externalities. We denote this result a 'private optimum' solution. These free market development paths are developments which are reached without corrections by the government as regards negative externalities in the environmental field and positive spillovers.

If economic and environmental policies correct for the positive and negative external effects by taking appropriate measures, optimum development paths can be reached. Here, the label 'optimum' corresponds to the utility maximisation of the present generation. We call these paths 'social optimum' solutions. The divergence of the private optimum from the social optimum development paths arises only from the existence of externalities. The divergence is the expression of economic inefficiencies which cause losses in social welfare of the present generation. In particular, externalities lead to a growth rate of welfare which lies below the optimum growth rate, as is shown in Figure 10.2.

Sustainable development paths are characterised by non-declining undiscounted welfare in the long run which adds the aspect of intergenerational distribution. It becomes clear from Figure 10.2 that private optimum as well as social optimum development paths can be either sustainable or non-sustainable.

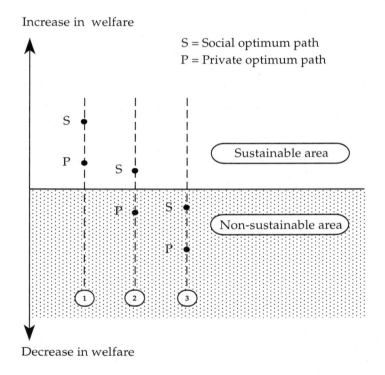

Figure 10.2 Scenarios for long-term development paths

In Figure 10.2, three different scenarios are shown. Scenario 1 concerns the case in which the private optimum path and the social optimum path are both sustainable. Internalisation of external effects leads to higher welfare growth in the long term, which is itself a desirable target. In scenario 2, the private optimum path is not sustainable. But by internalisation of the external effects, with externalities being valued according to the preferences of the present generation, sustainability is already achieved. This means that an environmental policy designed for the present generation brings, at the same time, a development which is favourable for future generations. The worst case is scenario 3, where neither path is sustainable, that is, even the social optimum path does not meet the requirement for sustainability. Here, it is not sufficient to correct for all externalities; more stringent measures are necessary to obtain sustainable development.

In the following section, the role of the discount rate is discussed. In Chapter 11, the decisive factors for sustainability in the context of growth theory will be represented more precisely. These factors concern the negative externalities in the environmental field as well as the characteristics of the exhaustible and the renewable natural resources. With the help of these additional elements, the different development paths can be analysed more thoroughly. Optimum development paths are non-sustainable, if, for example, in the long run natural resources can only be badly substituted by other production factors, but are available in an ever-lessening measure in the course of time (see Section 11.3). It can equally be the case that the resources which are important for production are renewable by nature, but are being overused by the present generation. In such a case, a non-sustainable development is also probable (see Section 11.4).

10.4 PRIVATE AND SOCIAL DISCOUNT RATES

Up to this point, the existence of positive discount rates in the individual utility function has been assumed. In the long term, this means that the wishes of future generations are less valued than the wishes of the present generation. In sustainability discussions, the opinion is often heard that, for 'fairness' reasons, social decision-making should ensure equal treatment of the generations. So one may deduce that the government should compensate for the short-sightedness of individuals with a correction of the discount rate.

Box 10.1: Sustainability in Bolivia

In the context of its economic policy in the mid-1990s, Bolivia concentrated on reaching a sustainable development. Policies have been modified since then but the original plan remains an illustrative example of applying the sustainability concept in practice.

On the administrative side, the responsibility was carried mainly by a specially created department (Ministerio de Desarollo Sostenible y Medio Ambiente). In contrast to the sustainability debate in Western industrialised countries, efforts lay mainly on the economic and political–administrative side. This is because the country with the weakest economy in Latin America is characterised by extreme poverty (which touches over 40 percent of the population) and a political marginalisation of a large part of the population.

The four goals of the Bolivian programme were economic growth, a more even income distribution, better protection of the environment and wider political participation. Points two and four broaden the concept of sustainable growth discussed in the main text to a more complete view of sustainable development in a Third World country. The distribution issue is a part of sustainability, when referring to the Brundtland definition (see main text) with an accent on the 'needs of the present generation'. Political participation is supposed to serve as a long-term insurance for the initiated policies in a relatively young democracy.

The support for growth is strived at mainly by 'capitalisation' of the most important state enterprises. To achieve this goal, half of the shares of these firms were sold to appropriate foreign investors and the proceeds were invested entirely in the enterprises concerned under the surveillance of a mixed supervisory board. In total, this has led to investments of about 60 percent of the present gross domestic product. Even after being taken over by private investors, the state enterprises are subject to state surveillance. The other half of the shares of the previously state-run enterprises is used for the construction of pension funds. Pension funds aim to diversify their portfolio, and the individual contributions of the working population were intended to complete the financing. A land reform and an educational reform, the content of which is the introduction of modern learning methods and up-to-date forms of instruction, are regarded as further important measures. Besides the effects on the formation of human capital, this measure was stressed as a path towards equal opportunities of all segments of the population.

As regards the environment, measures are planned in industrial fields even if there is some resistance. After a transition period, some of the European norms are intended to be imposed for the pollution level in this sector. For political reasons, traffic and heating were left untouched. As a basis for political decision-making, nationwide inventories of the forest stocks (mostly tropical forests) have been made. And finally, through a far-reaching decentralisation of state expenditure (about 50 percent of the tax revenues are distributed to the communities and regions by the central government) there has been an aspiration towards political integration.

The experience of Bolivia has shown that the application of the measures requires intensive communication between the different parties as well as between the central and the regional governments. From this viewpoint the capacities of the government are quickly exhausted in such surroundings. It also becomes clear that the significance of the financial sector in such a development should not be underestimated.

Things are not that simple, however. Lowering discount rates has, in some cases, undesirable effects, while in other cases it is simply not necessary to obtain sustainability. To establish the sustainability constraint is a more efficient way to reach sustainable development in no less than four different respects: (i) a very low or even zero discount rate may lead to investment rates that are so high that the present generation cannot survive, (ii) a low discount rate harms future generations by increased pollution if capital accumulation has a pollutant effect which is not internalised, (iii) social discount rates reflect intertemporal shadow prices which depend upon the adopted numéraire so that the measure is quite vague, and (iv) capital accumulation and the decline in natural resources both influence the level of welfare and have to be weighed against each other.

From a macroeconomic perspective, (iv) concentrates on the main point, on the well-being of future generations founded on basic macroeconomic relations. We cannot have a direct intuition about the validity of discounting future well-being unless we know something concrete about feasible development paths. The trade-offs between natural and man-made resources can, in principle, be calculated if appropriate weights are used. This will form the content of the following chapter.

If, in general, the effect of the positive discount rate is taken away, the growth rate of the goods production rises, according to the Keynes–Ramsey rule. And as long as not all negative externalities are internalised, an accelerated growth can have negative effects on the total welfare through heavy pollution. It should also be considered that the discount rates are not necessarily high in reality when the observable rates of consumption growth and real interest rate are compared with each other. As regards the political realisation, it must be mentioned that because of the limited time horizon in office, governments might discount even more than private households, and are therefore not necessarily interested in such policies. These remarks about the discount rate do not mean that discounting possibly very serious environmental catastrophes in the distant future are a valid procedure. In effect, even applying only a moderate discount rate seems to make the cost of these events very small today. But future environmental problems create costs for future generations and may thus contradict the sustainability criterion.

If, for example, the sustaining of a moderate climate costs a great deal in the future because today's emissions are too high, then a higher valuation of the future is necessary from the viewpoint of sustainability. In addition, the rising risk of environmental damage, for example in the field of species protection, demands more attention. But if a lower discount rate or even a zero discount is prescribed by the government as a guideline for policy, then some important policy options are neglected (see Chapter 12).

As an alternative to the private optimisation with the help of 'utilitarian' utility functions (as used in this book), another welfare criterion is sometimes mentioned in the literature. According to the so-called 'Rawls criterion' the growth path in which the minimum consumption (occurring in any time period) is the largest has to be chosen out of all possible paths in a very long time period. This procedure corresponds to a known decision rule in the case of uncertainty and is also known as the 'maximin criterion', which is here applied for the utility out of consumption. As a consequence of the application of this criterion, the total consumption is distributed as equally as possible over all generations. However, the criterion has strongly pessimistic and risk-averse aspects, since a consumption renunciation in a certain period in exchange for a higher future growth rate is not seen as advantageous. What is more, it remains unclear how this criterion could be realised in practice. The requirement of sustainability seems to be the better guideline in the long run.

SELECTED READING

- AGHION, P. and P. HOWITT (1998), *Endogenous Growth Theory*, Cambridge Mass.: MIT Press.

- BRETSCHGER, L. (1998a), 'The Sustainability Paradigm: A Macroeconomic Perspective', *Revue Région et Développement*, No. 7, 73–103.

- DALY, H.E. (1990), 'Toward some Operational Principles of Sustainable Development', *Ecological Economics*, **2**, 1–6.

- DASGUPTA, P.S. (1995), 'Optimal Development and NNP', in I. Goldin and L.A. Winters (eds), *The Economics of Sustainable Development*, Cambridge: Cambridge University Press.

- HOWARTH, R.B. and R.B. NORGAARD (1992), 'Environmental Valuation under Sustainable Development', *American Economic Review, Papers and Proceedings*, **82** (2), 473–7.

- PEARCE, D.W., A. MARKANDYA and E. BARBIER (1990), *Sustainable Development, Economics and Environment in the Third World*, Aldershot, UK and Brookfield, US: Edward Elgar.

- PEZZEY, J. (1989), 'Economic Analysis of Sustainable Growth and Sustainable Development', *World Bank, Environment Department Working Paper*, No. 15.

- SMULDERS, S. (1995): 'Environmental Policy and Sustainable Economic Growth, An Endogenous Growth Perspective', *De Economist*, **143** (2), 163–95.
- TOMAN, M.A. (1994), 'Economics and Sustainability: Balancing Trade-offs and Imperatives', *Land Economics*, **70** (4), 393–413.
- TURNER, R.K. (1988), 'Sustainability, Resource Conservation and Pollution Control: An Overview', in R.K. Turner (ed.), *Sustainable Environmental Management: Principles and Practice*, London: Belhaven Press.
- WORLD COMMISSION ON ENVIRONMENT AND DEVELOPMENT (1987), *Our Common Future*, New York: Oxford University Press.

11. Natural Resources

11.1 RESOURCE USE AND DYNAMICS

A first illustrative step in evaluating the consequences of the use of natural resources for the growth path is to consider an international cross-section of countries. In Figure 11.1, the growth rates of income are compared to the efficiency in energy use, where energy is oil, coal, electricity and so on. According to microeconomics, the more expensive (and the less abundant) energy is compared to its substitutes in production and consumption, the more efficiently it is used. Inspecting Figure 11.1, it can be seen that there is no clear evidence of countries with abundant energy and low energy prices having higher growth rates than others. In contrast, there are some prominent examples such as Japan, where high energy costs (a high efficiency in energy use) are parallel to high growth rates of the economy. It can be concluded that the relation between natural resource use and growth is more complex and involves several other economic variables.

It will next be asked how exactly the natural environment can influence welfare and the growth path of an economy. In the following, the different growth models of previous chapters are reconsidered in the light of environmental restrictions and the use of natural resources. There are, in principle, two channels through which welfare is influenced by the environment. First, there is a direct impact of the state of the environment on personal well-being, which applies, for instance, in the cases of air quality or the amenities of the landscape. Here it is obvious that ceteris paribus a better environment increases welfare. Second, environmental quality and natural resources affect the production process and hence, indirectly, future consumption possibilities.

A production sector influenced by the environment can be modelled in different versions, which is demonstrated in the following. Depending on what is assumed about the marginal productivity of capital, growth is generated either exogenously or endogenously in the model. Postulating decreasing returns to capital (with the decrease being strong enough, see Chapter 5), the growth process peters out in the long run. The assumption of constant returns to capital, however, ensures the feasibility of endogenous growth in the long run; also, it keeps incentives for savings and investments on a constant (positive) level. In addition, one can distinguish between one-sector models and multi-sector growth models. In one-sector

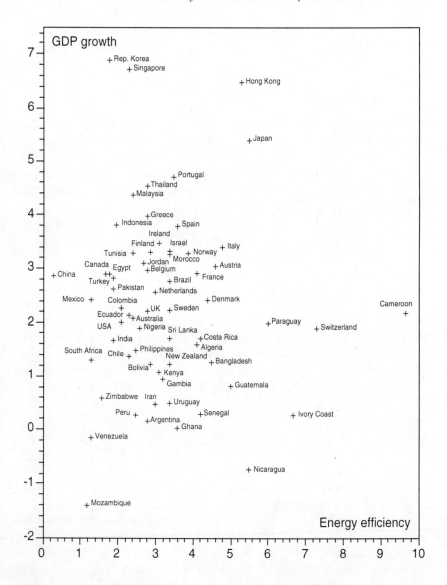

Figure 11.1 Energy efficiency and growth

Note: Average per capita GDP growth: real, per annum and in %: energy
          efficiency: GDP per unit of energy use 1980, 1987 $ per kg oil equivalent.
Source: Summers/Heston, Penn World Table 5.6; World Development Indicators
          1998 CD-Rom, World Bank.

models, the production technique for consumption and investment goods is the same. Multi-sector models usually have a dynamic sector, for example, research and development or education, and one or more sectors for the production of consumer goods. Here, the growth rate depends on the characteristics of the dynamic sector.

11.2 NEGATIVE EXTERNALITIES

In this section, the positive spillovers of the new growth theory will be brought together with the negative externalities caused by the pollution of the natural environment. From this, simple conditions for private optimum, social optimum, and sustainable development paths are deduced. The natural resource supply stays exogenous in this section; it will be endogenised in the following Sections 11.3 and 11.4.

a) Modelling of Externalities

Notation:

- K capital stock
- N natural resource as production factor
- M natural resource as consumption good
- X^* level of variable X when no negative externalities are effective.

We postulate the following (simplified) aggregate production function for the final goods Y (without time indices):

$$Y = A \cdot F(K, N) \tag{11.1}$$

or in the Cobb–Douglas form:

$$Y = A \cdot K^\alpha \cdot N^{1-\alpha} \qquad\qquad 0 < \alpha < 1 \tag{11.2}$$

The labour input is to be contained as human capital in the general capital term K. N is assumed to be a flow variable and a rival input. Furthermore, the following constant utility function of households is assumed for all generations:

$$U = U(C, M) \qquad\qquad (11.3)$$

or in the Cobb–Douglas form and per individual:

$$\frac{U}{L} = c^{\xi} \cdot M^{1-\xi} \qquad\qquad 0 < \xi < 1 \qquad\qquad (11.4)$$

For simplicity, the formulation here postulates that all individuals consume the same amount, namely the entire quantity of natural services M (meaning that M is non-rival). Positive externalities arise, as in Section 6.1, out of learning effects of the investments in physical capital, so that:

$$A = K^{\eta} \qquad\qquad 0 < \eta < 1 \qquad\qquad (11.5)$$

The negative externalities of pollution can be introduced analogously to the positive spillovers in (11.5). It is therefore assumed that the use of an input (for example, physical capital) decreases the used amount of another input (for example, natural resource). In order for the comparability with the positive externalities to be as direct as possible, the following relations will be used, the actuality of which depends on the environmental problem:

$$N = N^* \cdot K^{-\psi} \qquad\qquad N < N^*, \ \psi > 0 \qquad\qquad (11.6)$$

$$K = K^* \cdot N^{-\tilde{\psi}} \qquad\qquad K < K^*, \ \tilde{\psi} > 0 \qquad\qquad (11.7)$$

According to (11.6), the input of physical capital reduces the amount of available natural production factors N. An example of this is water pollution by one industry when at the same time clean water is an input for another industry. Or the input of the natural factor decreases the amount of physical capital as in (11.7). An example of this is the acid rain as a consequence of the burning of oil, which damages buildings. The quantities signed with a star correspond to the values for K and N which apply without negative externalities, the value for N^* being given exogenously for the moment. In these two expressions and the following expression, the figure values will be defined in such a way that $N < N^*$, $K < K^*$ and so on. The advantage of this way of modelling is that the one-sector structure in production can be retained in the model. Here, the intensity of the negative externalities is assumed as constant, for simplicity. Actually though, it is a relationship which depends on the abatement technology. As an extension of this approach, it would be possible to add a research sector for the development of abatement techniques which is capable of changing the technical relation of the negative externalities.

Negative externalities can also have an effect on consumption, that is, the use of nature for consumption purposes. These externalities start either from the input of the capital stock and the natural resources or from the total production. So, depending on the environmental problem, the model can be added to as follows:

$$M = M^* \cdot K^{-\upsilon} \qquad\qquad \upsilon > 0 \qquad\qquad (11.8)$$

$$M = M^* \cdot N^{-\tilde{\upsilon}} \qquad\qquad \tilde{\upsilon} > 0 \qquad\qquad (11.9)$$

$$M = M^* \cdot Y^{-\hat{\upsilon}} \qquad\qquad \hat{\upsilon} > 0 \qquad\qquad (11.10)$$

Examples of (11.8), (11.9) and (11.10) are noise emissions from industry, the pollution of the air by the use of oil, and waste deposits as a consequence of consumption goods production. As before, the condition to model endogenous growth is a constant marginal product of the broadly defined factor capital in the long term. When taking negative externalities in the production into consideration, the economic growth becomes smaller than if they are not considered. The welfare of the households also decreases if the negative external effects in consumption are taken into consideration.

Sustainability now refers to the constancy of certain model variables in time, or, expressed more precisely, to the fact that the values of these variables at least do not decline. The following variables are available up to now:

- The welfare or per capita utility of the population.
- The per capita output y (as important argument of the consumption possibilities).
- The aggregate value for N and M, which admits a substitution among the aggregate environmental media.
- Values for disaggregated entities N and M, such as amount prescriptions for the raw material forest or marginal value prescriptions for air.

For the aforementioned reasons, the per capita welfare is at the forefront here as an indicator of sustainability. An elemental influence factor for this variable is the per capita output. The application of a great number of dif-

Growth Theory and Sustainable Development

ferent growth models is possible for it to be determined in theory. An
exception is neo-classical theory, where the long-term growth rate is exogenous; to add more environmental aspects to the model therefore would
bring no new perceptions for the long term. In the context of the new
growth theory, where the growth rate is endogenous, one-sector models or
multi-sector models can be used. We shall start with a one-sector representation in the following example.

b) Externalities of Capital Use

We shall first simultaneously observe the positive externalities of learning
effects and the damage to the natural input caused by using the physical
capital stock. So the negative external effect of the capital input will be:

$$N = N^* \cdot K^{-\psi} \tag{11.6}$$

If we combine this relationship with the positive learning effects from
(11.5), the following results for Y in the Cobb–Douglas formulation (11.2):

$$Y = K^\eta \cdot K^\alpha \cdot [N^* \cdot K^{-\psi}]^{1-\alpha} \tag{11.11}$$

In order to simplify, we shall abstract from depreciation of physical capital
and from population growth. The value for the population L will be nor-
malised to one, so that the relation is also true for the per capita income:

$$y = k^\eta \cdot k^\alpha \cdot [N^* \cdot k^{-\psi}]^{1-\alpha} \tag{11.12}$$

   For the calculation of the growth rate under market conditions, the private marginal product of the capital is decisive. According to the Keynes–
Ramsey rule, the economic growth rate g depends on the marginal product of capital MPK, the discount rate ρ and the elasticity of intertemporal
substitution $(1/\gamma)$, that is, $g = (1/\gamma)(MPK - \rho)$, provided that the depreciation and the population growth rate are zero (see Section 4.3). For the
individual firm, total knowledge and negative externalities are exogenous,
that is, when deciding on how much to invest, the terms k^η and $k^{-\psi}$ in
(11.12) are constant for the firm. Thus in the presence of positive spillovers
and given (11.12), the private marginal product of capital here is (compare
with Section 6.1 and especially equation 6.6):

$$MPK_P = \left(\frac{\partial y}{\partial k}\right)_P = \alpha \cdot k^{(\eta + \alpha - \psi(1-\alpha))-1} \cdot (N^*)^{1-\alpha} \qquad (11.13)$$

Here the endowment with the natural resource functions acts as a scale variable: the marginal product of capital is higher with a higher (exogenous) endowment of N^*. Thus the higher the endowment, the higher the return on capital and the higher incentives for investments become. Accordingly, the higher the investments the larger the growth rate becomes. The per capita income develops in accordance with the changes of the marginal product in the course of time. Decisive in the assessment here are the sizes of parameters α, η and ψ. Whether a constant or increasing development of the per capita income is possible under these circumstances depends on the size of the parameters for the production elasticities. For sustainability, the question arises whether the marginal product of capital including all externalities is constant, decreasing or increasing. If the following is true:

$$\eta + \alpha + \psi(1 - \alpha) = 1 \qquad (11.14)$$

then the marginal product is exactly constant, which makes a constant long-term growth rate possible. In this steady state, the stock of physical capital increases and the natural input decreases according to equation (11.6). If the expression on the left-hand side of (11.14) is smaller than one, then the growth process peters out in the long run, because the incentives for the capital investments converge to zero. The effects of a decreasing input of natural resources on the development path is discussed in Section 11.3 in the context of exhaustible resources.

Because of positive and negative externalities, the calculated private marginal product is not identical to the social marginal product, which represents a measure for maximising total welfare and therefore for economic policy. The social marginal product of capital MPK_S is obtained by differentiating (11.12) with respect to k, which yields:

$$\left(\frac{\partial y}{\partial k}\right)_S = (\eta + \alpha - \psi(1 - \alpha))$$

$$\cdot k^{(\eta + \alpha - \psi(1-\alpha))-1} \cdot (N^*)^{1-\alpha} \qquad (11.15)$$

In this particular model, the question of optimum environmental policy depends on whether:

$$\eta > \psi(1-\alpha) \tag{11.16}$$

is true, or:

$$\eta < \psi(1-\alpha) \tag{11.17}$$

In the first case, the growth rate reached under market conditions is too low, and in the second case it is too high, since the negative externalities dominate the positive learning effects. If the social marginal product is higher than the private marginal product, then the government should subsidise the investments in this model; if the social marginal product is smaller, then the investments should be taxed.

c) Externalities and Utility Function

Now the negative externalities which have an effect on consumption can be added; for sustainability seen from an anthropocentric viewpoint means that, measured by the individual utility, including 'consumption' of the environment goods, welfare stays at least constant over time.

The negative externality from the consumption of natural resources, for example, in the form of pollution of the air through the burning of oil, can be represented as:

$$M = M^* \cdot N^{-\tilde{\upsilon}} \tag{11.9}$$

Taking logarithms of (11.9), totally differentiating (11.9) as well as the utility function (11.4) and observing that M^* is constant results in the percentage change of individual utility according to:

$$g_{(U/L)} = \xi \cdot g_c - (1-\xi) \cdot \tilde{\upsilon} \cdot g_N \tag{11.18}$$

The analysis of the production side gives us the growth of consumption c by calculating per capita income growth as shown above in (11.12)–(11.15). If N introduced into the production rises, then the negative relationship between M and N fixes a negative growth for the second part of the utility function. For sustainability, this negative influence has to be at least compensated for by income growth. An alternative is the development of abatement technologies to decrease $\tilde{v}$.

If we assume that the formation of physical capital exercises negative external effects on M in the utility function (see equation 11.8), then optimum growth is smaller than without this kind of environmental restriction. In this case, the accumulation of capital, important for the growth of the goods production, encroaches upon the utility of the individuals.

Depending on the model, the variables M and N are defined either as services of nature or as stocks of environmental capital. In certain cases, it is expressly the entire stock of the natural environment or the stocks of individual environment goods which appear in the utility function. For example, the natural amenity of a landscape is an entity which, as a whole, as a stock, brings utility. Then the utility loss, which arises because the natural capital stock is partially destroyed by the externalities of production or consumption, has long-term consequences for sustainable development.

In this model, the development of utility is decided by the force of the positive and negative externalities. To understand these externalities in reality, we should turn to empirical research. To determine the utility of the households from the environmental quality, many different direct and indirect procedures exist. Direct procedures are, for example, contingent valuation methods, market simulations or field experiments; in indirect procedures, the value of the environment is indirectly deduced from the – specifically observed – economic and political behaviour of individuals.

d) Externalities and Dynamic Sectors

Through negative external effects, the environment may alter the productivity of the inputs used in the dynamic sector of the economy. Dynamic sectors are those where 'growth' of an economy is generated. The education and the research sectors are the most important examples. The human capital model of Section 6.3 has a production sector producing consumption and physical investment goods, and an education sector where skills (that is, human capital) are generated. Growth is due to human capital accumulation, that is, it can only be created in the education sector.

Now, assume the use of physical capital to be polluting. In this case, negative environmental externalities influence the marginal value of physical capital in the steady state but not the efficiency of human capital in the education sector. As the growth rate of the economy only depends on the marginal product of human capital (see equation 6.30), and not on the marginal product of physical capital, the growth rate of the economy remains unaffected by this external effect. Accordingly, the growth rate of the economy is not influenced by environmental policy. However, the input intensities in the production function change as a consequence of environmental policy, which is due to changed relative prices of capital components.

If, however, one extends the human capital approach of Section 6.3 in the sense that pollution also affects learning abilities, that is, the marginal returns to education, then the effects of environmental quality on the growth rate are different. Assume pollution to be caused by the use of capital and to decrease learning abilities (which has been observed empirically in regions with heavy air pollution, for example, in Mexico City). If the natural resource N (for example, clean air) is important for learning, a simple formulation is:

$$\mu = N^{\phi} \qquad\qquad \phi > 0 \qquad\qquad (11.19)$$

where μ is the productivity in the education sector as in Section 6.3. Applying the growth formula of Section 6.3 and again using g for the growth rate, $(1/\gamma)$ for the elasticity of intertemporal substitution and ρ for the discount rate gives:

$$g = \frac{1}{\gamma}(\mu - \rho) \qquad\qquad (11.20)$$

which together with (11.19) results in:

$$g = \frac{1}{\gamma}(N^{\phi} - \rho) \qquad\qquad (11.21)$$

The natural environment, expressed by N, now has a direct impact on the growth rate. A better environmental quality stimulates human capital accumulation and, as a result, the growth rate of the whole economy.

This positive effect can also be modelled for the R&D sector. Assuming the productivity of the research laboratories to be negatively affected by pollution, a decrease in pollution increases both the productivity of research and the growth rate of the economy. It has to be noted, however, that the assumptions to derive these results are rather restrictive and will only be applicable for special fields of education and research.

11.3 EXHAUSTIBLE RESOURCES

In Section 11.2, the available quantities of N and M were exogenously given in a constant amount. It is, however, typical of many natural resources that they cannot, or can only partly be regenerated, which has a direct impact on the available supply. An important field in environmental economics is therefore the problem of the non-renewable or so-called exhaustible resources, most prominently represented by the raw material oil.

a) Hotelling Rule

If the stock of a natural resource is limited, then the price development, which is called the 'Hotelling rule', will result in the steady state of a simple growth model. For simplicity we shall here consider an owner of resources who owns a fixed amount of resources and maximises his/her rent over two periods; the same result can be obtained when considering more than two periods. Now exhaustible resources will be denoted by R in order to use a different notation compared to natural resources in general (denoted by N), as used up to now.

Notation:

- R exhaustible resource
- π^R rent from selling the resource
- p^R market price of the natural resource
- c^R extraction costs
- W financial wealth
- r market interest rate.

In period 1, the rent from selling the resources is:

$$\pi^R_1 = p^R_1 - c^R_1 \tag{11.22}$$

An alternative financial asset W will have an exogenous interest rate r, so that:

$$W_1(1+r) = W_2 \tag{11.23}$$

In the capital market equilibrium, the returns are equalised, then:

$$\pi^R_1(1+r) = \pi^R_2 \qquad (11.24)$$

The increase in the price can be calculated as follows from the relationship between the rents:

$$\frac{\pi^R_2}{\pi^R_1} = 1+r = \frac{p^R_2 - c^R_2}{p^R_1 - c^R_1}$$

$$1+r = \frac{(p^R_2 - p^R_1) - (c^R_2 - c^R_1) + (p^R_1 - c^R_1)}{p^R_1 - c^R_1} \qquad (11.25)$$

From this and using d for the difference between the two periods, it follows that:

$$r = \frac{dp^R - dc^R}{p^R_1 - c^R_1}$$

The growth rate of the resource price is:

$$g_{PR} = \frac{dp^R}{p^R_1} = \left(\frac{p^R_1 - c^R_1}{p^R_1} \cdot \frac{dp^R - dc^R}{p^R_1 - c^R_1}\right) + \left(\frac{c^R_1}{p^R_1} \cdot \frac{dc^R}{c^R_1}\right)$$

$$g_{PR} = \left(\frac{p^R_1 - c^R_1}{p^R_1}\right) \cdot r + \left(\frac{c^R_1}{p^R_1}\right) \cdot g_{c^R}$$

Through further transformations, we arrive at the equation known as the Hotelling rule:

$$g_{PR} = r + \left(\frac{c^R_1}{p^R_1}\right)(g_{c^R} - r) \qquad (11.26)$$

If extraction costs c^R are not of too great an importance (as for example, with the oil from the Middle East), the second term in (11.26) is unimportant compared to the first. Then, the percentage price increase of the natural resource g_{PR} is given by the level of the market interest rate r. It is then possible to write the price of the resource in time according to:

$$p^R(t) = p^R(0) \cdot e^{r \cdot t} \tag{11.27}$$

where t is the time index and 0 is the starting point of the observation. Adding a simple constant elasticity demand function for the natural resource in the form of:

$$R(t) = p^R(t)^{-a} \tag{11.28}$$

and observing the restriction that the sum of all quantities R cannot exceed the total stock of the resource denoted by S_0, one arrives at a diagram like the one in Figure 11.2 for the use of exhaustible natural resources.

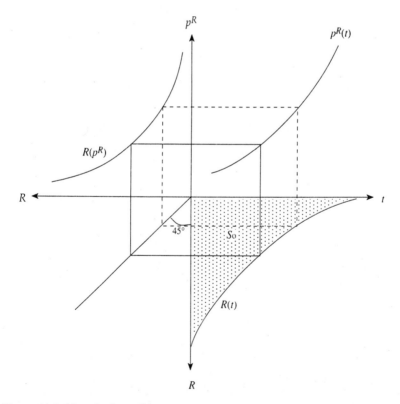

Figure 11.2 Use of exhaustible resources

The first quadrant (north-east) of the figure shows the price path according to the Hotelling rule (11.27). The quadrant in the north-west is the demand relation (11.28). Then, the time path of the use of the resource can be derived in the south-east. As the price of the resource increases in time, the quantity used decreases continuously. The shaded area under the curve represents the total stock of the resource S_0.

In reality, however, the prices of several exhaustible raw materials have not developed according to the Hotelling rule in the past, but have even declined to some extent. This has to do with the following facts, which deviate from the assumptions of the used model:

- Lack of a long-term ownership guarantee for natural resources, which shortens the time horizon for optimisation.
- Varying monopoly power on the resource markets.
- Increasing known reserves because of successful explorations.
- Falling extraction costs in the course of time through technical progress.
- Information problems: economic agents do not have perfect foresight.
- Survival of the present generation: certain countries are totally dependent on the sales of resources in order to ensure the continued existence of their inhabitants.
- Political sector: governments often optimise only within the horizon of their governmental period.
- Existence of so-called backstop technologies, which can completely take over the role of the natural resources in production from a certain resource price onwards.

These points can also be seen as points of criticism of the simple Hotelling rule, at least when it is used for forecasting. Nevertheless, it is easily possible to include several of the additional elements in the theory. If known reserves increase, this means, in the model, that stock S_0 rises, which shifts the $R(t)$ curve in Figure 11.2 away from the origin. This leads to a decrease in the price of the resource, so that the price path in Figure 11.2 shifts downwards. Introducing backstop technologies means that the price of the natural resource has a price 'ceiling'. If the resource price exceeds the ceiling, then demand for the resource will be zero. For example, solar energy is seen as a possible backstop technology as regards the use of oil.

An interesting issue is the influence of monopoly power. In static theory, the price of the monopoly is always higher than the price under perfect competition. But in this intertemporal optimisation problem of exhaustible resources, there is a dynamic restriction which dominates static optimisation. If total reserves are fixed, it cannot be that the price of the monopolistic supplier is always higher than the price under perfect competition. If it were so, then the monopoly could not sell the entire reserves at the end. Depending on the demand function, the price path of the monopoly differs in general from perfect competition, but there must be a period in which prices of perfect competition are higher because of the stock restriction. Given constant elasticity demand functions, the optimum price of the monopoly is even the same as the price under perfect competition (see, for example, Hartwick and Olewiler 1986, p. 98). The theory assumes that the time horizon of agents is long enough so that they are aware of the stock restriction, which is not always the case, as noted above.

To conclude, it can be said that the increase in known reserves and decreasing extraction costs have greatly influenced the price of many exhaustible resources in the past. But it is probable, in the future, that the limitation of the entire stocks will influence the price development increasingly. Then the substitution of these resources will become a problem of increasing economic importance.

b) The Substitution Process

When the input of natural resources in production continually becomes more expensive in relation to the other production factors, the relative amount of these resources which is employed continually decreases. A substitution takes place in the production. So it is logical to examine more closely the value of the elasticity of substitution in the aggregate production function. For this purpose, we have to use the CES production function.

Notation:

- σ elasticity of substitution
- $\phi_{1,2}$ fixed parameters
- K capital.

The greater the elasticity of substitution between the exhaustible resource and the accumulated capital, the easier it is to maintain sustainable growth. This can be shown with the help of the following CES production function (omitting time indices):

$$Y = [\phi_1 \cdot K^{(\sigma-1)/\sigma} + \phi_2 \cdot R^{(\sigma-1)/\sigma}]^{\sigma/(\sigma-1)} \qquad (11.29)$$

From (11.29), the quotient Y/R is now calculated. If this quotient is bounded above, then in the limit with $t \to \infty$, Y can be calculated by multiplying R by a constant term. Since the sum of all the Rs in the course of time is at maximum equal to the given stock of exhaustible resources, the sum of all incomes which are attainable over time is also constant. This renders exponential growth impossible. In this case, the income has to decrease over time and to converge towards zero. Following (11.29), the relation Y/R is:

$$\left(\frac{Y}{R}\right)^{(\sigma-1)/\sigma} = \phi_1 \cdot \left(\frac{R}{K}\right)^{(1-\sigma)/\sigma} + \phi_2 \qquad (11.30)$$

Under the assumption that the elasticity of substitution is smaller than one, that is, $\sigma < 1$, the following is true:

$$\lim_{R \to 0} \left(\frac{Y}{R}\right) = (\phi_2)^{\sigma/(\sigma-1)} \qquad (11.31)$$

Here the right-hand side is a constant. For $\sigma < 1$ then, the statement is valid that the income development becomes negative in the course of time. So with small substitution possibilities of the exhaustible resource, sustainability is not possible with this kind of production function.

From (11.30), it also becomes clear that the quotient Y/R is unbounded above with $\sigma > 1$, which makes an unlimited exponential growth of the income possible. R then is a so-called inessential factor, the meaning of which asymptotically disappears for production in the course of time. In this case, sustainability represents no particular problem.

The variant which lies between these two cases is where the substitution elasticity is one. Here, the income share spent for natural resources remains constant over time. This leads us to the known Cobb–Douglas form of the production function:

$$Y = K^\alpha \cdot R^{1-\alpha} \qquad (11.32)$$

Here R appears as an 'essential' production factor, the meaning of which does not disappear asymptotically in the course of time. At the same time, the quotient Y/R is not bounded above. A sufficiently strong capital accumulation can compensate for the falling input of R. In this case, for sustainability, it depends whether the savings of the household suffice for the accumulation of enough capital. This is shown in the following subsection.

c) Hartwick Rule

If the savings rate is assumed to be constant, for simplicity, as in the neo-classical model, a savings rate can be derived for the Cobb–Douglas production function (11.32) which guarantees a constant income and therefore sustainability. Following (11.32), the growth rate of Y can be expressed as follows:

$$g_Y = g_K - (1-\alpha)(g_K - g_R) \tag{11.33}$$

From the assumption of a constant savings rate then it follows that:

$$g_K = s \cdot \left(\frac{Y}{K}\right) \tag{11.34}$$

According to the Hotelling rule, the growth of the resource price is equal to the interest rate. Furthermore, with perfect competition the resource price corresponds to the marginal product of the resource R and the interest rate corresponds to the marginal product of capital. Expressed with (11.32), the marginal product of capital is:

$$\frac{\partial Y}{\partial K} = \alpha \cdot \left(\frac{K}{R}\right)^{\alpha-1} = \alpha \cdot \left(\frac{Y}{K}\right) \tag{11.35}$$

The marginal product of the resource, that is, the price of the resource, then is:

$$\frac{\partial Y}{\partial R} = (1-\alpha) \cdot \left(\frac{K}{R}\right)^{\alpha}$$

which yields for the percentage increase of the resource price:

$$g_{(\partial Y/\partial R)} = \alpha \cdot (g_K - g_R) \tag{11.36}$$

Equating expressions (11.35) and (11.36) suggested by the Hotelling rule and inserting into (11.33) together with (11.34), we have:

$$g_Y = [s - (1-\alpha)] \cdot Y/K \tag{11.37}$$

According to Section 3.2 the quotient Y/K is constant in the long-term steady state. An income which is constant over time ($g_Y = 0$) then becomes possible by the savings rate:

$$s = 1 - \alpha \qquad (11.38)$$

This is the so-called 'Hartwick rule'. In this model, sustainability is attained because the following generations are exactly indemnified, as regards their income, for the decreasing stocks of R, since the existence of sufficient savings enables a strong enough growth of K.

d) Interest-dependent Savings

Following the explanations in Chapter 4, the Keynes–Ramsey rule for an optimum consumption growth yields the growth rate g_C as a function of the marginal product of capital, the discount rate and the elasticity of intertemporal substitution, provided that the depreciation and the population growth rate are assumed to be zero. Using the production function (11.32), this yields:

$$g_C = \frac{1}{\gamma}\left[\alpha \cdot \left(\frac{K}{R}\right)^{\alpha - 1} - \rho\right] \qquad (11.39)$$

where $1/\gamma$ is the elasticity of intertemporal substitution and ρ the discount rate as in the previous chapters. The quotient K/R rises over time, since R decreases and K either increases or stays constant, if depreciation is ignored. Since the coefficient $\alpha - 1$ is negative under neo-classical assumptions, the marginal product of capital falls in the course of time. Only a declining capital stock could hinder a fall in the marginal product of capital. But even this would not mean sustainability, because income and consumption would necessarily also decrease with a declining capital stock.

This has shown that – without technical progress – interest rate-dependent saving leads to a falling consumption in the long run for the given production function. In this model, it can be shown that a low discount rate only makes it possible for consumption to rise to the steady state in a first phase of transition. However, in the long term, every discount rate which is greater than zero combined with intertemporal optimisation leads to a worsening situation for future generations. An exception arises when the individuals are extremely risk-averse, that is, when the elasticity of the intertemporal substitution $1/\gamma$ is practically zero. Then it becomes clear from (11.39) that consumption assumes a constant value ($g_C = 0$) independent of the right-hand-side expression in brackets. But this theoretical case has to be excluded on the grounds of the empirical evidence regarding the attitude towards risk.

The situation is slightly different when one departs from the neo-classical form of the production function and assumes a constant marginal product of capital according to the new growth theory. A corresponding production function with a constant D is:

$$Y = D \cdot \tilde{K} \cdot R^{1-\alpha} \tag{11.40}$$

Here $\tilde{K}$ is an aggregate of the accumulated kinds of capital such as physical, human and knowledge capital. Now the course of the marginal product of capital MPK ($\partial Y / \partial \tilde{K}$) depends only on the variable R:

$$MPK = D \cdot R^{1-\alpha}$$

Since R decreases in the course of time with increasing scarcity, a sustainable development cannot even be attained with the production function (11.40), when interest rate-dependent saving is assumed, because the readiness of the households to accumulate savings disappears with a falling marginal product.

According to the Keynes–Ramsey rule, the growth rate is:

$$g_C = \frac{1}{\gamma}(D \cdot R^{1-\alpha} - \rho) \tag{11.41}$$

As soon as the marginal product of capital falls below the value of the discount rate, there is no more positive growth. In this example, sustainability is possible only if measures are taken by the government in favour of accumulating savings.

In the context of a one-sector model, sustainability is achieved without such an active policy, that is, under market economic conditions, only if strong enough increasing marginal products of capital $\tilde{K}$ are postulated or if an exogenous technical progress is adopted into the model (see also Box 11.1).

Box 11.1: Technical Progress and Sustainability

For the question how substantial technical progress has to be for a sustainable development in a situation of a dwindling input of exhaustible resources, Nordhaus (1992) presents the following calculation, based on a 'realistic' production function of the Cobb–Douglas form with the following inputs:

$$Y = A \cdot K^\alpha \cdot R^\theta \cdot L^\omega \cdot O^\xi \tag{1}$$

Here A represents the (exogenous) stock of technical knowledge, K the physical capital, R the exhaustible natural resources, L the labour and O the input of land. The temporal decrease in input of exhaustible resources in time is given by the following condition:

$$R_t = b \cdot S_0 \cdot e^{-b \cdot t} \tag{2}$$

t is the time index, S_0 is the given initial stock of R and b is a constant. Condition (2) for R is inserted into production function (1). In the long-term steady state, it can be taken into consideration that the quotient Y/K is constant ($g_Y = g_K$). Furthermore, the amount of land is assumed as fixed. Taking logarithms and differentiating the production function results in the following for the growth rate of the per-capita income:

$$g_y = -[1 - \omega/(1 - \alpha)] \cdot g_L - [\theta/(1 - \alpha)] \cdot b \tag{3}$$
$$+ [1/(1 - \alpha)] \cdot g_A$$

Now the following 'realistic' values are inserted for the parameters: ω: 0.6, α: 0.2, g_L: 0.01, θ: 0.1, b: 0.005. The parameter values g_L and b are per annum values.

By dissolving, we can conclude that the growth of y is greater than zero if technical progress amounts to 0.25 percent per annum, that is:

$$g_y > 0 \text{ if } g_A > 0.0025$$

Nordhaus concludes that in reality it is not very difficult to reach this value. From his point of view then, sustainability is relatively easily guaranteed by technical progress. This strong statement can become relative if one observes the restrictive form of the chosen production function, the neglect of uncertainty, the lack of an explanation for the sources of technical progress and the rather low values for parameter b.

It has already become clear in Chapters 6, 7 and 8, however, that the application of multi-sector models is more useful for certain questions. It is then possible, for example, to introduce a sector for research and development or an education sector (see next subsection).

e) Multi-sector Approach

The basic idea of substitution in a multi-sector model with endogenous knowledge forming can be illustrated using the following example (see Bretschger 1998). In accordance with the R&D models of Chapter 7 and 8, we consider an economy with two consumer sectors and a sector for R&D (see Figure 11.3). The two consumer goods are homogeneous traditional goods Z, which are produced under constant returns to scale, and high-technology consumer goods Y^H, which are assembled from differentiated intermediate inputs x.

R&D provides the know-how for the production of intermediate inputs. The model assumes production to be based on two primary inputs, labour L and natural resources N, which have to be allocated to the three sectors. R&D is assumed to be the sector that is most intensive in labour, whereas the traditional sector is most intensive in the natural input, and the production of differentiated goods lies in between.

Long-term growth is driven by a continuous expansion-in-varieties in the Y-sector, which is possible due to the ongoing invention of new designs. Each design contains the know-how to produce a variety of differentiated goods. R&D is assumed to generate positive spillovers to knowledge capital, which is, in turn, an input into R&D. The more knowledge is available, the more efficient R&D is, which leads the economy on to a constant growth path. In a steady state, the relation between the growth rate of consumer outputs and the growth rate of designs is constant. Due to the positive spillovers of R&D and the absence of negative externalities in the model, the welfare-maximising growth rate is higher than the rate resulting under free market conditions. At the same time, a positive growth rate of output implies a steady increase in welfare, that is, sustainable development as defined above. So it is given that a small increase in the steady-state growth rate of designs yields an increase in welfare.

Sustainable growth requires an increase in man-made capital large enough to compensate for the declining input of natural resources into production. To provide sufficient incentives for savings and capital investments, the return on capital must be constantly on a level exceeding the discount rate of households. In the three-sector models used here, the return on R&D investments is decisive for long-term growth. An increase in the price of the natural resource raises the costs of the innovative sector. This negative growth impact can only be countered by a decrease in the labour wage. The decisive point here is that this occurs only with an elasticity of substitution between natural resource and labour which is smaller than unity.

Primary inputs   **Sectors**

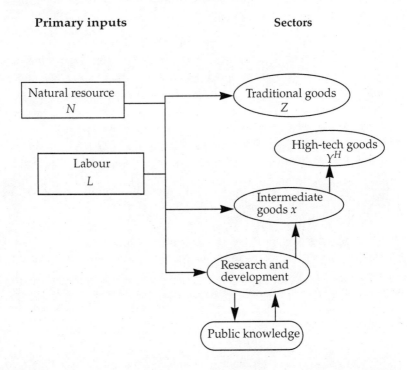

Figure 11.3 Substitution in a multi-sector model

In this approach, an elasticity of substitution that is smaller than unity decreases the labour share of total income which is favourable for growth. The reason is that, with decreasing N, labour appears as a cost factor in the innovative sector so that lower wages are positive with regard to dynamics. A low elasticity means that labour is released from the resource-intensive sectors and can be used more in the dynamic sector.

This demonstrates that, with a declining input of natural resources being the main impulse, an economy's sectoral change can be regarded as one of the main propagation mechanisms to effectuate the substitution of natural inputs that is required for sustainability. The multi-sector approach has more realistic features than the one-sector model. First, it is seen that not only the substitution between inputs, but also the substitution between different sectors of the economy has an impact on the growth path. This requires the formulation of a multi-sector model where the elasticities of input substitution are measured on the disaggregated level. Second, it is considered that man-made capital is not only an input, but is also an output of specific sectors of the economy.

The relation between the return on capital and the cost of capital goods is the centre of the analysis, as it governs the savings decisions and therefore the growth rate of the economy. In a multi-sector model, the return on capital has to be valued with the price of the output, whereas the capital good has to be valued with the price of the capital good. The different behaviour of these prices is one of the key elements in determining the macroeconomic substitution process under consideration. It has been emphasised that in the one-sector model, an elasticity of substitution between capital and natural resources of unity leads to an ever declining growth rate, that is, to non-sustainable development. In the multi-sector model, however, an elasticity of substitution between labour and natural resources that is equal to unity still leads to positive growth rates in the long run, as the cost in the research sector remains constant in this case. Thus, using multi-sector models to characterise real development sheds a more optimistic light on the issue under consideration: it suggests that sustainability can indeed be achieved under realistic conditions.

In this three-sector model, it is postulated that traditional production generates no learning effects, but uses the environment most intensively, while research and development generate positive spillovers, but need only few natural inputs, that is, do only minimal harm to the environment. Also under the assumption of more than three sectors in the economy, the sectors realistically show different intensities in the use of the natural resources in production. On the other hand, learning effects or knowledge spillovers also arise in different sectoral intensities. It would favour sustainability if, in general, the industries which use natural resources intensively create little additional knowledge, whereas the learning-intensive sectors of the economy are extensive in the use of natural resources. Then, a structural change involving a shift in weights of the different sectors can serve two purposes at the same time. This is illustrated in Figure 11.4.

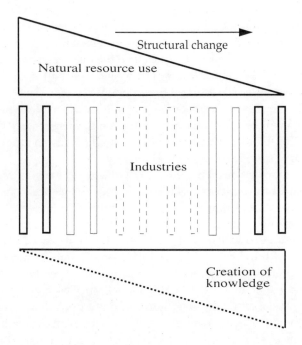

Figure 11.4 Effects of structural changes

Given the favourable conditions in the figure, the fact that natural resources become more expensive leads to a transformation of the structure inside the economy. The faster the prices of the natural resources rise, the faster this change happens. Since the production factors, such as labour or knowledge capital, which are used intensively in innovative sectors, become cheaper in comparison to the natural resources, the costs in the innovative sectors have a below-average development compared to the total economy. As a consequence, the results in the multi-sector approach are more optimistic regarding sustainability than in the one-sector model.

The described sectoral transformation leads to intensified stimuli for the accumulation of additional knowledge by investments in research and development or education. So here, in the context of multi-sector growth models, we have found a basis for policy which is dedicated to the principle of sustainability (see Chapter 12).

11.4 RENEWABLE NATURAL RESOURCES

For the case of renewable natural resources, we arrive at another analysis, which plays an important role especially for less developed economies, but also for industrialised countries. Here the demand for sustainability concentrates on the determination of a 'harvest rate', which makes a constancy in the biomass possible and therefore a sustainable use and sustainable growth, together with the other sectors of the economy. Here the regeneration function of nature, which describes the natural renewal of the stock of resources, is decisive. The market price is determined by the quantities supplied in the market steady state together with the demand for the renewable resource.

a) Regeneration Function

With renewable natural resources such as forests and fish, natural growth depends on the stock of the resources. The example of fish is illustrative. If the stock of fish is low in certain waters, regeneration will be substantial without outside intervention, since the food supply is abundant. The growth rate of the stock will become smaller with a growing fish stock, since the access to food becomes increasingly difficult. The total stock increases until the regeneration rate of the fish reaches the natural death rate.

Notation:

- V stock of the renewable natural resource (biomass)
- Z 'harvest' of the renewable natural resource
- F natural regeneration.

Natural time-dependent regeneration can be algebraically expressed as a function of the total stock as follows:

$$dV/dt = F(V) \tag{11.42}$$

Following the above verbal explanations, the graphic representation of expression (11.42) is shown in Figure 11.5.

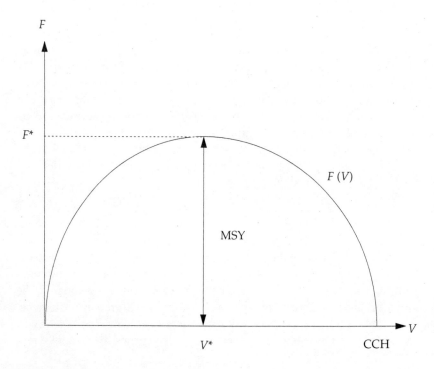

Figure 11.5 Regeneration function

b) Harvest of the Natural Resource

Every point of the function $F(V)$ describes an amount which can be harvested by human beings, without the total stock of biomass V decreasing or increasing by natural regeneration. With a stock of V^*, a maximum harvest is possible ('maximum sustainable yield' = MSY). If there is no harvesting at all, the system reaches the point CCH ('carrying capacity of the habitat'), where the regeneration rate corresponds to the natural 'death' rate.

A special form of regeneration function arises when a minimum amount of biomass has to be present in order for a positive growth of the natural resource to take place. Such a threshold value is shown, for instance, by swarm fish, which can survive only from a certain population size on. In a similar sense, one can argue with threshold values given by natural science for other natural resources and environmental problems too.

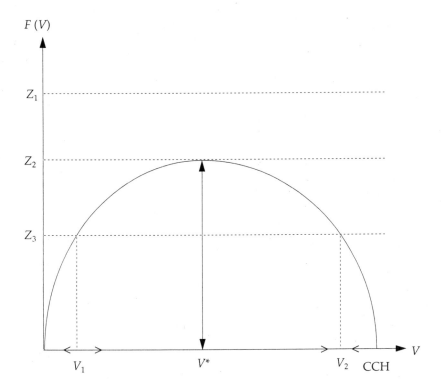

Figure 11.6 Different harvest rates

We shall now examine the consequences of three different harvest rates on stock V. Figure 11.6 will serve as our reference here:

- The harvest amount Z_1 means that the harvest surpasses the natural renewal rate. In this way, the natural resource will be completely used up.

- Z_2 is the biggest sustainable harvest rate. If there were no economic expenditure for the harvest, this would be the optimum amount in a static consideration. However, this statement is valid only if the stock is at least V^* before the beginning of the harvest, otherwise even this harvest amount leads to the exhaustion of the natural resource.

- For harvest amount Z_3, two different steady states exist. If one assumes nature to be untouched (state CCH), then the stock V_2 in biomass occurs after an adjustment phase. If the original stock is bigger than V_1, the system reaches the same steady state from the other side. Point V_2 then is a stable steady-state. In contrast, the steady-state in point V_1 is unstable, because, with this harvest amount, if the stock is even slightly bigger or smaller, then the development gains a distance from the starting point.

c) Intertemporal Optimum

For the optimum harvest rate, the expenditure for the harvest or harvest costs as well as the discount rate of the households has to be taken into consideration in addition to natural regeneration. At every moment, the net benefit of the harvest of natural resources consists of the difference between the consumption benefit for the households and the expenditure for the harvest. For the determination of the intertemporal optimum, the net benefit of the future is discounted with the discount rate; after which a maximum over the total time has to be sought for the net utility.

Society can 'invest' in the biomass by renouncing a certain amount of harvest, thus ensuring the stock of the natural resource or even enhancing the growth of the biomass. In analogy to the Keynes–Ramsey rule in Chapter 4, a constant consumption of Z is reached when the marginal product of the 'investment' (the non-consumption) is equal to the discount rate.

This maximisation occurs under the restriction of the natural regeneration function. In this case, the society wants to use a greater amount than can grow again naturally; this restriction is binding for the attainment of an optimum. In order to prevent an overuse in this case, the harvest has to be made more expensive through environment political measures.

Notation:

- E harvest costs
- U consumption utility of the harvest.

This context is represented in Figure 11.7. It is assumed here that the marginal utility of the harvest shows the falling course usual in microeconomic theory, and the marginal costs of the harvest show a course which rises with the harvested amount. In the upper half of the figure, the static optimum in the equalisation of marginal utility and marginal costs for the harvest can be seen. However, in the example shown, the static optimum harvest amount leads to overuse of the natural resource and does not correspond to the intertemporal optimum.

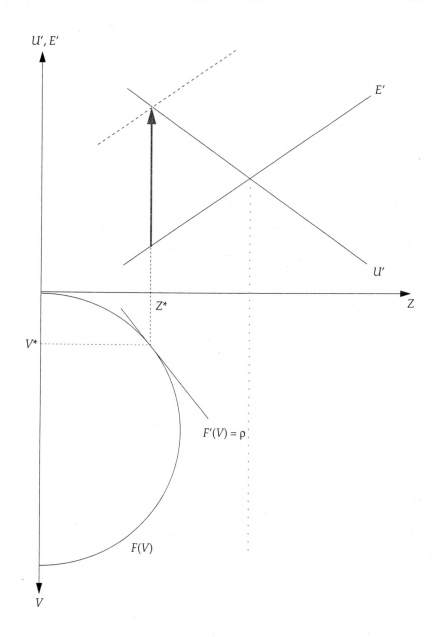

Figure 11.7 Intertemporal optimum

The intertemporal optimum is given at the point where the marginal product of the investment (the non-harvest) $F'(V)$ is placed on the level of the discount rate ρ. If harvest prices are raised by means of economic policy, which is indicated by an arrow in the figure, a harvest amount Z^* can be reached, which, on the one hand, is intertemporally optimal, and on the other hand, guarantees sustainability in the use of nature. The optimum harvest point is unstable, however. To sustain the optimum, one must therefore constantly take care that the stock does not fall below V^*. If it deviates in the upward direction, then the system converges towards the stable equilibrium point.

If a situation occurs where the marginal product in the natural regeneration is smaller than the discount rate in any case, a divergence of the optimum use from the sustainable use might occur, for then it is the exhaustion of the natural resource which is optimum. But if the natural resource has an important role in the entire ecosystem and its loss would have serious or maybe still uncertain consequences, then the exhaustion is not sustainable. Then a smaller harvest amount which is adjusted to the natural regeneration must be imposed through corresponding measures in order to safeguard sustainability.

In the case of renewable resources, there is also another kind of externality, which arises through incomplete distribution of owner rights (paired with the property of excludability) and which plays an important role. For example, it is a consequence of free market access to fishing on the world's seas that the individual fishing boat calculates only its own costs and ignores the fact that the 'catch probability' of the other fishing boats is diminished through its catch. Here, it is a question of a congestion problem, because the sea is freely accessible but the catch of fish is rival, a similar case to congestion on the streets. Here again political intervention is necessary in order to internalise this kind of externality between users. In certain fields of environmental problems, this internalisation step could lead to sustainability without the introduction of further measures.

SELECTED READING

- BOVENBERG, L.A. and R.A. DE MOOIJ (1996), 'Environmental Tax Reform and Endogenous Growth', *Journal of Public Economics*, **63**, 207–37.

- BOVENBERG, L.A. and S. SMULDERS (1995): 'Environmental Quality and Pollution Augmenting Technical Change in a Two-sector Endogenous Growth Model', *Journal of Public Economics*, **57**, 369–91.

- BOVENBERG, L.A. and S. SMULDERS (1996), 'Transitional Effects of Environmental Policy in an Endogenous Growth Model', *International Economic Review*, **37**, 861–93.

- BRETSCHGER, L. (1998b), 'How to Substitute in Order to Sustain: Knowledge Driven Growth Under Environmental Restrictions', *Environment and Development Economics*, **3**, 425–42.

- DASGUPTA, P.S. and G.M. HEAL (1979), *Economic Theory and Exhaustible Resources*, Oxford: Cambridge University Press.

- GRADUS, R. and S. SMULDERS (1993), 'The Trade-off Between Environmental Care and Long-term Growth – Pollution in Three Prototype Growth Models', *Journal of Economics*, **58** (1), 25–51.

- HARTWICK, J.M. and N.D. OLEWILER (1986), *The Economics of Natural Resource Use*, New York: Harper & Row.

- NORDHAUS, W.D. (1992), 'Lethal Model 2: The Limits to Growth Reconsidered', *Brookings Papers on Economic Activity*, 1–59.

- SMULDERS, S. and R. GRADUS (1996): 'Pollution Abatement and Long-term Growth', *European Journal of Political Economy*, **12**, 505–32.

12. Achieving Sustainability

12.1 ENDOGENOUS WELFARE INCREASE

In the past two centuries, many countries have experienced an unprecedented increase in living standards. At the same time, the stock of various natural resources has declined and the environmental conditions have changed substantially. To analyse the properties of the observed development paths, growth theory plays an important role. A better understanding of the mechanics of economic growth helps to direct the development process in a direction which is desired by today's generations. There is little to be gained in speculating on future development paths if they are not predictable in some way by theory. Similarly, one cannot have a direct intuition about the dynamic consequences of the different policies unless something concrete is known about the properties of feasible development paths. Thus, a profound study of sustainable growth is not possible without a sound theory of endogenous economic growth.

In the recent debate, sustainability has emerged world-wide as a main guideline for economic and environmental policy. By demanding a long-term constancy or increase in welfare, sustainability is more than survivability, which only requires that consumption be kept above some subsistence minimum. Both fairness and efficiency criteria are crucial to determine sustainable growth paths. Regarding the efficiency of development paths, positive and normative aspects can be analysed using economic theory. Concerning fairness, that is, the intra- and intergenerational distribution of income, the main contribution of economics is to show the relation between ethical constraints and the development of welfare. Therefore, in the interdisciplinary study of the distributional aspects of sustainability, economic theory should, in the first place, provide a positive analysis of the different redistribution policies which are discussed in the context of sustainability.

The different theories summarised in this book shed light on the different problems and potential solutions that arise when seeking to achieve long-term economic growth and sustainable development. The study of the older theory in Chapter 2 shows the consequences of limited substitution possibilities for the employment of factors and for the growth rate. The neo-classical growth theory in Chapter 3 provides insights about the growth rate in the medium term as well as about the determination of capital intensity. As saving is an important part of capital accumulation, inter-temporal optimisation in Chapter 4 is a further important ingredient to understand the development process.

Chapters 5 to 9 emphasise why, in the older growth theory, the long-term growth rate is a variable which cannot be explained by theory; this is the reason why the dynamic effects of environmental policy cannot be analysed with this approach. Then it is shown how, in the research pro-gramme of the new growth theory, the long-term growth rate is deduced directly from the theory. The dynamic consequences of learning by doing, public infrastructure, education, research and development as well as the openness of the economies are demonstrated in different approaches.

Chapters 10 and 11 show how the possible trade-offs between economic growth and an environmental policy oriented towards sustainability can be thoroughly examined with the help of endogenous growth theory. A comprehensive view suggests the concentration on welfare targets. The term welfare not only includes economic aspects such as aggregate con-sumption or production output but also the whole variety of environmen-tal services. Accordingly, a sustainable growth path is characterised by non-declining welfare between generations, welfare being measured as average undiscounted individual utility. Society's beliefs regarding income distribution and social factors are prior constraints for long-term economic optimisation. However, these beliefs are not independent of the economic environment.

To apply the theoretical concepts in practice, it is easiest to refer to cer-tain rules concerning the use of natural resources. First, one should not use more renewable resources than nature is able to regenerate. Second, non-renewable resources can be used but one must ensure that appropriate substitutes or alternative technologies exist or can be developed. In the course of time, a decreasing quantity of non-renewable resources will be available. The possibilities of substitution are elucidated in different mod-els to show the complexity of this crucial issue.

12.2 SUBSTITUTION POLICY

If welfare is to be sustained or increased, the decreasing amount of natural inputs has to be sufficiently compensated for by the accumulation of man-made inputs consisting of different forms of capital. The greater the saving effort of the present generation, the more possible the substitution of natu-ral resources in production and consumption becomes. But saving means consumption renunciation, and this renunciation is economically attractive only if the proceeds of the savings and of the investments financed by saving are sufficiently high. In this way, the return on capital is connected with sustainable development.

To guarantee a sufficient return on man-made capital, the steady-state income share of capital in all versions of the growth models must either remain constant or rise. In the one-sector model using capital as a symmetrical input, this can only be accomplished by an elasticity of substitution among input factors that is larger than unity. Then, natural resources are an inessential input in the long run and the income share required for the compensation of the natural input declines steadily.

Provided that the elasticity of substitution among input factors is unity, it follows from the one-sector representation that the declining input of natural capital stock diminishes the return on investments in non-natural capital. Because of the positive discount rate of the households this causes the income path to fall.

If the 'blame' for the lack of sustainability in present-day development is attributed to the positive discount rate, government encouragement to save can represent a possible measure. However, this is not to the point, since subsidising savings is an imprecise instrument. As long as investments in heavily polluting industries benefit from the subsidies, the interests of sustainability are not served. An exclusive orientation of the policy towards drastic reduction in the input of natural resources is also one-sided, as it does not necessarily correspond to economic efficiency.

Better guidelines for policy result from multi-sector growth models. The fact that the intensities in natural resource use and the size of learning effects which lead to the formation of knowledge are not the same in all sectors of an economy can only be studied in a multi-sector approach. On average it is not learning-intensive activities which are intensive in the use of the environment; on the contrary, it can be seen that learning-intensive activities usually damage the environment only marginally. This opens up a wide range of policy options to support the sustainability requirements for development.

It should be noted that incorporating environmental values in decision-making per se will not bring about sustainability unless each generation is committed to transferring to the next sufficient natural resources and capital assets to make development sustainable. Put another way, the problem of intergenerational equity must be viewed as an issue of ethics that is distinct from economic efficiency in the Pareto sense. Sustainability criteria should be imposed as prior constraints on the maximisation of individual preferences in order to take into account the distribution of welfare between present and future generations. Consequently, each successive generation ensures that the expected welfare of its children is no less than its own perceived well-being.

Thus one should distinguish carefully between efficient allocations of resources – the standard focus of economic theory – and socially desired allocations that may reflect other intergenerational as well as intragenerational equity concerns. In other words, because of physical limits and ethical constraints on resource use, a sustainable development path may not be the same as the efficient path predicted by standard economic theory.

The various theoretical models give mixed results concerning the influence of environmental restrictions on dynamics. Predictions of one-sector models are, in general, rather pessimistic, in particular if the elasticity of substitution between the natural resource and accumulated capital is low and/or the learning effects determining the growth potential of an economy are unimportant. But the more realistic the theoretical models become, the more the impression of a rather weak relation between the state of the environment and economic growth emerges.

We observe that there are more substitution possibilities when using multi-sector models, so that the economy can adjust flexibly to changed prices of natural resources. Furthermore, the possibility of pollution diminishing the productivity in education and research opens up an interesting field for measures promoting growth and at the same time protecting the environment. The study of more complex models, including elements such as different sectors, the open economy and abatement activities, suggests even a negative relation between natural resource use and long-term dynamics. Still, there remain critical areas where future generations could be faced with high costs of repairing environmental damage if the present generation does not engage in enough activities to substitute accumulated capital and knowledge for natural resources.

12.3 ADMITTING STRUCTURAL CHANGE

It is clear from the discussion on the multi-sector approach that for the substitution process to be successful, there must be a long-term change in relative prices: environment-damaging goods have to be made more expensive, and learning-intensive sectors have to be relieved in comparison with the present situation. With these price changes the desired transformations of sectoral structure in an economy are reached efficiently.

In this way, enough new knowledge capital and human capital which substitute the natural resources in the long term can be formed. New knowledge also makes it possible to realise the massive increase in efficiency in the treatment of the environment which is demanded today by ecologists. The return on savings and investments stressed in economics is maintained at an attractive level, since the continuous progress influences investment returns positively. Such a path towards sustainability presents the best possible conditions for the substitution of natural resources to be combinable with economic prosperity in the long term.

An adjustment of the relative prices under the title 'removal of external costs' is already advisable in the name of present-day environmental protection. An environmental policy which meets the purpose contains an internalisation of the negative external effects which is as complete as possible and which generates the smallest possible costs. Market-conforming instruments such as environmental taxes, environmental subsidies or certificates are usually very efficient in this respect. However, with internalisation sustainability is not yet guaranteed. Even stronger measures are sometimes necessary in certain fields. An additional acceleration of the substitution of natural resources in the production can be indicated in certain cases.

Sustainability is a world-wide political aim. Moreover, the state of the environment and economic growth are both largely influenced by the economic relations between economies and world regions. Thus the combination of dynamics, trade and environment is a promising field for further economic research. An examination of the existing literature indicates that more interesting results can be expected in the future. Many results of growth theory are valid only for closed economies; by opening the economies, one should try to confirm, reject or refine these model outcomes. In many cases, results on the closed economy are expected to be confirmed, as free trade, under appropriate conditions, leads to a more efficient allocation of resources in general.

The impact of international know-how transfers requires more careful study. Moreover, a more subtle analysis of the implementation of environmental policy, for example, the dynamic consequences of the international joint implementation of environmental policy, should be a focus in future research. Finally, more empirical results on the relation among environmental policy, natural resource use and growth in open economies are highly desirable.

With the global orientation of the sustainability debate, a new kind of international labour distribution comes to the fore. Less developed countries have a comparative advantage in the supply of natural resources. The expenditure for the protection of the environment is smaller in less developed countries, and the benefit is substantial for everybody, even industrialised countries. Through international compensation for services to protect the environment, the resulting income transfer acts as a stimulus to development of lower income countries. When additional knowledge transfers are added, Third World countries are better equipped to realise a sustainable development under these new circumstances.

To conclude, it should be remembered that in the case of market failures, the increase in prices of natural resources has to be effectuated by political measures. The same applies for price increases necessary for sustainability. This all has to be accomplished as a primary target. Moreover, and even more importantly, the sectoral change that is required for sustainable development has to take place at low economic costs. If adjustment costs are high, there is a slowdown in the growth process and the development path may become non-sustainable. The lower the cost of the reallocation in the direction of sectors that generate many spillovers and do not use natural resources intensively, the better the chances of sustainable development. Therefore, the political aim to lower these adjustment costs is the best measure to achieve sustainable development by supporting the necessary changes in the economy.

Author Index

Subject Index